...bert S. Wistrich is Neub... ...ropean and Jewish Histo... ...rusalem. He previously he... ...at ...niversity College, London,... ...at ...arvard, Brandeis and Oxfor... ...ities, and at the Royal ...nstitute of Advanced Study in the Netherlands. An editor of *East European Jewish Affairs* and a regular contributor to the ...*Literary Supplement*, Professor Wistrich is the author ...of many highly regarded books, including the award-winning *Socialism and the Jews* (1982) and *Antisemitism: The Longest Hatred* (1992). He has also scripted, edited or presented several acclaimed documentary films for British television, ...cluding *The Longest Hatred* and *Good Morning, Mr Hitler*.

*By Robert Wistrich*

Revolutionary Jews from Marx to Trotsky
Trotsky: Fate of a Revolutionary
Who's Who in Nazi Germany
Socialism and the Jews: The Dilemmas in Germany and
Austria-Hungary
Hitler's Apocalypse: Jews and the Nazi Legacy
The Jews in Vienna in the Age of Franz Joseph
Between Redemption and Perdition: Antisemitism and Jewish
Identity
Antisemitism: The Longest Hatred
Weekend in Munich: Art, Propaganda and Terror in the Third
Reich
Demonizing the Other: Antisemitism, Racism and
Xenophobia *(as editor)*
Hitler and the Holocaust: How and Why the Holocaust
Happened

*Other titles in the Phoenix Press*
*Universal History series*

The Renaissance *Paul Johnson*
The Balkans *Mark Mazower*
Islam *Karen Armstrong*
Communism *Richard Pipes*
The German Empire 1871–1919 *Michael Stürmer*
The Catholic Church *Hans Küng*
Peoples and Empires *Anthony Pagden*

# HITLER AND THE HOLOCAUST

## HOW AND WHY THE HOLOCAUST HAPPENED

Robert S. Wistrich

PHOENIX

5 UPPER SAINT MARTIN'S LANE
LONDON
WC2H 9EA

A PHOENIX PAPERBACK

First published in Great Britain in 2001
by Weidenfeld & Nicolson
First published in paperback in 2002
by Phoenix Press
an imprint of Orion Books Ltd,
Orion House, 5 Upper St Martin's Lane,
London WC2H 9EA

Reprinted in Phoenix paperback
Second impression 2003

Copyright © Robert S. Wistrich 2001

The right of Robert S. Wistrich to be identified as the author of
this work has been asserted by him in accordance with the
Copyright, Designs and Patents Act 1988.

A CIP catalogue record for this book
is available from the British Library.

ISBN 1 84212 486 2

Printed and bound in Great Britain by
Clays Ltd, St Ives plc

*To my mother, Sabina,*
*who lived through it all*
*without losing faith*

# Contents

# Jewish Death Toll by Country of Origin 1939-1945

Neutral territory

FINLAND
7

NORWAY
762

ESTONIA
1,500

*North
Sea*

SWEDEN

LATVIA
70,000

DENMARK
60

*Baltic
Sea*

LITHUANIA
140,000

NETHERLANDS
100,000

GERMANY
134,500

POLAND
2,900,000

SOVIET
UNION
1,000,000

BELGIUM
28,900

LUXEMBOURG
1,950

BOHEMIA AND
MORAVIA
78,150

SLOVAKIA
68,000

FRANCE
77,320

SWITZERLAND

AUSTRIA
50,000

HUNGARY
550,000

ROMANIA
271,000

ITALY
7,680

YUGOSLAVIA
56,200

*Adriatic Sea*

BULGARIA
0

*Mediterranean Sea*

GREECE
60,000

# The Camps

- (E) Extermination Camp
- (C) Concentration Camp
- (O) Official Reception and Holding Centre
- (T) Transit Camp
- (F) Fortress Town and Show Camp
- (S) Slave Labour and Work Camp

GREAT BRITAIN

Channel Islands
Sylt (S)

FRANCE

Neutral territory

SWEDEN

Kaiserwald (C)

DENMARK

Baltic Sea

Provieniskis (C)

North Sea

Neuengamme (C)

Westerbork (T)

Ravensbrück (C)

Stutthof (C)

Vught (C)

NETHERLANDS

Sachsenhausen (C)

Treblinka (E)

Bergen-Belsen (O)

Chelmno (E)

POLAND

Dora/Nordhausen (C)

Gross Rosen (C)

Sobibor (E)

Buchenwald (C)

Plaszow (S)

Majdanek (EC)

Drancy (T)

GERMANY

Theresienstadt (F)

Auschwitz/Birkenau (EC)

Flossenbürg (C)

CZECHOSLOVAKIA

Belzec (E)

Natzweiler (C)

Dachau (C)

FRANCE

Mauthausen (C)

AUSTRIA

HUNGARY

SWITZERLAND

San Sabba (C)

ROMANIA

ITALY

Jasenovac (C)

YUGOSLAVIA

Adriatic Sea

Mediterranean Sea

# Acknowledgements

The research for this book was conducted over a number of years in many archives, libraries and research institutes in Israel, Europe, Britain and America. My indebtedness to the work of countless scholars, too numerous to mention here, will be apparent from the notes. As one of the six historians appointed to the Vatican Historical Commission to study the role of Pius XII during the Holocaust, I also benefited from access to many sources in at least seven languages that proved helpful in the writing of this book. During the first six months of the millennial year, 2000, I was fortunate enough to be a visiting professor at the Netherlands Institute for Advanced Studies (NIAS) in Wassenaar. I wish to thank Professor Wesseling and his gracious staff for their hospitality and assistance. This project was originally proposed to me by Toby Mundy and supervised by Rebecca Wilson of Weidenfeld and Nicolson, whose suggestions were most useful. I gratefully acknowledge the efforts of Frances Bruce in deciphering my handwritten text and putting it into a readable format. I owe a special debt to Trudy Gold, Director of Holocaust Education at the London Jewish Cultural Institute for help and encouragement in facilitating my task at critical moments. I also learned much from my earlier work with the Institute in writing the text for the educational pack *Lessons of the Holocaust* (1997), now widely used in British schools; and in collaborating with Rex Bloomstein in co-making the film *Understanding the Holocaust* for which I also wrote the script. As always, I owe a debt of gratitude to my wife Daniella and my three children for their patient understanding in accepting my single-minded dedication to completing this project. This book is dedicated to my mother Sabina, born in Cracow ninety years ago, who always set me an example of how one can overcome adversity with fortitude and spirit.

Robert Solomon Wistrich
London/Jerusalem
December 2000

# Introduction

The missionaries of Christianity had said in effect: You have no
right to live among us as Jews. The secular rulers who followed
had proclaimed: You have no right to live among us. The German
Nazis had at last decreed: You have no right to live.

**Raul Hilberg** *The Destruction of the European Jews* (1961)

The Holocaust was an unprecedented crime against humanity,
which aimed at the total annihilation of the entire Jewish population of Europe, down to the last man, woman and child. It was
the planned, deliberate policy decision of a powerful state, the
Nazi Reich, which mobilised all its resources to destroy an
entire people. The Jews were not condemned to die for their
religious beliefs or for their political opinions. Nor were they
an economic or military threat to the Nazi state. They were
killed not for what they had done but for the simple fact of their
birth.

To be born a Jew in the eyes of Hitler and the Nazi regime
meant that one was defined *a priori* as not being a human being
and therefore as unworthy of life. There were other innocent
victims of Nazi racial ideology: gypsies who were considered to
be racially impure were sent to the gas chambers; Russians,
Poles and other occupied nations in the East were reduced
to slavery. Even those ethnic Germans who were branded as
mentally or physically defective were put to death until a public
outcry moderated this policy. We know that under the Nazi
regime, the SS, the *Einsatzgruppen*, the Wehrmacht, the Order
Police and the guards in the death camps practised brutality on
a hitherto unknown scale; that they mowed down row upon
row of shivering, half-naked adults and smashed to pieces the
heads of Jewish infants without pity or remorse; that they built

a vast system of concentration camps and death camps whose sole purpose was the production of corpses on an industrial scale.

The question is, why? Why were Jews worked to death on senseless, unproductive tasks, even when the Reich was suffering an acute labour shortage? Why were skilled Jewish armaments workers killed in the camps despite the pressing military needs of the Wehrmacht? Why did the Nazis insist they were fighting an omnipotent 'Jewish' power even as their mass murder of the Jews revealed the powerlessness of their enemy?

At the heart of this seeming mystery lay a millenarian ideology or *Weltanschauung* (world-view) which proclaimed that 'the Jew' was the source of all evils – especially internationalism, pacifism, democracy and Marxism; that he was responsible for Christianity, the Enlightenment and Freemasonry. The Jew was branded 'a ferment of decomposition', formlessness, chaos and 'racial degeneration'. Jews were identified with the inner fragmentation of urban civilisation, the dissolving acid of critical rationalism and the loosening of morality. They stood behind the 'rootless cosmopolitanism' of international capital and the threat of world revolution. They were the *Weltfeind* – the 'world enemy' against which National Socialism defined its own grandiose racial Utopia of a Thousand-Year Reich.

In Hitler's genocidal racist ideology, the redemption (*Erlösung*) of the Germans and of 'Aryan' humanity depended upon the 'final solution' (*Endlösung*) of the 'Jewish Question'. Unless the demonic 'world enemy' was finally annihilated, there would be no 'peace' in a Europe that had to be united under Germanic leadership; a continent in which Germany fulfilled its natural destiny and expanded to the East to create *Lebensraum* (living space) for its own people. The Second World War that Hitler initiated was simultaneously a war for territorial hegemony and a battle against the mythical Jewish enemy.

War made the Holocaust a concrete possibility. The victories of the Wehrmacht brought millions of Jews for the first time under the heel of German power. The task of annihilating them in cold blood was delegated by Hitler to the SS under the Reichsführer Heinrich Himmler and his closest subordinate Reinhard Heydrich. As early as 1939 a so-called 'euthanasia programme', responsible to Hitler and the Führer Chancellery, was initiated to eliminate nearly 90,000 ethnic Germans deemed 'unfit to live' because they were physically or mentally 'defective'. This programme, temporarily halted in 1941, proved to be a training ground for the 'Final Solution'. In late 1941 its personnel, apparatus and experience in killing by poison gas were transferred to death camps in Poland to be used against the Jews.

The Holocaust required more than an apocalyptic ideology of anti-Semitism in order to be implemented. It was equally the product of the most modern and technically developed society in Europe – one with a highly organised bureaucracy. The streamlined, industrialised mass killings carried out in death camps like Auschwitz and Treblinka were a *novum* in European and world history. But millions of Jews were also killed by the Germans and their helpers, using more primitive, 'archaic' methods in Russia, eastern Europe and the Balkans. The *Einsatzgruppen* and police battalions hunted down Jews and executed them in gruesome pit-killings, in forests, ravines and trenches. Russians, Poles, Serbs and Ukrainians, although not earmarked for *systematic* mass murder, also suffered decimation in large numbers. Three million Soviet prisoners of war would die in German captivity.

Some, like Daniel Goldhagen, have argued that the Germans carried out these murders because they were Germans; their political culture and mindset had already been pre-programmed by an 'eliminationist anti-Semitism' that existed since the mid-nineteenth century. That proposition seems to me unconvincing. Before Hitler, *völkisch* racist anti-Semitism had not made great inroads in Germany, though it was far from being a negligible quantity. Anti-Semitism had been much stronger and more influential in Tsarist Russia, Romania or the Habsburg Monarchy and its successor states, especially Poland, Slovakia and Austria. Germany before 1933 was still a state based on the rule of law, where Jews achieved remarkable economic success, were well integrated into society, enjoyed equal rights and decisively shaped its modernist culture.

Hitler's rise to power would not have been possible without the carnage of the First World War, the traumatic impact of German military defeat, the humiliation of the Versailles Treaty, the economic crises of the Weimar Republic and the fear of communist revolution. Anti-Semitism, while central to Hitler, Goebbels, Himmler, Streicher and other Nazi leaders, was not the main vote-catcher of the movement. But once racist anti-Semitism became the official state ideology of the Third Reich, reinforced by an extraordinarily powerful propaganda apparatus and a barrage of anti-Jewish laws, its impact was devastating.

The receptiveness of Germans (and other Europeans) to the demonisation of the Jews after 1933 owed a great deal to the much older tradition of Christian anti-Judaism, which went back to the Middle Ages. The Nazis did not need to invent the prevailing images of 'the Jew' as a usurer, blasphemer, traitor, ritual murderer, dangerous conspirator against Christendom and deadly threat to the foundations of morality. Both secular rulers and the Christian churches had ensured that (until the French Revolution) Jews were pariahs in European society, condemned to a position of inferiority and subordination. Racism, too, had been used in Catholic Spain in the fifteenth century to justify the removal even of converted Jews from public functions and positions of economic influence.

The Protestant Reformation, especially in Germany, brought little improvement in the status of the Jews. Luther's anti-

Jewish diatribes would indeed be a contributing factor in later German Protestant complicity with Hitler's deeds and the prevailing silence during the Third Reich's anti-Semitic persecutions. Catholics, too, were increasingly implicated in anti-Semitic political movements in France, Austria, Hungary, Slovakia, Poland and other European states in the nineteenth and twentieth centuries. During the Holocaust, many Catholic clerics, like the Protestants, were often indifferent or even hostile to Jews, though there were also cases of heroic resistance to Nazism and rescue by 'righteous Gentiles'. The deep ambivalence of the Vatican and the Christian churches cannot, however, be understood without taking into account the long-standing 'teaching of contempt' that had deep roots in the New Testament itself and in the teachings of the Church Fathers. Nazism, though ultimately determined to uproot Christianity, could build on the negative stereotypes about Jews and Judaism that the Churches had disseminated over centuries.

The Germans did not carry out the Holocaust alone, although under Nazi rule they were undoubtedly its spearhead and driving force. They found many willing collaborators and 'helpers' among Lithuanians, Latvians, Ukrainians, Hungarians, Romanians, Croats and other European nationalities, especially when it came to killing Jews. Austrians (who had been annexed to the German Reich in 1938) formed a wholly disproportionate number of the SS killers, death camp commandants and personnel involved in the 'Final Solution'. Even official France 'collaborated' eagerly, not in the killing of Jews but in their deportation eastwards and in the passage of draconian racist legislation.

The Holocaust was a *pan-European* event that could not have happened unless millions of Europeans by the late 1930s had not wished to see an end to the age-old Jewish presence in their midst. This consensus was especially strong in the countries of east-central Europe where the bulk of Jewry lived and still retained its own national characteristics and cultural distinctiveness. But there was also a growing anti-Semitism in western Europe and America, tied to the hardships caused by the Great Depression, increased xenophobia, fear of immigration and the influence of fascist ideas.

This hostility would influence the unwillingness of British and American decision-makers to undertake any significant rescue efforts on behalf of European Jewry during the Holocaust. Already in the 1930s the quota-system in the United States had precluded any mass immigration of Jews from central and eastern Europe that might have relieved some of the enormous pressures on Jewry. British concerns about Arab unrest in Palestine following increased Jewish immigration in the 1930s to the 'Jewish National Home', led to another major refuge being denied and sealed off. Hitler duly noted these responses and the appeasement policy of the West before 1939, drawing his own conclusions: that his expansionist ambitions could be implemented without too great a risk and that the West would not interfere with his increasingly radical anti-Jewish measures.

The Jews of Europe, on the eve of the Holocaust, found themselves in a trap from which there appeared to be no escape. They were faced by the most menacing and dangerous enemy in their history – a dynamic great power in the heart of the European continent that openly sought their destruction. Its influence was felt in neighbouring states, especially to the east and southeast of Europe which were passing anti-Semitic laws of their own to restrict Jewish rights and pushing for the removal or emigration of their Jewish populations. Moreover, the three million Jews in Communist Russia were cut off from the rest of the Jewish world; yet the identification of Jews with Bolshevism had become a highly dangerous political myth that would eventually fuel the mass murders carried out by the Nazis and their allies on the Eastern Front after June 1941.

The Jews of America were also limited in what they could do

for European Jewry, by a combination of their own insecurity, fear of anti-Semitism and the reality of American isolationism prior to late 1941. The Jews of Palestine were still a relatively small community under British control and faced with a hostile Arab majority. The Zionist movement, while growing in the 1930s, was too fragmented politically and fractious to be effective.

The Nazi myth of the Jews as a well-organised, international power with clearly defined goals and common 'racial' interests could not therefore have been further removed from reality. The Jews were in fact disorganised, relatively powerless, lacking in solidarity or any agreed political agenda. Before and during the Holocaust they did not have a State, an army, a common territory or flag, let alone a coherent organisational centre.

With rare exceptions, such as Denmark, Finland, Italy or Bulgaria (which had only relatively small Jewish populations), the Jews would moreover be cruelly disappointed by the lack of solidarity of most of their Gentile neighbours once the dark night of persecution descended upon them. Even more bitter was the ease with which the protection of European states and governments, which they had loyally served and trusted, was withdrawn and their rights sacrificed as if they were absolute pariahs, beyond the pale of civilisation. Many Jews were reluctant to confront these harsh facts and draw the necessary conclusions before it was too late. Hitler's war found them trapped and virtually defenceless against a ruthless enemy bent on their total destruction in a world largely indifferent to their fate.

From this searing and potentially shattering trauma, the Jewish people nonetheless rose up after the Second World War to establish their own independent state. Other nations and minorities also learned the price of powerlessness after the Second World War and have fought to achieve their freedom from totalitarian tyranny and foreign oppression. But the Holocaust also has more universal lessons. It reminds us that xenophobia, racism and anti-Semitism can lead to group violence and atrocities on an unimaginable scale; that any society, however culturally, scientifically and technologically advanced, can become totally criminal once it loses its ability to distinguish between right and wrong. The Holocaust underlines the danger of trusting in the idolatry of power when it lacks any ethical restraint. It drives home the lesson that each individual is responsible for his or her own conscience and fate. It is a warning from history that obeying orders can be no excuse for criminal acts.

If there is a general lesson, then we must learn that evil can and must be resisted in its early stages; that we always have choices and there can be no place for racism and anti-Semitism in a civilised society. Thinking about the Holocaust is like staring into an abyss and hoping it will not stare back. It is the ultimate extreme case, a black hole of history that not only challenges our facile assumptions about modernity and progress but questions our very sense of what it means to be human.

# I    *Anti-Semitism and the Jews*

After Satan Christians have no greater enemies than the Jews ...
They pray many times each day that God may destroy us through
pestilence, famine and war, aye, that all beings and creatures may
rise up with them against the Christians.

**Abraham a Sancta Clara (1683)**, Viennese Catholic preacher

I hold the Jewish race to be the born enemy of pure humanity and
everything noble in it. It is certain that it is running us Germans
into the ground, and I am perhaps the last German who knows
how to hold himself upright in the face of Judaism, which already
rules everything.

**Richard Wagner (1881)**

We therefore raise our voice, Polish Catholics. Our feelings towards
the Jews have not undergone a change. We have not stopped
regarding them as the political, economic and ideological enemies
of Poland ... [but] we do not wish to be Pilates. We do not have
the means to act against the German murders, we cannot advise,
we can save no one – but we *protest* from the depths of our hearts,
overcome with pity, indignation, and dread. This protest is
demanded of us by God. God who does not permit murder ... The
blood of the defenceless cries out for vengeance to heaven. He
among us who does not support this protest is not a Catholic.

**Zofia Kossak-Szczucka**, *Protest* (A pamphlet of August 1942)

Mass killings go back to the dawn of human history. Throughout
recorded time there have been countless massacres, some on
religious grounds, others for political or territorial reasons.
Native peoples have been exterminated in colonial wars. Millions of black Africans were sold into slavery. The colonisation
of North America, Australia, Africa and other parts of the globe

by expanding Western societies involved constant dis-
placement, despoliation and sometimes even the genocide of
indigenous populations in the name of empire, plunder and
'progress'. In the early twentieth century, the Turkish massacre
of over a million Armenians during the First World War marked
a new stage of brutality.[1] However, if the number of victims
alone were to be our point of departure, then pride of place
might go to those unfortunate Soviet citizens who were shot,
starved or worked to death in the Gulags of Stalinist Russia as
'enemies of the people', in the name of Marxist ideology.[2] The
victims of this 'auto-genocide' that a totalitarian regime
inflicted on its own subjects may have been as many as twenty
million people. (While staggeringly high, this was a much lower
percentage of all Soviet citizens than the one-third of all Jewish
people in the world who were killed by the Nazis.) No less
horrifying were the events in Maoist China (the full story has
yet to be told) and on a much smaller scale in Communist
Cambodia during the 1970s. The slaughter in Rwanda and
'ethnic cleansing' in ex-Yugoslavia in the 1990s further demonstrate that the dark genocidal chapter in human history is far
from over.

Even during the Second World War, several genocides
occurred, though of different magnitudes. Approximately three
million Polish Gentiles fell victim to the Nazis, as did a similar
number of Russian prisoners of war who were starved to death by
the Germans. Both groups were used as guinea pigs at Auschwitz
before the gassing of Jews began. The German war in the east
involved much more than exterminating the Jews – it was
initially conceived as part of a larger grand design for a radical
and complete racial restructuring, in which Poles, Russians and
Ukrainians would be expropriated, deported or killed.[3] Gypsies,
too, were earmarked for destruction if they were deemed racially
impure. Between 250,000 and half a million gypsies were sent
to their deaths between 1939 and 1945, coterminous with the

Holocaust. Gypsies (Roma and Sinti) did not, of course, hold the same place as did Jews or Judaism either in Christian consciousness or in the Nazi world-view. Prejudice and hostility towards their nomadic way of life was nonetheless widespread and in some ways comparable to the perception of Jews as aliens in Christian Europe.[4]

The Nazis were particularly hostile to the gypsies as an 'anti-social' element and as 'people of different blood' who fell under the Nuremberg race laws of 1935. A year later, some groups of gypsies were sent to Dachau concentration camp. Heinrich Himmler's decree of December 1937 permitted their arrest on the extremely elastic grounds of asocial behaviour, even without the commission of any criminal act. Further legislation in 1938 to deal with the 'gypsy plague', aimed at a strict separation between 'pure' and 'mixed blood' gypsies, as well as between Germans and gypsies.[5] During the war, Nazi policy became even more radicalised and in the autumn of 1941, 5000 Austrian gypsies were deported to the Lodz ghetto. Then, in early 1942, some gypsies were murdered along with Jews in the Chelmno death camp. Gypsies started arriving in Auschwitz-Birkenau on 26 February 1943. A great many died of hunger, disease and from 'medical experiments'; later in 1944, women and children were gassed. In the Baltic States and the Soviet Union, gypsies were murdered by the *Einsatzgruppen*; in Yugoslavia by the Ustashe regime; in Hungary they were persecuted and rounded up the Arrow Cross fascists. In France, they were interned and later sent to camps in Germany. Two thirds of the Polish gypsies died under Nazi occupation.

The Nazis regarded 'the fight against the Gypsy Menace' after 1939 as 'a matter of race' and insisted on the need to 'separate once and for all the gypsy race (*Zigeunertum*) from the German nation (*Volkstum*)', to prevent the danger of miscegenation. In that respect, there was an ideological link between the murder of Jews and gypsies, both of them forming part of a composite

Nazi vision of radical ethnic cleansing or 'purification' of the *Volksgemeinschaft*. Indeed, the settlement of the 'Gypsy Question' was conceived from the outset in the framework of 'knowledge stemming from ethnological research' under the jurisdiction of Heinrich Himmler as Reichsführer SS and chief of the German police. The fate of the gypsies, as Himmler made clear in September 1942, was not a matter for the law or the courts, any more than that of the Jews. Hence they were totally at the mercy of the police and SS and liable to be thrown at any time into concentration camps. The accusations against them of hereditary racial inferiority, economic parasitism or sexual 'immorality' threatening to the general German population overlapped with the demagogy of anti-Semitism.

As with the Jews, it was wartime that provided the cover for the annihilation of all gypsies, except those Sinti and Lalleri tribes classified as 'racially pure'.[6] This was, then, a case of genocide comparable at some points to the Holocaust yet different in its motivation and scale. The gypsies were deemed a 'social menace' though never a total and universal enemy like the Jews, engaged in a universal conspiracy against Germany and the 'Aryan' world. The 'Gypsy Question' had, for example, only marginal importance in the Nazi political agenda and Hitler himself referred to gypsies on only two occasions, in stark contrast to his relentless obsession with the Jews.[7] Moreover, 'racially pure' gypsies were never regarded as a danger to the German people and were even thought of as having noble blood. Thus, the horrible crime against the gypsies as a social group did not aim in principle at the *total* annihilation of an entire people.

The Holocaust was unprecedented – as compared to other genocides – because it was the planned, deliberate policy decision of a powerful state that had mobilised all its resources to destroy the *entire* Jewish people. In this diabolical aim the Germans were almost successful in Europe and only their mili-

ANTI-SEMITISM AND THE JEWS

tary defeat prevented its gruesome completion. By 1945 two thirds of European Jewry had been wiped out by the Nazis, leaving only a remnant of the ancient Jewish culture that had existed on European soil for nearly two millennia. One of the more remarkable aspects of this mass murder was that Jews never constituted (except in the paranoid Nazi mindset) any economic, political or military threat to the German state. On the contrary, had there been a Nobel Prize for passionate identification with German language and culture before 1933, the Jews would surely have won it. During the First World War they made great efforts to demonstrate their patriotic loyalty and validate their Germanness (*Deutschtum*) on the battlefield. Before the rise of Hitler, they had felt very much at home in what they regarded as a well-ordered state, based on the rule of law.

If anything, there were striking affinities between Germans and Jews that seemed to augur well for their common future: a great respect for education, hard work, the importance of the family and a marked talent for abstract, speculative thinking. Both Germans and Jews were considered highly musical and often regarded by other nations as being both indispensable and troublesome, aggressive and prone to self-pity. *Judenhass* (Judaeophobia) and *Deutschenhass* (Germanophobia) had more than a few attributes in common. But, as Freud shrewdly observed, the 'narcissism of little differences' can produce great hatreds; proximity, affinity and assimilation may in certain circumstances give rise to an intense and irrational backlash. The German 'Jewish Question' of the nineteenth and twentieth centuries was precisely such a case. It was an amalgam of false perceptions, stereotypes and delusions that had many sources: Christian anti-Judaism, neo-Romantic *völkisch* mysticism and a racist obsession with Jews and other 'aliens' that assumed a special virulence in Nazi ideology.[8]

This shadow-boxing with imaginary demons and projective

*Angst* persuaded the novelist Jacob Wassermann that Judae-ophobia was *the* German national hatred – a self-induced patho-logical delusion that was not only irrational but impenetrable. Germans, he concluded in 1921, were emotionally resistant to accepting Jews as their equals and given to scapegoating them for every crisis, setback or defeat. Jew-hatred embodied every conceivable sexual frustration, social anxiety, jealousy, ani-mosity, bloodlust and greedy instinct that Germans were other-wise unable to exorcise.[9] Thirty years earlier, the German philosopher Friedrich Nietzsche had been equally severe, heaping aristocratic contempt on the Jew-baiters of the 1880s as *Schlechtweggekommene* – life's losers and born misfits, bungled, botched and envious creatures, eaten up with neurotic *ressentiment*.[10]

This verdict was all the more remarkable since Nietzsche had at one time been under the spell of the composer Richard Wagner – the *fons et origo* of modern German anti-Semitism. Moreover, to compound the irony, his own rhetoric about the *Übermensch* (Superman), the 'blond beast' and the 'will to power' would later be eagerly annexed by fascists and Nazis. Indeed, Nietzsche's relentless assault on Judaeo-Christian mor-ality did provide one of the deeper sources of inspiration for the Nazi Revolution. It was, after all, Nietzsche who had branded priestly Judaism and the teachings of the Gospels as the begin-ning of 'the slave-revolt in morals'. The Jews, he explained with oracular certitude, had engineered the greatest *transvaluation of values* in world history, two thousand years earlier in Roman-occupied Palestine. It was a most fateful and catastrophic event – responsible in his eyes for all the 'decadent' modern ideologies of liberalism, rationalism, socialism and levelling mass dem-ocracy.[11] In the 1930s it would not be difficult for fascists and Nazis – intoxicated with the hubris of self-deification – to adapt Nietzschean ideas about modern decadence to their own totali-tarian-nihilist agenda.[12]

It mattered little that few Nazis had actually read Nietzsche or paid attention to his contempt for the Germans and admiration for Jews. The attraction lay in the prospect of transgression on a grand scale, the Nietzschean smashing of those remaining taboos that still reined in the barbarian warrior-lust lurking under an increasingly thin 'civilised' veneer. Nazism, (mis)understood as a Nietzschean experiment, seemed to be offering to the German people a Faustian pact with the Devil. In return for destroying traditional Christian moral restraints, perhaps they would be granted future hegemony over the earthly kingdoms which other European powers had already partitioned among themselves.

The demonisation of the Jews and Judaism assumed immense symbolic importance in this endeavour. The Nazi leaders (and especially Hitler) were obsessed with the doctrine of the 'Chosen People' and its imagined secret power. They read into it a prefiguration of their own will to set the races apart under an iron law, until the end of time.[13] The singularity of the Jews, and the mystery of their survival over thousands of years, was treated as if it were a vindication of the eternal truths of blood and race.[14] Nazi racism can indeed be seen as a blasphemous gloss on, or perhaps even as a grotesque parody of, Judaic chosenness. To put it bluntly, there could not be two chosen peoples. The character of Hitler's messianic pretensions necessitated the removal of that very people who had embodied chosenness for three millennia. The Jews were responsible (or rather guilty) in his eyes for having invented the very notion of a moral conscience, in defiance of all healthy, natural instincts.[15] They had bequeathed this noxious ideal to Christianity and communism, with their contending dreams of the brotherhood of man, human equality and justice. Though outwardly incompatible, these world-views were for the Nazis two sides of the same Judaic coin – egalitarian ideals that had caused incalculable suffering, persecution and intolerance. Moreover, the Jews were accused of having deliberately encouraged the mixing of races and devitalising doctrines of democracy that could only destroy the foundations of human culture itself. For the Nazis, the world had to be liberated from such 'evil' principles so that mankind could return once more to its pristine natural order. Thus the planned, systematic eradication of Judaic values *preceded* the physical annihilation of the Jewish people and was its necessary prerequisite.

In its own perverse way, Nazism did indeed grasp something fundamental about Judaism and the Jews. For at the heart of Judaism stood the belief in a single, all-powerful deity who had created the universe and installed mankind at its heart to uphold the *moral* law. The revelation of the Divine Law and the Ten Commandments at Mount Sinai had made the Biblical Israelites into a covenanted people, chosen by God for a distinctive ethical mission. They had been chosen not to conquer an empire but to carry a divine revelation which affirmed that man was created in the image of his Maker; that each human being carried a divine spark, and that each life was sacred. 'Thou shalt not kill' rang out as the clarion call for any civilised moral code of mankind (one that Nazism would exactly invert) along with universal injunctions against adultery, theft, blasphemy and the worship of false gods. In the Mosaic teaching, special attention was paid to the rights of the weak and oppressed, the orphan, the widowed, the enslaved and the stranger within the gates. Judaism was in that respect the antithesis of the xenophobic racist nationalism espoused by fascists and Nazis. At the heart of the Torah (the Five Books of Moses) was the demand for 'justice, and only justice'. Whenever the biblical Israelites were in danger of backsliding and whoring after false gods, a prophet would arise to call them back to the straight path. The cry of Amos: 'Let justice roll down as waters, and righteousness as a mighty stream,' is the leitmotif of biblical prophecy. The Amidah prayer of *Rosh Hashanah* (the Jewish New Year) makes the fulfilment of God's kingdom *in this world* conditional on the disappearance of arrogance, injustice and oppression from the face of the earth. In the Judaic conception it is that ideal which is the ultimate goal of human history, one wholly incompatible with the Nazi vision of the world. The Torah (completed by the Talmud and rabbinical teachings through the centuries) became the constitution and 'law of life' of the Jewish people, holding it together through two millennia of dispersion. It was their 'portable homeland' in the profound words of the German-Jewish poet Heinrich Heine and also the mark of their vocation as a distinct people among the nations.

Only in the era of emancipation in the nineteenth century (primarily in the democratic societies of the West) did Jews begin to redefine themselves as a denationalised *religious* group, comparable in certain respects to Catholics or Protestants.[16] Yet the bulk of the Jewish diaspora, concentrated as it was in compact and dense settlements in eastern Europe, continued to preserve its distinct languages (Yiddish, Ladino, etc.), a social code, a value system, customs and laws very different from the surrounding peoples' as well as stubbornly maintaining its separate religious beliefs. The Jewish self-understanding of being a 'people apart' was further reinforced by a strong sense of continuity of persecutions to which they had been subjected during their long exile, following the destruction of the Second Temple (AD 70). Thus a sense of being linked in a common community of suffering and fate reinforced their diasporic identity.

Even before the loss of national independence nearly two thousand years ago, Jews had already displayed formidable powers of resistance and survivalist instincts against the sway of vast ancient empires such as Egypt, Assyria, Babylon and Persia. Under Judah Maccabee and the priestly clan of the Hasmoneans, they had revolted against the cultural and political yoke of an all-conquering Hellenism, leading in 142 BC to the brief re-establishment of Jewish political sovereignty in Judea. Subsequently the Jews would rise in a series of unsuccessful revolts against the military might of imperial Rome, preferring martyrdom to the betrayal of their heritage and faith. It was in this messianic atmosphere of repeated Jewish rebellions against a fiercely repressive Roman rule that Christianity emerged in first-century Palestine, as the teaching of a dissident sect originating out of Judaism. Not only Jesus of Nazareth but also his mother Mary, all of his disciples and the apostle Paul were born as Jews. The new faith that grew out of the teachings of Jews (as recounted in the Gospels) was to have a powerful influence on the subsequent fate of the dispersed and exiled Jewish people in what would become, after Constantine the Great, an increasingly Christianised Europe from the fourth century AD.[17] On the one hand, Jews were permitted to exist with some protection from the Church and secular rulers in the Middle Ages; the other side of the same coin was their abject theological status as an 'accursed people' and 'murderers of God'.[18]

In the New Testament one can find a number of references to 'the Jews' as children of 'your father the Devil' or to the 'synagogue of Satan'. Nor is it an accident that Judas, the disciple alleged to have betrayed Jesus for filthy lucre, would eventually emerge as the collective incarnation of the Jewish people and a universal byword for treachery and cowardice. In the writings of the Church Fathers from the fourth century onwards, Jews are consistently and malevolently depicted as 'murderers of the prophets', 'adversaries and haters of God', 'enemies of the faith' or 'advocates of the Devil'; they were portrayed as vipers, slanderers, scoffers, 'leaven of the Pharisees'; carnal, sensual, dissolute, mercenary, and corrupt; they were supposedly driven exclusively by sex, money and power – the things of *this* world that Christianity professed to despise.[19] This language of invective continued to echo down the centuries, with greater or lesser intensity (according to country and circumstances) throughout most of the lands of Christendom. The main effect of these savage polemics was to humiliate, discredit and *delegitimise* the Judaic parent religion from which Christianity itself had sprung.[20] Such a comprehensive negation demonstrated that Judaism had no *raison d'être* after the appearance of Christ, for the Church had now become the 'true' Israel and repository of the New Covenant. The divine blessings and promises given to the Israelites in the Hebrew Bible (appropriated as Christian Holy Scriptures and revered as the anticipation and validation of the Gospels) were reserved for the Church itself and for 'God's people' (the Gentile Christians). The curses and the maledictions were applied to the reprobate Jews. Had they not been abandoned and punished by God with permanent wandering and exile, for their blindness in failing to recognise Jesus as Messiah? Would they not continue to be persecuted until they converted to the true faith?

After the First Crusade of 1096 (when the crusading armies massacred Jews in the Rhineland as 'infidels' and 'Christ-killers', before slaughtering both Muslims and Jews during their conquest of Jerusalem), the theological charge of deicide became increasingly explosive, blending with irrational popular superstitions.[21] The so-called blood libel that spread from Norwich in England (in the eleventh century) to the European Continent, was based on the pure fabrication that Jews required the fresh blood of Christian children to make their *matzot* (unleavened bread) at Passover time, which usually coincided with the Christian Easter.[22] The unexplained disappearance of any Christian child at Easter could, as a result, provoke suspicions that it had been kidnapped and killed by Jews. Such counter-factual myths produced ritual murder trials, pogroms and violence against Jewish communities even in the nineteenth and twentieth centuries. No less destructive was the irrational fantasy that Jews deliberately and malevolently pierced Holy Communion wafers to make them bleed (the so-called 'desecration of the Host') as if they were compulsively repeating and re-enacting the crucifixion of Christ. Other ominous medieval accusations included the allegation that Jews had poisoned the wells in order to provoke the bubonic plagues of the 'Black Death', which decimated European society in the fourteenth century. Jews in the Middle Ages were also persistently depicted as bloodsucking usurers, as sorcerers, blasphemers, insatiable enemies of Christ and agents of the Devil, secretly plotting the downfall of Christendom. Only on a soil watered for centuries by such a fearsome demonology could the Holocaust have been conceived, let alone carried out with so little opposition.[23]

Even the great German Protestant reformer Martin Luther, despite his devastating assault on the corruption, falsehoods and superstitions abounding in the papal Rome of his day, could not free himself of the demonic anti-Jewish image that he had inherited from the medieval Church.[24] In his diatribe of 1543, 'Concerning the Jews and their Lies' (cynically used to justify the Nazi burning of synagogues in 1938), Luther began by reiterating the traditional Christian view of the Jews as a 'damned' and 'rejected' people. His 'honest advice' to German rulers was to set Jewish houses of worship on fire, break down their homes, deprive them of prayer books, forbid their rabbis to teach ('under threat of death') and confiscate their passports and travelling privileges. The Jews had to be 'stopped from usury' by being made 'to earn their bread by the sweat of their noses' through hard labour in the fields. Luther proposed that the secular rulers of German principalities follow the example of other nations such as France, Spain and Bohemia by expropriating the property of the Jews, to 'drive them out of the country for all time'. This programme of 'severe mercy' (as Luther called it) 'ought to be done for the honour of God and of Christianity in order that God may see that we are Christians, and that we have not wittingly tolerated or approved of such public lying, cursing, and blaspheming of His Son and His Christians...'[25]

Like the relentlessly negative stereotypes of medieval Catholicism that had shaped his outlook, Luther's Protestant Reformation in Germany with its hateful depiction of the satanic Jews, created a powerful arsenal of myths, images and fantasies on which Nazi anti-Semitism could build. Long before the Nazis, the Jews had been demonised in theological polemics, in sermons, medieval mystery plays, in the visual arts, in fiction and in popular folklore as mysterious and threatening incarnations of evil. They were the most potent and hated collective 'other' against which Christian Europe could define itself.[26] At times, they seemed raised to the status of a metaphysical abstraction, embodying the most sinister forces of heresy, carnality and black magic. 'The Jew' resembled a creature of a different order, scarcely human at all. Nazism secularised and sharply radicalised this image but invented relatively little that was new at the level of basic stereotypes.

The biological racism of the Nazis did introduce a relatively new element into Judaeophobia, though this apparent innovation also had Christian precedents. For example, in fifteenth century Catholic Spain, the 'purity of blood' statutes had been introduced to distinguish 'Old' from 'New Christians' (conversos or Jewish converts) and to help root out 'Judaising' influences.[27] The manic hunt by the Spanish Inquisition for crypto-Jews, the violent pogroms that began in the late fourteenth century, the autos-da-fé and the terrifying persecution which led to the mass expulsion of 150,000 Jews in 1492, were an early modern foregleam of the Nazi genocide.[28] It was surely significant that this witch-hunt occurred in precisely that European society where Jews had enjoyed the most remarkable 'Golden Age, a success story that anticipated the German-Austrian-Jewish 'symbiosis' of the nineteenth and twentieth centuries. In medieval Spain, too, Jews had already gone far down the road of acculturation, social integration and extensive conversion. They had attained remarkable heights in literature, philosophy, commerce, the professions and even in government. The prosperity and success of the Spanish Jews and 'New Christians' aroused the envy of their rivals as well as the hostility of the Catholic Church, which feared the seeds of heresy. No less importantly, the decision to exclude both Jews and Muslims provided a focal point for Spain's ambitious rulers to proclaim the unity of the nation, which had completed its 'reconquest' from Islam under the banner of the Holy Catholic faith. As elsewhere, in Europe, the imminent prospect of expropriating substantial Jewish wealth provided a decidedly material incentive for both rulers and populace alike.

In contrast to the expulsions of Jews from England (1290), France (1306, 1332), from the German principalities and then from Spain and Portugal (end of the fifteenth century), the kingdom of Poland was initially very welcoming to the Jews as an urban, commercial element who could help rebuild its shattered economy after the Mongol invasions. From the fourteenth century until the partitions of Poland in the late eighteenth century, Jews would enjoy an unprecedentedly wide degree of autonomy under the protection of charters of liberty, guaranteed by successive Polish rulers. They were frequently employed by the Polish nobility as estate managers and tax collectors, often served as middlemen between landowners and peasants and played a similar intermediary role in the towns as traders and craftsmen. Poland would become in its imperial heyday, and still remain even in its decay, a leading centre of Ashkenazi Jewish scholarship and spirituality. On the other hand, the massacres associated with the name of Bogdan Chelmnicki, leader of a Ukrainian peasants revolt in 1648–9 against the Polish nobility, were a frightening reminder of the vulnerability of the Jews' position in the Polish lands. Between a quarter to a third of the Jewish population in the Ukraine and southern Poland were slaughtered by rampaging Ukrainian Cossacks. They were put to the sword as 'Christ-killers' and as tax-collecting middlemen serving the interests of the hated Polish landlords.²⁹

In western Europe, Jews definitively entered the modern era with the French Revolution of 1789. By sweeping away all the feudal privileges of the *ancien régime* (including the special position of the Catholic Church) the French National Assembly for the first time established Jewish civic equality in Europe. The revolutionary generation who emancipated the Jews in 1791 had been influenced by universalist Enlightenment ideals, an optimistic faith in reason, a generally cosmopolitan outlook and the belief that human beings could be made perfectible through education and a change in social conditions. The more radical strand of the Enlightenment offered to the Jews the promise of a new beginning, as long as they were willing to throw off the shackles of their own Judaic tradition. As the Comte de Clermont-Tonnerre pointedly told the French National Assembly in 1789: 'The Jews should be denied everything as a nation, but granted everything as individuals ... if they do not want this ... we shall then be compelled to expel them.'³⁰ In the course of the nineteenth century the Jews of France and western Europe were ready to accept this emancipation contract (orthodox Jews were an exception) although it involved abandoning a separate group identity. The attractions of unrivalled individual opportunities, freedom of movement, new career prospects and untrammelled entry into a modern secularised society proved difficult to resist.

By the end of the nineteenth century there was, however, a distinct backlash by conservative forces in France against the legacy of the 1789 revolution and its emancipation of the Jews. The Catholic Church linked the Jews with the secularising, anti-clerical Third Republic that had become dominant after 1880. The monarchists (who dreamed of a royalist restoration), aristocratic army officers bitter at their defeat by Prussia in 1870 and a motley crew of anti-Semites and nationalists hoped to overthrow the hated Republic. Their best opportunity came when a Jewish army officer from Alsace, Alfred Dreyfus, was accused in 1894 of betraying French military secrets to the German enemy. Dreyfus's guilt became a dogma not only for intransigent anti-Semites, convinced that every Jew was a potential 'Judas', but also for those on the Catholic and nationalist Right who believed that there had been a deliberate conspiracy to destroy the French nation.[31] The plot was supposedly hatched by Jews, helped by Freemasons, Protestants, anticlerical republican radicals and socialists. The myth of the all-powerful Jew (embodied by the Rothschild family and by 'Jewish' international high finance) acquired a new lease of life in the 1890s. The Dreyfus Affair in *fin de siècle* France proved an ideological matrix for the emergence of a wide variety of ultranationalist and proto-fascist ideas in Europe.[32] It was also a kind of dress rehearsal for the mob politics of Nazi-style anti-Semitism.

The term 'anti-Semitism' had itself been coined by the radical German journalist Wilhelm Marr in 1879, to mark it off from more traditional Christian forms of animosity towards Judaism. Indeed, Marr's 'anti-Semitism' (directed against Jews as an alien race of 'Semitic' exploiters) was noticeably hostile to supranational Catholicism and to monotheistic religion in general. In a mediocre if sensational pamphlet of 1879, he claimed that German society had already become 'judaised' (a code word for the victory of materialism, Mammon and laissez-faire capitalism); gloomily, he asserted that the Jews had conquered Germany by seizing control of its press and stock exchanges.[33] Similar charges were made in the same year by the Protestant court preacher, Adolf Stoecker, a powerful anti-Semitic orator who had just founded the lower middle-class Christian-Social party in Berlin, and by the illustrious Prussian conservative historian, Heinrich von Trietschke, who coined the anti-Semitic slogan much favoured by the Nazis: 'The Jews are our misfortune.' Imperial Germany would emerge as the favoured laboratory for ideological anti-Semites – both Christian and anti-Christian – in the years between 1880 and 1914.[34] While this Judaeophobia was by no means 'eliminationist' (in the sense claimed by Daniel Goldhagen), its extent and obsessive quality played a part in preparing the way for the tragedies to come.[35]

There were other fully fledged racist propagandists like the anticlerical Theodor Fritsch (1852–1933) whose *Handbook on the Jewish Question* was familiar to the young Hitler in Vienna before 1914. Fritsch was an indefatigable publicist, active in Saxony, who had founded the Hammer Publishing House for anti-Semitic literature in 1883 and a decade later produced a popular racist decalogue ('Ten Commandments for an Anti-Semite').[36] His catechism sternly warned Germans against having social, sexual, business or professional intercourse with Jews or consuming any Jewish writings, 'lest their lingering poison may unnerve and corrupt you and your family'. Fritsch's handbook went through more than forty editions, inspiring a number of Nazis, who later honoured him as an elder statesman. Other pre-1914 ideological anti-Semites highly regarded in the Third Reich included the orientalist scholar Paul de Lagarde (advocate of a virile Germanic and de-Judaised Christianity) who denounced the evils of Western liberalism, capitalism and parliamentarianism;[37] and Eugen Dühring, a former socialist and a vehement anti-Christian, who demanded radical measures to return Jews to the ghetto, by placing them under a discriminatory aliens' legislation. Dühring insisted that the Germanic-Nordic race could only fulfil its evolutionary destiny when it had finally thrown off the yoke of a 'Semitic' Judaeo-Christianity.[38] Even more influential was the expatriate Teutomaniac Englishman Houston Stewart Chamberlain, whose best-selling book, *The Foundations of the 19th Century* (1899), greatly appealed to the bombastic imperialism of the German emperor, Wilhelm II. Chamberlain, a passionate Wagnerian and philosophical dilettante, lived long enough to hail Hitler in 1923 as the future 'saviour' of Germany.[39]

Despite the growing weight of anti-Semitic ideologies in imperial Germany before 1914, the Second Reich still appeared to most Jews as a stable, prosperous and highly cultured society where their civil rights were respected. Similarly, in the rest of western and central Europe (including the more than 2 million Jews in Austria-Hungary), the prospects of integration seemed promising before the First World War. Yet, for many Jews, the war and its consequences would prove to be a cruel disappointment. The Jews in Galicia and those along the Russian war front soon found themselves fleeing for their lives, often punished as spies and traitors by the Tsarist high command or deported into the Russian interior. In Poland, at the end of the war in 1918, the proclamation of national independence was accompanied by the jarring music of pogroms against Jews, especially in places of mixed population, where their loyalties were deemed by Poles to be suspect.[40] Although the German army on the eastern front treated Jews reasonably well, a special census (*Judenzählung*) of Jewish soldiers engaged in active duty was undertaken in 1916 by the High Command. This was supposedly intended to verify rumours of shirking and black-marketeering. The results were never published, though 12,000 German Jews laid down their lives for the fatherland and a relatively high number won awards for bravery on the battle-field. Such sacrifices did not prevent the pernicious legend from circulating that Jews (and Marxists) had 'stabbed Germany in the back' during the war – a myth that became such a powerful propaganda weapon for Hitler and the German nationalist Right after 1918.

In November 1917, two events of decisive importance for modern Jewish history took place, which also have a bearing on events to come. The Bolshevik revolution in Russia overthrew the brief experiment in parliamentary democracy, led primarily by moderate Russian liberals and socialists. Although it consolidated the emancipation of Russian Jewry granted ten months earlier with the fall of tsarism, the immediate consequences of communist revolution were disastrous for Jews. They resulted in the worst pogroms hitherto recorded in Jewish history, with over 100,000 fatalities among the Russian and Ukrainian Jewish population between 1918 and 1921.[41] Most of the atrocities were committed by the anti-Bolshevik White reactionaries and by the Ukrainian nationalist army, for whom Jews had become synonymous with the communist revolution. Though this amalgam was plainly a myth, there were a disproportionate number of leading Bolsheviks of Jewish origin in key positions during the early days of the Russian Revolution. None of these 'non-Jewish' Jews identified in any way with Judaism, Jewish nationalism or Russian Jewry.[42] Similarly, most Russian and Ukrainian Jews did not sympathise at all with Communism. But the anti-Semitic savagery of the anti-Bolshevik pogromists eventually drove them into the arms of the Red revolution.[43] The impact of the Bolshevik spectre on Germany was to prove particularly fateful. After 1919, the newly created Nazi Party, along with the many right-wing forces in Germany (and far beyond its borders), assiduously propagated the myth of a Jewish-Bolshevik conspiracy to destroy Germany and Western Christian civilisation. This ideological fantasy was to become a central driving force of the Holocaust.

Almost simultaneously with the Bolshevik triumph in Russia, the British government (through its Foreign Secretary, Lord Balfour) issued on 2 November 1917 what came to be known as the Balfour Declaration. The announcement that the British government publicly favoured 'the establishment in Palestine of a national home for the Jewish people', coincided with the conquest by British troops of Palestine from the Ottoman Turks. It laid the foundations for what would officially become the British Mandate for Palestine in 1922 and eventually the state of Israel in 1948. Through the Balfour Declaration, the Zionist movement gained its greatest success yet on the international stage, achieving political recognition by what was then the leading imperial power in the world. Ironically, this anticipation of a restored Jewish statehood for the first time in nearly two thousand years occurred at the same historical moment as unprecedentedly large numbers of Jews were killing each other in the trenches of the First World War. Zionism, however, offered the prospect of a new centripetal force that might transcend the centrifugal and disintegrating influences of modernisation on traditional Jewish society.

The attitude of Nazis, nationalists and anti-Semites in Germany and elsewhere to the Zionist experiment was more ambivalent than it would be towards Communism. At one level, Zionism could appeal to anti-Semites as a movement seeking Jewish emigration. Palestine even appeared to be a convenient dumping ground for unwelcome Jews, in the eyes of the Nazi regime between 1933 and 1939. However, there was also a more sinister view of Zionism as a political tool in the Jewish bid for 'world-domination', put forward in the 1920s by Hitler and the leading Nazi ideologue Alfred Rosenberg.[44] Zionism for them simply reinforced the stereotype of Jewish dual loyalties and fed the conspiracy myth of an insatiable Jewish lust for power.

After 1918, with the break-up of the Ottoman, the Russian, the Austro-Hungarian and German Empires, the map of Europe irrevocably changed. New independent nation-states such as Poland, Czechoslovakia, Yugoslavia, Romania, Hungary and the Baltic states, emerged or were restored. Most of them contained numerous ethnic and religious minorities as well as sizeable Jewish populations. These old-new nations spawned fiercely exclusivist, ethnic nationalisms and increasingly illiberal authoritarian regimes, deeply suspicious of the Jews as 'outsiders'. Not only were Jews still regarded as 'different' and as having group loyalties of their own but they were seen either as unwelcome economic competitors or as dangerously subversive radicals. In Poland, Romania and Hungary alone (which between them contained $4\frac{1}{2}$ million Jews in the 1930s) harsh quotas were introduced soon after the First World War, to restrict Jewish attendance at the universities. Jews found themselves squeezed by government fiscal policy, subject to discrimination in employment, and were frequently vulnerable to the effects of the Wall Street Crash and the Great Depression of the 1930s.[45] The impoverishment of the Jewish masses reinforced the effects of hostile legislation and nourished the increasingly nationalist and anti-Semitic climate that sought to exclude Jews as much as possible from economic life.

Among the nations in inter-war Europe most eager to encourage a massive removal of Jews from their midst was Poland. In October 1938 the Polish ambassador to Great Britain proposed that Polish Jews be allowed to go to Northern Rhodesia and similar colonies at a rate of 100,000 a year; otherwise, he declared, the Polish government would feel itself 'inevitably forced to adopt the same kind of policy as the German government, and indeed draw closer to that government in general policy'. Polish anti-Semitism, despite some similarities, did in fact differ from the German Nazi variety in a number of significant ways. In the first place, the 'Jewish question' existed in Poland as a genuine *minorities* problem in an insecure, multi-ethnic state where Poles in 1931 still made up less than 65 per cent of the population.[46] Furthermore, threatened by such powerful neighbours as Germany and Bolshevik Russia, many Poles developed decidedly paranoid sentiments about ethnically non-Polish groups in their recently restored state, viewing them as a potential fifth column. Jews, who accounted for between a quarter and a third of the population in the large cities such as Warsaw, Lodz, Lwow, Cracow and Lublin, were particularly suspected of disloyalty or indifference to Polish national interests.[47] This produced some very ugly results. To the nascent

Polish middle class, the highly urbanised Jews were dangerous business competitors; in the eyes of the dominant conservative and clerical elites, they were invariably seen as crypto-Bolsheviks; to the peasantry and small traders they were alien exploiters.[48]

For the Primate of Poland, Cardinal Hlond (speaking in 1936), it was allegedly a fact that 'Jews oppose the Catholic Church, are steeped in free-thinking, and represent the avant-garde of the atheist movement, the Bolshevik movement and subversive action'. Cardinal Hlond did not fail to mention the classic allegation that Jews engaged in 'white slavery', in dispensing pornography, committing fraud and usury as well as undermining Christian morality in general.[49] Biological and racist anti-Semitism of the pseudo-scientific kind was admittedly less prevalent in Catholic Poland than in neighbouring Nazi Germany. Equally, violence against the Jews was frowned upon. But once Hitler had come to power in 1933, the mood against Jews in Poland became more bellicose, especially on the nationalist Right (among the 'National Democrats' or *Endecja*) and in the ranks of its fascist hooligan offshoots.[50] By the late 1930s there were mini-pogroms in the countryside, and 'ghetto-benches' reserved for Jewish students at Polish universities.[51] Worse still, there was a growing competition among Polish politicians to see who could propose a more far-reaching solution to the 'Jewish question' whether through economic boycott, social exclusion, legal discrimination or mass expulsion.

Not only in Poland but also in Romania, Hungary, Slovakia and even Italy in the late 1930s, steps were being taken to restrict Jews in the professions and reduce them to second-class citizenship. This was an ominous sign of things to come. The Jews found themselves increasingly powerless against this pan-European trend to strip them of their hard-won civic and political rights. Massive pressure was building to impose a sweeping *numerus clausus* that would block their educational as well as their economic opportunities, thereby forcing them to emigrate in large numbers.

The relative feebleness of the Jewish response reflected a long-standing disinclination and inability of Jews before the Holocaust to act politically in an organised and effective way to defend their vital interests as a group. In the West, the politics of the emancipation contract (and subsequently of assimilation) permitted individual lobbying behind the scenes and phil-anthropic activity, but no self-assertive ethnic politics. The Jewish national movement, which did advocate precisely such a course, remained a minority trend in the Jewish world, until the success of Hitler began to vindicate many Zionist argu-ments. By then, however, it appeared to be too late to do any-thing positive beyond desperately organising a legal (or illegal) immigration to British-controlled Palestine. Decision-making in the Middle East still rested, however, in the hands of a British elite preoccupied with reasons of state and its own considerations of imperial expediency.[52] They were faced in Palestine with a well-organised Jewish community, but one which still lacked a sovereign Jewish state, a Jewish army, or a clearly agreed set of political objectives. The Palestine *Yishuv* was numerically small, economically weak, divided into warring political factions, dependent on British goodwill and facing a hostile Arab majority.

Even American Jewry, though by 1939 the richest, largest and strongest Jewish community in the world, was still far from being the organised, vigorous, disciplined, cohesive lobby of the post-war era, able to influence the foreign policy of the United States government. On the contrary, it was so lacking in unity or self-confidence and so cowed by the rise in American anti-Semitism during the Depression years, that it was unable to seriously challenge the draconian immigration restrictions that helped to seal the fate of European Jewry.[53] Much the same could be said of the smaller Anglo-Jewish community (330,000), even though a few individual Jews did achieve prominence in British public life during the inter-war years.[54]

Equally powerless were the more than three million strong Polish Jews, despite their organised representation at local and national parliamentary levels in Polish society. Polish Jewry was a microcosm of the wider Jewish world with its turbulent, fractious, ideologically polarised politics – replete with internecine quarrels between Right and Left, religious and secular, Zionist and anti-Zionist extremes. The 'nationality' politics of Polish Jews had little chance to succeed in the face of Gentile hostility, though there was an energetic self-defence against anti-Semitic violence by the Jewish Socialist Bund.[55] But whether they were law-abiding or revolutionary, nationalist or integrationist, central and east European Jews before 1939 had little chance of warding off the rising anti-Semitic tide. After 1939, the unequal struggle would become increasingly hopeless with one side (the Germans) heavily armed and the other (the Jews) essentially defenceless. This huge disparity in strength, if anything, increased the sadism of the Nazis, who claimed to be fighting against an omnipotent enemy, yet one which was manifestly not equipped to protect itself.

The powerlessness of the Jews was exacerbated after 1939 by the hostility of local populations, especially in Eastern Europe, and their readiness to collaborate with the Germans in the 'solution to the Jewish question'. This was true even in Poland, which fought the Nazis from the first to the last day of the war, produced no Quislings and developed the largest resistance movement in Europe. There were some Polish anti-Semites who not only fought against Hitler but even rescued Jews, though this was an act punishable by death. But though the scale of Polish suffering was second only to that of the Jews under Nazi occupation, the Poles, too, were hostile, indifferent or else committed hideous acts against their Jewish neighbours – as did Lithuanians, Latvians, Estonians, Ukrainians, Belorussians, Romanians, Hungarians and many other European nationalities.

Writing in 1944, while hiding on the 'Aryan' side of Warsaw, the Polish-Jewish historian, Emanuel Ringelblum, bitterly observed:

'Last summer, when carts packed with captive Jewish men, women and children moved through the streets of the capital, was it really necessary for laughter from wild mobs to resound from the other side of the ghetto walls...?'[56]

Already in October 1940 he had confided to his diary that there were 'a considerable number of anti-Semitic elements who collaborated with the Germans in waging war on the Jews.'[57] The German-controlled radio, public loudspeaker system, special exhibitions, brochures, leaflets and posters, spread a message of hate which struck a powerful chord with the local population, already intoxicated by the anti-Semitism of the Polish-language 'reptile press'.[58]

Mordekhai Tenenbaum, commander of the Jewish Fighting Organisation in the Bialystok ghetto, was even more critical about Polish behaviour as the death-trains rolled to Treblinka and other places of slaughter. Had it not been for the passive and active aid of Poles, he maintained, 'the Germans would never have been as successful as they were' in locating Jews. 'It was the Poles who called out "Yid" at every Jew who escaped from the train transporting him to the gas chambers, it was they who caught these unfortunate wretches and who rejoiced at every misfortune.'[59]

The intrepid Polish courier, Jan Karski, in a report to the Polish government-in-exile, had observed in 1940 that the 'Jewish Question' was like 'a narrow bridge upon which the Germans and a large part of Polish society find themselves in agreement.'[60] Zofia Kossak-Szczucka, a fervently Catholic member of the Council For Aid to the Jews (Zegota) founded in late 1942, was profoundly shocked by the demoralisation created in Polish ranks by the 'universal, ominous silence' surrounding the massacre of millions of Jews. She also noted with horror the lack of protests in England, America, in the international Jewish organisations and the Catholic Church, but it was above all for the soul of Poland that she worried. 'The compulsory participation of the Polish nation in the bloody spectacle that is taking place on Polish soil can easily breed indifference to crime, sadism and above all the perilous conviction that it is possible to murder one's neighbour without punishment.'[61]

Murder most foul is exactly what the Polish population of Jedwabne (about 100 kilometres from Bialystok) perpetrated against nearly all of their 1,600 Jewish neighbours on July 10, 1941, shortly after the German invasion of the Soviet Union. While the Germans looked on and limited themselves to filming the proceedings for propaganda purposes, the Polish villagers slaughtered Jews with axes, poles, knives and nail-studded clubs. Men had their tongues or eyes cut out, women were raped and murdered, babies thrown to the ground and trampled to death. Jews, after being savagely beaten, were lined up in the market square and forced to sing that they 'had caused the war'; other groups of Jews were forced to undress, sing, dance and perform 'insane exercises' while Polish peasant onlookers, including women and children, applauded. A group of young Jews was ordered to lift a giant statue of Lenin (from the time of the Soviet occupation) and drag it to the Jewish cemetery, where they were promptly butchered. All the remaining Jews, reeling from savage blows, were then forced into a nearby barn, which was set alight with kerosene, so that they burned alive.[62]

The ordinary Poles who carried out these barbarities, described in Jan Gross's short book on Jedwabne, were no different in their brutal sadism from the German perpetrators analysed by Daniel Goldhagen, who tended to exaggerate the uniquely German elements in the Holocaust. Resentment against collaborators with the Soviet occupiers who had fled after the German invasion in June 1941, and the stereotypical Polish identification of the Jews with Communism, was perhaps an exacerbating factor but not the cause of the massacre.[63] More important was the potent cocktail of pre-war anti-Semitism embedded in the radical nationalism of the *Endecja* and a deeply reactionary, primitive Catholicism, mixed with sheer greed and the desire to plunder Jewish property, opened up by the German war against the Soviet Union.[64] Similarly bestial pogroms were carried out by rural Poles elsewhere in the Bialystok region, with enthusiastic spectators laughing loudly and applauding as Jews fell under the merciless blows of the murderers. As one eyewitness put it: 'The seed of hatred fell on well-nourished soil, which had been prepared for many years by the clergy. The wild and bloodthirsty mob took it as a holy challenge that history had put upon it – to get rid of the Jews. And the desire to take over Jewish riches whetted their appetites even more'.[65]

This was already the Holocaust in miniature, revealing the more archaic layers of the monstrous enterprise and its use of primitive, ancient weapons. It was but one small episode in the murderous war of Hitler against the Jews, but similar scenes would soon occur all over Europe.

# II    *From Weimar to Hitler*

As for the final goal and mission of the Germanic *völkisch*
movement, as far as the Jews are concerned ... it is to wipe out the
East European and vermin Jew with an iron broom. A perfect job
needs to be done.

*Völkische Beobachter* (editorial), 10 March 1922

... we want to point the finger at the Jew as the inspirer, the
originator, and the beneficiary of this terrible catastrophe [the
Spanish Civil War] ... this is the enemy of the world, the destroyer
of cultures, the parasite among the peoples, the Son of Chaos, the
incarnation of evil, the ferment of decomposition, the plastic
demon of the decay of humanity.

**Joseph Goebbels**, Nuremberg Party Congress, September 1937

And when I heard that the Jews were being driven from their
professions and homes and imprisoned in ghettos, the points
switched automatically in my mind ... It was only 'the Jew' who
was being persecuted and 'made homeless'.

**Melita Maschmann**, Head of the League
of German Girls in the Hitler Youth

The ill-fated Weimar Republic was established after 1918
against the background of unparalleled national traumas. The
unexpected defeat in the First World War, the abdication of the
Emperor, the threat of communist revolution at home, the
humiliation of the Versailles Treaty and the prospect of the huge
reparations payments to the Western Allies weighed heavily on
the Germans. The spectre of economic and political chaos could
only benefit the enemies of the Republic, especially those on
the nationalist Right.[1] They damned it with the responsibility

for signing a treaty that had accepted German 'War Guilt'; blamed it for the substantial loss of territory, the 'shame' of an emasculated army and dependence on foreign loans. A further blow to the Republic was the massive inflation of 1923 and the consequent monetary collapse, which had a devastating effect on the working classes as well as on many in the middle strata of German society, who lost their life savings. Although the Weimar Republic would enjoy a brief period of economic and political stability between 1924 and 1928, important changes beneath the surface were already weakening the middle ground in German politics. More liberal parties like the Democrats and German People's Party were steadily losing support. So, too, were the conservative Nationalists whose share of the vote by 1928 had declined from 20 per cent to 14 per cent. The Social Democrats, the dominant party in the early years of the Republic, also began to lose votes – mainly to the Communists – who never forgave them for having crushed in 1919 (with the aid of the army and paramilitary *Freikorps*) the possibility of proletarian revolution in Germany.[2] For its part, the Catholic Centre Party, whose electoral base remained stable, was no longer willing to form a coalition with the socialists and began to move to the Right.

German Jews, who numbered slightly more than half a million persons, were a very small group in the population (less than 1 per cent in the 1920s), clearly oriented to the liberal-left wing of the German spectrum. They had little political influence, despite anti-Semitic legends to the contrary. They were, however, disproportionately prominent in publishing, journalism, the arts, the free professions, trade, private banking and commerce, including the ownership of the new department stores. In 1933, 11 per cent of all Germany's doctors were Jews and about 16 per cent of its lawyers – a degree of visibility that was all the greater in the big cities such as Berlin. Middle-class anti-Semitism in Germany – especially rampant among doctors, lawyers, shopkeepers, artisans, small businessmen, academics and students – was undoubtedly stimulated by professional jealousy and envy at more successful competitors.[3] It was also nourished by the intensive post-1918 propaganda of *völkisch* (racist) anti-Semitic organisations who branded Jews with the stigma of wartime profiteering, black-market dealings, stock-exchange speculation and responsibility for defeat in the First World War. A series of economic and political crises between 1918 and 1923 exacerbated these embittered feelings and brought them to a fever pitch.[4]

A constant refrain of the political Right was to single out the prominent role of radical socialists and communists of Jewish origin in the abortive German Revolutions of 1918/19. This seemed to accredit the idea in the minds of many Germans that Jews were a ferment of subversive activity and revolution. The Spartacist revolt in Berlin (a communist uprising) was led, for example, by the Polish-born internationalist Rosa Luxemburg, who like a number of the early leaders of the KPD (German Communist Party) was Jewish, though thoroughly alienated from her origins. In the Bavarian capital, Munich, the first Independent Socialist Prime Minister, Kurt Eisner was not only a Jew but also a bohemian intellectual, a Berliner and a pacifist who had published documents attributing responsibility for the First World War to Germany.[5] These attributes made him almost perfect as a hate symbol for the conservative and anti-Republican elements in Bavarian society. The middle classes were even more panic-stricken when a short-lived Munich Soviet Republic was established in 1919 that also featured a number of Russian Jews in leading positions. It was soon crushed by the local *Freikorps* (on instructions from the Social Democrats) who exacted a murderous revenge. In the course of 1918–19, some of the most prominent Jewish revolutionaries such as Rosa Luxemburg, Gustav Landauer, Kurt Eisner, Eugen Leviné and a number of other radical Jews such as the independent socialist

Hugo Haase were either brutally assassinated or shot – a fate that also befell the Spartacist leader Karl Liebknecht, who was not a Jew.[6] This wave of assassinations culminated in the killing of Germany's first ever Jewish foreign minister, the highly assimilated and versatile industrialist Walter Rathenau, by youthful right-wing, nationalist fanatics in 1922. Rathenau, an ardent Prussian patriot who had contributed much to the efficiency of the German economy during the war, was demonised as an 'Elder of Zion' and a 'Jewish Bolshevik' by his blonde, blue-eyed murderers. Rathenau's death was a worrying omen for German Jewry.[7]

The stream of impoverished Polish Jews arriving in Berlin in the early 1920s was another troubling development. These *Ostjuden* (eastern Jews) were frequently unemployed and disoriented by the post-war upheavals and revolutions in eastern Europe. Moreover, they were cultural outsiders and an easy target for xenophobic accusations (made also by Social Democrats) of economic parasitism. In the Weimar Republic they made up approximately a fifth of the German Jewish population. The more assimilated and established members of German Jewry tended to believe that the revival of anti-Semitism was directed primarily or even exclusively against the failings of the *Ostjuden*, but this turned out to be a tragic self-deception.

The most militant of the many disparate *völkisch* anti-Semitic sects and groupings that mushroomed in the aftermath of war and defeat was the German National Socialist Workers' Party (NSDAP or Nazi Party for short), founded in Munich in 1919. Its official party programme of 24 February 1920 stood for 'the uniting of all Germans within one Greater Germany', on the basis of national self-determination. The party called for the annulment of the Versailles Treaty, demanding land and soil for the excess German population; it advocated that the 'yoke of interest-capital' be broken, favouring widespread nationalisations and profit-sharing, land reform, the communalisation of department stores and other radical-sounding measures. Article 4 of the NSDAP programme made it clear that only 'persons of German blood' could be nationals (*Volksgenossen*) and therefore citizens of the state. This automatically excluded Jews, who in the future would only be permitted to live in Germany as guests 'subject to Legislation for Aliens'. Article 23 insisted that publishers, journalists and 'all editors and editorial employees of German-language newspapers must be German by race'. It also called for laws against 'trends in art and literature that have a destructive effect on our national life' (an implicit reference to Jews). Article 24 observed that the NSDAP stood for 'positive Christianity' and fought 'against the Jewish-materialistic spirit *within* and *without* us'.[8]

Until 1930 the Nazi Party remained a minor although highly vocal *völkisch* grouping that continued to advocate (without much success) a nationalist form of socialism underpinned by strong anti-Semitic foundations. Between 1919 and 1924 it remained confined to Bavaria, appealing mainly to ex-soldiers, anti-Communists, anti-Semites, and a hodgepodge of déclassé elements who were attracted to the vague slogans of a 'national revolution'. Nevertheless its leader, Adolf Hitler, a raucous, spellbinding Austrian agitator in his early thirties, who had been a corporal in the German army during the First World War, had already attracted some national attention. On 8–9 November 1923, together with the old war-hero General von Ludendorff, the thirty-four-year-old Hitler had attempted to seize power in Bavaria, hoping eventually to march on Berlin and overthrow the Weimar Republic. The planned *putsch* failed miserably when Hitler and his followers were fired on by the Munich police while marching through the city centre. The putschists dispersed in some confusion. Following his arrest, Hitler managed, with the help of a sympathetic judge, to turn his trial into a harangue against the 'traitors of 1918', a public indictment of Weimar democracy and a platform for his own extreme nationalist and anti-Semitic views. Though guilty of high treason, he was sentenced to a mere five years' imprisonment, of which he served just nine months in Landsberg prison, where he wrote *Mein Kampf* (My Struggle) in 1924. This sprawling, poorly written and primitive book was to become the bible of the Nazi movement and a core anti-Semitic text as well.

As a political autobiography, *Mein Kampf* offers us a vital insight into Hitler's own background and the formative influences that moulded his world-view. Adolf Hitler had been born in the small town of Braunau on the Inn, which lay on the border between Austria and Bavaria, on 20 April 1889. In his adolescent years, spent partly in Linz, he had come under the influence of the pan-German ideology of the extremist politician Georg von Schönerer, the leading German nationalist in Austria who advocated the *Anschluss* (union) of the two German states into one Greater German Reich. (This was a boyhood dream that Hitler himself would fulfil in 1938.) The rancorous Schönerer passionately hated the cosmopolitan Habsburg ruling dynasty of Austria, the Czechs and other neighbouring Slav nationalities (who threatened German hegemony), the Roman Catholic Church and especially the Jews.[9] As Hitler freely acknowledges in *Mein Kampf*, he was strongly influenced by Schönerer's uncompromising racial anti-Semitism. The Austrian pan-German leader had in 1885 proclaimed anti-Semitism as the 'main pillar of a true folkish mentality, and thus as the greatest achievement of this century'.[10] Schönerer turned his advocacy of 'Germandom' into a matter of faith and early in his political career, had added an 'Aryan' clause excluding even the most ardent German nationalist Jews from membership in his movement. Hitler fully accepted Schönerer's radical views on the need for an intransigent ethnic anti-Semitism (rooted in blood and race), adopted his hatred of the 'Jewish press' and the

'Jewish-led Social Democracy', and shared his loathing for universal suffrage. He was no less scathing about parliamentarianism, liberal democracy and the House of Habsburg, which he held responsible for betraying the German *Volk*. The young Hitler learned to identify with the Germanic cult of the *Führer* (leader) and adopted Schönerer's German greeting of 'Heil!'[11]

Another important Austrian role model for the young Hitler, to whom he devoted many pages in *Mein Kampf*, was the extremely popular and elegant Mayor of Vienna, Karl Lueger, leader of the Christian-Social Party. The Viennese Mayor had come to power largely through the skilful, demagogic use of anti-Semitism, focusing his attacks on the prominent role of Viennese Jews in the liberal press, the stock exchange, banking and industrial capitalism.[12] In his propaganda, he fused Catholic prejudice against the 'Christ killers' with the more modern anti-capitalist resentments of a declining lower middle class faced with economic crisis. Lueger cleverly mixed this religious and economic anti-Semitism with the xenophobic feelings of many Viennese towards the eastern Jews, who by 1900 already formed about 25 per cent of Vienna's 175,000 strong Jewish community. Hitler greatly admired Lueger's political virtuosity and his reforming zeal as Vienna's Mayor.[13] He absorbed from him the lesson that anti-Semitism could be an extremely effective instrument of mass mobilisation in crystallising the resentments of the 'little man'. But he disliked the easy-going opportunism behind Lueger's policy towards Jews and Slavs, the Viennese Mayor's refusal to embrace the racial principle and his tight alliance with the Catholic Church, though he did appreciate the tactical shrewdness behind this strategy in a pre-war Austrian context. According to Hitler, the main problem was that Lueger's Catholic anti-Semitism still allowed Jews the escape-route of baptism. It was simply not radical enough. 'Lacking was the conviction that this was a vital question for all humanity, with the fate of all non-Jewish peoples depending on its solution.'[14]

The other great influence on Hitler's view of the Jews was the German nationalist composer Richard Wagner, whose operas he knew by heart and whose writings he avidly consumed at an early age.[15] The intensity of Hitler's emotional identification with Wagner, whose diatribes against the corrupting role of Jews in music and art were certainly familiar to him, gave special weight to this connection. Those passages in *Mein Kampf* which claim that the Jew had never had produced any creative art of his own – least of all in music(!) and architecture – and which portray his 'parasitic' cultural activity in exceptionally malevolent language could have been lifted verbatim from Wagner's writings.[16] For Richard Wagner, the Jews represented the 'evil conscience of our modern civilisation' or, to quote a phrase much repeated by the Nazis, 'the plastic demon of the decline of mankind'.[17]

Nevertheless, there were distinctive features to Hitler's anti-Semitism that should not be overlooked. One element, which he himself directly related to 'the visual instruction of the Vienna streets', was his stylised encounter with the caftan-wearing orthodox Galician Jews from eastern Europe. The way he tells it, this 'apparition in a black caftan and black hair locks' first made him wonder about the foreignness of the Jew and whether this strange being could possibly be a German?[18] The impact was apparently instantaneous: 'For a few pennies, I bought the first anti-Semitic pamphlets of my life.' Once he had begun to take cognisance of the 'Jewish Question', Hitler tells us that wherever he went he 'began to see Jews, and the more I saw, the more sharply they became distinguished in my eyes from the rest of humanity'.[19] The climax of this psycho-drama, which turned him (by his own somewhat hysterical account) from a 'weak-kneed cosmopolitan' into a 'coldly rational' anti-Semite, was the realisation that the internationalist Austrian

Social Democracy was 'Jewish' in character: 'When I recognised the Jew as the leader of the Social Democracy, the scales dropped from my eyes. A long soul struggle had reached its conclusion.'[20]

Of course, not *all* of Hitler's 'autobiographical' account of how he picked up his Judaeophobia on the streets of pre-war Vienna needs to be taken literally. No doubt he had an interest in projecting back and rationalising his anti-Semitism, demonstrating its iron logic and continuity. We know that Hitler did in fact mix quite freely with Jews in pre-war Vienna and relied on them to sell his picture-postcard sketches and paintings.[21] Yet much of what he writes still rings true and reflects the greater saliency of the 'Jewish Question' and of anti-Semitism in the Austrian capital, especially if compared to imperial Germany. The repressed sexual dimension to Hitler's Judaeophobia also seems striking: 'With satanic joy in his face, the black-haired Jewish youth lurks in wait for the unsuspecting maiden whom he defiles with his blood, thus stealing her from her people. With every means he tries to destroy the racial foundations of the people he has set out to subjugate.'[22] Hitler drew a direct parallel between this highly personal racist fantasy drawn from the back streets of imperial Vienna and the post-war occupation of the Ruhr by black French-colonial troops. In both cases, he saw a Jewish conspiracy behind a presumed threat to 'bastardise' and thereby enslave the 'Aryan' race. 'It was and it is Jews who bring the Negroes into the Rhineland, always with the same secret thought and clear aim of ruining the white race by the necessarily resulting bastardisation...'[23]

*Mein Kampf* is permeated by obsessions with 'racial purity' as well as by the social Darwinist principle of a relentless battle of each nation (*Volk*) for its own self-preservation. In the case of the German *Volk*, its foremost vital need must be to acquire more living space (*Lebensraum*) in the East, at the expense of Soviet Russia – the menacing citadel of international Communism. Thus for ideological, economic and geo-political reasons, Hitler called from the early 1920s for an all-out war against 'the Jewish doctrine of Marxism'. It contradicted 'the significance of nationality and race', denied the value of personality and negated the 'eternal laws of nature' with its egalitarian doctrines.[24] In an apocalyptic prophecy of the kind that he would frequently invoke after 1939, whenever he referred to the 'Final Solution' of the 'Jewish Question', Hitler wrote in *Mein Kampf*: 'If, with the help of his Marxist creed, the Jew is victorious over the other peoples of the world, his crown will be the funeral wreath of humanity ... Hence today I believe that I am acting in accordance with the will of the Almighty Creator: by defending myself against the Jew, I am fighting for the work of the Lord.'[25]

Though Hitler had abandoned the simple Catholic faith of his boyhood, one can find in these and other passages crude echoes of popular Christian beliefs, transmuted into the new 'political religion' of National Socialism.[26] In claiming 'divine' sanction for his fight against the Jews and 'Jewish Marxism', Hitler was signalling that he considered this political battle to be a crusade or Holy War in which there could be no compromises. The 'war against the Jews' was an existential matter of life and death, an 'either-or' question in which the future of civilisation itself was at stake.[27] There were also other related themes that in retrospect seem to prefigure the Holocaust, such as the statement in *Mein Kampf* that between 12,000 and 15,000 Jews ('Hebrew corrupters') ought to have been gassed in the First World War, so that 'the sacrifice of millions at the front would not have been in vain'.[28] Of course, this does not necessarily mean that Hitler envisioned gassing the Jews in 1924. But it is important to understand his peculiar kind of logic in order to grasp its full implications. Like many de... VIEW OF OTHERS FROM HITLER'S GENERATION his generation, he was convinced that ... had been betrayed in 1918 by pacifists and M... incited by the Jews. This 'betrayal' must never be allowed...

recur, as Hitler made abundantly clear to the Czech Foreign Minister in early 1939: 'We are going to destroy the Jews. They are not going to get away with what they did on 9 November 1918.'[29] The ninth of November symbolised for Hitler not only the disgrace of the German defeat and surrender but the chaos of communist revolution and the advent of the hated 'Jewish Republic'. He had, after all, entered politics to make sure this would never happen again. By implication, only the preventive strike of putting the Jews under the gas in order to destroy them could forestall a repetition of 'the stab in the back' and ensure a future German victory.

War, revolution and the Jews were inseparably locked in Hitler's mind. Revealingly enough, his first known statement about political affairs comes in a letter on the 'Jewish Question' dated 16 September 1919, which defines Jewry strictly as a 'racial' and not a religious group. He describes its actions in a horrifying metaphor as resulting 'in a racial tuberculosis of peoples'.[30] Rejecting mere pogroms as a purely 'emotional' response to the Jewish problem, Hitler called instead for a 'rational anti-Semitism' that would impose an aliens' law on the Jews in order to revoke their 'special privileges'. The final objective, he wrote to his correspondent, 'must be the complete removal (*Entfernung*) of the Jews'.[31] This ambiguous term could mean either their forced emigration, their extermination or perhaps a mixture of these solutions.

Hitler's speeches of the early 1920s, like those of other leading Nazis in southern Germany such as Alfred Rosenberg, Julius Streicher or Hermann Esser, constantly hammer away at the need to take ruthless, systematic measures against the Jews; to remove them from all government employment, newspaper offices, theatres, cinemas; to 'eliminate' the Jewish spirit from German culture and the economy; to break their imagined political power by sweeping away the Marxist parties. In *Mein Kampf* as in many of his speeches, Hitler would conjure up the spectre of Bolshevik Russia where 'the Jew' (frequently compared to a vampire or giant parasite) had 'killed or starved about thirty million people with positively fanatical savagery, in part amid inhuman tortures, in order to give a gang of Jewish journalists and stock-exchange bandits domination over a great people'. In his unpublished *Secret Book* of 1928, Hitler elaborated still further on the meaning of the 'Jewish-Bolshevik' tyranny: 'The end of the Jewish world struggle therefore will always be a bloody Bolshevisation. In truth this means the destruction of all the intellectual upper classes linked to their peoples so that he can rise to become the master of a mankind become leaderless.'[32]

Marxism was thereby reduced to a weapon of terror that the Jews had ruthlessly applied to destroy an 'inherently anti-Semitic Russia' and to extirpate the Russian national intelligentsia along with the Russian upper classes. The massive atrocities in 'this Jewish struggle for hegemony in Russia amounted to 28–30 million people in number of dead. This is fifteen times more than the World War cost Germany.'[33] The Bolshevik revolution had not only destroyed marriage, sexual morality and the bonds of social order, it had deliberately created a 'chaotic bastardisation', which left the Jews as its 'only intellectual cement'. Hitler's unbending conclusion from this so-called Jewish–Bolshevik *genocide* – which he regarded as the 'most terrible crime of all times against mankind' – was that only the National Socialist movement could prevent a similar victory for Jewry in the bitter struggle that 'is being waged in Germany at the present time'.[34] For Hitler, Germany was always the pivotal land that would determine whether Communism (and Jewry) would triumph or not. The problem was that even the bourgeois parties were tools of Jewry. Behind 'the Jew' stood not only Marxism, democracy and 'the so-called Christian Centre' but also 'the bourgeois national parties of the so-called national fatherland leagues' – in a word, the entire parliamentary political spectrum. Hence, National Socialism in its *total war* against the Jews would have to completely destroy the Weimar 'system' and replace its rotten foundations by a ruthless racist dictatorship.

It is evident that Nazi discourse on these issues had qualitatively moved some distance beyond the familiar themes of pre-1914 anti-Semitism, whether Christian or anti-Christian. Hitler had adopted a political conception of Jewry which was ultimately derived from the *war* experience; he had embraced a mental universe of *Sieg oder Untergang* (Victory or Downfall) in relation to Communism and the Jews. Moreover, the latter were consistently dehumanised in zoological language either as an inferior race, or as 'vermin' to be cleansed, or else as germs, bacillae and microbes that attack and poison the organism until they are eradicated.[35] Jewry is presented as the equivalent of a bubonic plague in the Middle Ages, only the medical metaphors in this case have become more modern, invoking killer diseases such as cancer and tuberculosis. 'The Jew' was invariably referred to in Nazi discourse as a type to which *all* Jews conformed – whether western or eastern, men or women, secular or religious, assimilated or unassimilated, bourgeois or proletarian. Even baptised Jews were irrevocably tainted in Nazi ideology by the stigma of degenerate blood. Jews as a 'counter-race' were perceived as the polar opposite to the German 'Aryans', being inherently destructive, parasitical and agents of decomposition (*Zersetzung*).[36]

By virtue of their abstract intellect, mercenary egoism and corrupt mentality, the Jews were a special danger to German women. Julius Streicher in *Der Stürmer*, the most pornographic of all Nazi anti-Semitic publications, specialised (much to Hitler's delight) in elaborating on the presumed sexual pathology of the 'Jewish peril'. Streicher regularly accused Jews of rape and exploiting German girls for prostitution; he revived the medieval blood libel that Jews abducted German children for ritual murder purposes; he even claimed that Jews deliberately sought to poison the blood of German women through sexual intercourse.[37] Der Stürmer revelled, for example, in the absurd theories put forward by the racist author Arthur Dinter in his best-selling novel The Sin Against the Blood (1918). Dinter had claimed in all seriousness that a German woman would transmit Jewish hereditary characteristics even to children conceived by German fathers, if she ever, at any time, had engaged in sexual relations with a Jew. The sexually charged quality in Nazi anti-Semitism came out in the insistence that the Jew deliberately (and in a planned way) pursued 'blood poisoning' in an attempt to destroy the German family and Volk. For Hitler, with his gnawing doubts about his own 'racial purity' and the possible taint of Jewish blood in his family background, such obsessions had a special significance.[38] Intense, guilt-ridden sexual puritanism, the deeply rooted desire to avenge himself for early deprivations and social humiliation, together with a morbid fixation on blood and race heightened the irrational extremist dimension in his Judaeophobia.

But how far could such personal obsessions be shared by other groups in German society? To what extent, if any, did paranoid anti-Semitism help Hitler to win power? It is probably impossible to measure its conscious or subconscious impact on Germans in any convincing way. We do know that the consequences of the First World War encouraged many disillusioned former soldiers not only to despise the post-war Republic and its democratic politicians but also to blame the Jews for the debacle of 1918. Right-wing nationalists, conservative monarchists and members of the old elites, frightened by the Bolshevik revolution in Russia and the prospect of a repeat performance in Germany, were often receptive to the myth of a Jewish conspiracy. Among the lower classes, there were many who did indeed believe that Jews had profiteered from the war or the reparations. There were others, too, who resented Jewish immigration from the east; or believed that the stock-exchange and banking capital were mainly in the hands of Jewish financiers. Such arguments were hardly new. They had long attracted impoverished artisans, craftsmen and small traders.[39] But now, in the overheated atmosphere of the early post-war years, extreme anti-Semitism did seem to burst through traditional restraints. It extended from the semi-respectable DNVP (Deutschnationale Volkspartei, German National People's Party) to the student fraternities, where it was especially violent; it penetrated the churches and found an echo in communist efforts to play the nationalist card by denouncing 'Jewish finance capital'.[40] The notorious Russian anti-Semitic forgery, the Protocols of the Elders of Zion, translated into German shortly after the war, briefly became a best-seller.[41] By 1933 there were over 400 anti-Semitic associations and societies in Germany, along with some 700 anti-Jewish periodicals. Some of the pamphlet literature was scurrilous and portrayed the Jews in the hysterical tones reminiscent of Der Stürmer, not only as an economic and political threat but as a menace to German womanhood and the purity of the race. More respectable, conservative opinion deplored the permissive mores, modernist culture and radical politics of Berlin in the 1920s, which was attributed to Jewish and Marxist influence.[42]

On the other hand, throughout the 1920s the Nazi vote remained modest. Even in the 1928 Reichstag elections they had obtained only 800,000 votes and a mere twelve seats in parliament. National Socialist success in using anti-Semitism seemed limited outside of certain regions where there was already a pre-existing historical tradition or local factors favoured it. Thus anti-Semitism found a strong echo in Franconia, Hesse, Westphalia and some areas of Bavaria but was relatively muted in the Rhineland, Baden, Württemberg or Schleswig-Holstein. Even among ordinary Nazi Party members, only a hard core minority (though a very vocal one) regarded anti-Semitism as the critical issue. It was probably less important than anti-Communism, nationalism or unemployment, in attracting new adherents to the movement. Nevertheless in Nazi agitation among high school and university students, anti-Semitism was undoubtedly a crucial weapon in recruitment, helping the Nazis to 'capture' a commanding position at German universities by 1930.[43] Similarly, they had achieved some success among professional associations of physicians and teachers in spreading the anti-Jewish message. Since Jews in the Weimar Republic were well represented in the free professions, the universities and cultural life, it was relatively easy to ignite competitive envy against them in these sectors.

Nazi penetration of the countryside and of urban middle-class groups just as the Great Depression began to bite in Germany after 1929 helps to explain the remarkable increase in their vote during the September 1930 elections. The movement dramatically leapt from twelve to 107 seats (18.3 per cent of the total vote) in the Reichstag, making it the second largest party in Germany. Two years later, in July 1932, the Nazis definitively emerged as the biggest party in the Reichstag, with 37.3 per cent of the vote (230 seats), which was their peak performance under strictly democratic conditions. The staggering shift in their fortunes had coincided with their emergence as a 'catch-all' party appealing to the unifying ideal of *Volksgemeinschaft* (national community). They appeared to be a movement which, unlike all its rivals, was able to transcend regional, class, religious and party political barriers. Though the Nazis made little impact on the solid electoral base of the Catholic and Socialist parties, they did win over much of the youth vote, the disaffected *Mittelstand*, disillusioned supporters of the weakened middle-class parties, some sections of the unemployed, unskilled workers and much of the farming constituency.[44] To achieve such a broad appeal, Hitler focused his message more intensely around integral nationalism. Between 1930 and 1933, he began to temporarily tone down the full-blooded anti-Semitism that lay at the core of his world-view.

Hitler had no difficulty in tailoring Nazi propaganda to the supreme prize of attaining power by legal means, once he recognised that anti-Semitism was not his most effective vote-winner or the central issue that faced the German electorate in the early 1930s. Instead, he underlined his unswerving rejection of a parliamentary democracy that had palpably failed. He acknowledged the urgent need to regenerate economic life in the face of mass unemployment and adapted his message to the longing for stability, law and order felt by so many ordinary Germans. Hitler knew how to play with uncanny skill on the chord of wounded German pride and national humiliation since 1918 while holding out the promise of a redemptive reawakening that would lift Germans from the depths of their despair. Anti-Semitism in this political context was a crucial adjunct but it was not decisive. Nonetheless, it was employed with great effectiveness to exacerbate local grievances, to satisfy the radical anti-capitalist urges of the SA rank and file and to reinforce street campaigns against the Marxist parties. Hitler was far too shrewd to allow it, though, to interfere in the complex political game that would bring him power in January 1933.

It was the backstage manoeuvrings of authoritarian conservative politicians, wealthy industrialists and army leaders that unexpectedly opened the road to Hitler.[45] For a brief moment when the Nazi vote fell in the November 1932 elections, reducing their representation to 196 seats in the Reichstag, it seemed that they might have passed their peak. The conservative camarilla who hoped to manipulate the Nazis for their own narrow purposes, dreamed of dealing the death-blow to the Weimar parliamentary system and finally smashing the left-wing parties. They unwisely gambled on their ability to control events. These reactionary elites who had always despised the Republic thought they could tame Hitler and convince him to do their bidding. Especially naïve in this respect was the former Chancellor and Catholic Centre Party politician, Franz von Papen. He desperately needed Hitler's electoral appeal to further his ambitions since he lacked any popular support himself. Determined to take revenge on his hated rival, General von Schleicher, and to remove him from the Chancellorship, von Papen was eager to promote a coalition of Nationalists and Nazis. He persuaded the ageing President von Hindenburg to reluctantly accept this coalition. On 30 January 1933 Hitler became Chancellor and von Papen his deputy in a cabinet that contained eight more conservatives and only two additional Nazi ministers. But in the new age of mass politics, such cabinet arithmetic counted for relatively little. During these backstage manoeuvrings by Germany's right-wing conservative cliques, the Nazi 'war against the Jews' – not for the first or the last time – was temporarily suspended. The 'Jewish Question', so central to Hitler's own concerns, was quietly subordinated to the immediate task of 'seizing power'. But any illusions that the assumption of office might moderate Nazi policy toward the Jews were to be swiftly and cruelly dashed.

Hitler's accession to power in January 1933 marked the end of Jewish emancipation in Germany. In the next six years a whole century of Jewish integration into German society and culture would be comprehensively and brutally reversed. From the outset, the Nazis instituted an orgy of terror directed against political opponents and Jews, who were subjected to random violence by marauding gangs of SA thugs. On 1 April 1933, the German government officially proclaimed a one-day economic boycott of Jewish shops and businesses, organised by the fanatical Julius Streicher. It was ostensibly designed as a form of 'self-defence' and a response to anti-German 'atrocity stories' allegedly inspired by Jews abroad. The Propaganda Minister, Josef Goebbels, asserted that the boycott was a 'spontaneous' grassroots action but this was belied by the public response of Germans, which was decidedly mixed. For German Jews, it was, however, a tremendous shock to suddenly become the targeted victims of government-inspired hate and to be turned into hostages whose safety would henceforth be conditional on the 'good behaviour' of their co-religionists in the outside world. Within less than a week, the new 'Law for the Restoration of the Professional Civil Service' pensioned off civil servants of 'non-Aryan' origin. In deference to President Hindenburg's sensitivities as a field marshal and war hero, Jewish war veterans (whose relatively large number appears to have surprised the Nazis) were temporarily exempted from this legislation. Separate laws disbarred fourteen hundred lawyers as well as 381 Jewish judges and state prosecutors. By the end of 1934, 70 per cent of all Jewish lawyers and 60 per cent of all Jewish notaries had been dismissed. By mid-1935 more than half the Jewish doctors in Germany had also been removed from their profession. Within less than five years the medical purge had become total.[46]

Goebbels moved rapidly against thousands of Jewish academics, artists, journalists and writers – some of whom were Nobel laureates or enjoyed an international reputation. Albert Einstein was only the most celebrated among the many prominent scientists and intellectuals who emigrated. No less than two hundred Jewish academics followed suit in 1933 alone. Altogether in the first year of Nazi rule, about 40,000 Jews left Germany, those who were young and single having the best chance to begin a new life abroad. The purge in the artistic and cultural sphere was especially swift. The new Reich Chamber of Culture, established by Goebbels in September 1933, immediately excluded Jews from employment in theatre, the film industry and the music profession and a National Press Law likewise prevented Jews from being journalists. The result was an unprecedented haemorrhaging of talent with Germany's loss

to me,' he observed, 'if specifically Jewish states are now to be set up in Rhodesia or somewhere. That would be letting the Nazis throw us back thousands of years.'[49]

But it was those like Klemperer, clinging on at all costs in Germany, who seemed increasingly out of touch with events. Nearly 10 per cent of German Jews had already fled the country by the end of 1933, mostly turning to neighbouring countries such as France, Belgium, Switzerland and Holland, though these lands were themselves in the grip of economic depression and Jewish refugees were not exactly welcomed. Moreover, as refugees they had to forfeit much of their property, which had been confiscated by the German authorities, making their emigration much more difficult. The Nazis cynically judged that the more destitute Jewish refugees appeared to be, the more of a burden they would become on potential host countries, thereby stirring up anti-Semitic sentiments in the outside world. The immigration quotas and closed door policy of the United States and many other countries – including those like Canada, Australia and South Africa that had large territories and sparse populations within the British dominions – seemed to confirm their assessment. Nevertheless, about 200,000 Jews left Germany within the first six years of Nazi rule and another 82,000 emigrated from Austria in 1938. Out of all these Jewish refugees the largest single group (numbering 132,000) found new homes in the USA. Fifty-five thousand Jews emigrated to British-controlled Palestine, 40,000 to England, 20,000 to Argentina and Brazil; 9,000 went to Shanghai, 7,000 were accepted in Australia and another 5,000 in South Africa. But the absolute figures are deceptive unless one takes into account the size, population and resources of the host countries.

Palestine, as the 'Jewish National Home' designated by the League of Nations Mandate, appeared for the first time as an increasingly realistic prospect to many German Jews after 1933. Alternative options were already shrinking fast. Jewish emigration to Palestine was indeed encouraged by the Nazis as a way of making Germany *judenrein* (free of Jews).[50] The Third Reich even signed a 'transfer' agreement (*Ha'avara*) with the Zionist leadership of Palestinian Jewry (the Jewish Agency), which permitted Jews to take out a portion of their capital in the form of German goods. This much criticised deal would enable thousands of German Jews to emigrate to Palestine, where they significantly strengthened the Jewish community through an influx of numbers, educated manpower, technical and organisational skills. Although the new immigrants only received a part of their money back, they were nonetheless better off than if they had emigrated to other destinations, where no such arrangements were in place. Above all, their lives would be saved since they were physically more removed from the Nazi Reich than in neighbouring European countries. Of course, had the British Eighth Army not defeated Rommel in late 1942 in the deserts of North Africa, even that outcome might have been less fortunate.

In the economic sphere, Hitler still proceeded cautiously against the Jews, following the expert advice of his Economics Minister Hjalmar Schacht.[51] He was well aware of Germany's financial vulnerability and the vital importance of overcoming mass unemployment. Hence government legislation mainly targeted small Jewish traders and professional people rather than Jewish-owned banking houses, department stores or companies that were important to the German economy. Nevertheless, despite these constraints, by 1935, about a quarter of all Jewish businesses had already been dismantled or 'Aryanised' at knock-down prices. It was only after June 1938, when the German economic recovery had been fully achieved (and the Nazis were more or less indifferent to international opinion), that the systematic dispossession and expropriation of Jewish property was finally undertaken. This definitive elimination of the Jews from the German economy would oblige about 120,000 Jews to leave the country, almost penniless, within just over a year.

Hitler's anti-Jewish policy in the early years of Nazi rule had to take account of the limitations of his domestic and international situation. He could not initially afford to ignore President Hindenburg and the more conservative ministers in this cabinet like von Papen, Hugenberg, Foreign Minister von Neurath and Schacht, who expected him to preserve law and order while keeping in check the plebeian anti-Semitism of the more radical Nazis. The conservative nationalists were hardly 'philosemites' or defenders of Jewish rights. They had no problem with the *numerus clausus* law, which had limited Jews to 1.5 per cent of the intake in high schools and universities, nor with the formal cancelling of the Jews' citizenship on 23 March 1934. Strictly *legal* measures that aimed at isolating and excluding the Jews appeared perfectly acceptable to them as they did to much of German public opinion, including the Protestant and Catholic Churches.[52]

Violent anti-Jewish street actions were another matter. Leading Nazi party officials themselves euphemistically referred to such gangsterism as *Einzelaktionen* – the kind of SA rowdiness and sadistic hooliganism that was giving Germany a bad name abroad. Hence the deputy *Führer*, Rudolf Hess, citing Hitler's need to refute 'allegations of atrocities and boycotts made by Jews abroad', gave a confidential order in April 1935 to party militants not to engage in acts of terror against individual Jews.[53] It was not easy, however, to pacify the Nazi rank and file, who could not understand why *any* Jewish banks, department stores, export houses or industrial enterprises were permitted to function in a National Socialist state reputedly at war with world Jewry.[54] The 'little Nazis' greedily anticipated the liquidation or 'Aryanisation' of Jewish property, which they believed had been promised to them by the party programme and by their own leaders' anti-capitalist demagoguery. But while Hitler profoundly sympathised with the violent impulses of the more fanatical anti-Semites, he knew that the time was not yet ripe to implement a truly radical approach.

The Nuremberg Race Laws of September 1935 were a kind of compromise between these countervailing pressures to which the Nazi leadership was subject by party radicals and the more conservative state bureaucracy. The laws 'for the Protection of German Blood and German Honour' formally stripped the Jews of their remaining rights as citizens.[55] They also forbade marriages and extramarital sexual intercourse between Jews and subjects of the state 'of German or related blood'; they prohibited Jews from employing female German servants under forty-five years of age in their households (presumably out of fear that Jewish men might seduce younger German women and father their children); they forbade Jews from flying the national flag (the swastika), or Reich colours. The Reich Citizenship Law also provided a new definition of who was, and who was not, a Jew. It differentiated between three categories: 1) Full-blooded Jews were designated as persons descended from at least three fully Jewish grandparents; so, too, were those who belonged to, or had later joined, the Jewish religious community, had two Jewish grandparents or had married a Jew. 2) The *Mischlinge* (part-Jews or persons of mixed descent) were defined as being 'first degree' if they had two Jewish grandparents but had not married a Jew or been a member of the local synagogue. 3) The 'second degree' *Mischlinge* were those who had only one Jewish grandparent. According to the somewhat inflated Nazi statistics, in 1935 there were no less than 750,000 Germans who fell into the category of first or second degree *Mischlinge*, in addition to the estimate of 475,000 'full Jews' who practised their religion and another 300,000 who did not do so. Thus, there were more than 1.5 million Germans of 'Jewish blood' in 1935, according to the peculiar Nazified categorisations. Time would show that differences in these categories could become life-and-death issues.

The declared objective of the Nuremberg Race Laws, according to Hitler's own Reichstag speech, was 'to find a separate secular solution (*eine einmalige säkulare Lösung*) for building a basis upon which the German nation can adopt a better attitude towards the Jews' (*eine erträgliches Verhältnis zum jüdischen Volk*).[56] The Nazi leader could simultaneously claim both that he was seeking to solve 'the Jewish problem by *legal* means' and that, by disenfranchising the Jews, he was finally fulfilling a cardinal point in the NSDAP programme of 1920 – namely that no Jew could ever be a *Volksgenosse* (racial comrade) or a *Reichsbürger* (citizen of the Reich). No less important, Hitler starkly warned that if workable arrangements with the Jews broke down, he might have to pass a law 'handing the problem over to the National Socialist Party for final solution' (*zur endgültigen Lösung*).[57] Yet top Nazi officials, such as the Interior Minister Wilhelm Frick, also made more reassuring remarks at this time. In December 1935 he declared that 'the Jews will not be deprived of the possibility of living in Germany.'[58] The Director of the German press agency even suggested that 'Germany is helping Judaism to strengthen its national character and is making a contribution towards improved relations between the two peoples.'[59] The correspondent of the London *Times* summarised the official commentary on the Nuremberg racial laws as follows: 'The members of the Jewish minority in Germany received through the new legislation the right to live their own cultural and national life. They can have their own schools, theatres and sports clubs ... But the participation of Jews in the political or social affairs of the German people is now and for ever (says the commentary) prohibited.' The correspondent even noted that Hitler had informed party leaders that he was against arbitrary 'individual actions'.[60]

Although German Jews had been reduced to the humiliating position of second-class citizens, they had not yet given up hope that they might find a small niche within the Third Reich. They clutched at the straw that racial separation could stabilise their position, as some official rhetoric seemed to imply, by offering them a 'legally protected' framework.[61] German Jews might be isolated from the rest of the population but their means of livelihood had not yet been destroyed. Some German Zionists also managed to find a few positive aspects to the Race Laws, though for different reasons. They particularly welcomed its contribution to the collapse of 'assimilationist' delusions. There were even those among them who misguidedly believed that the principle of racial separation offered good prospects for an increased and more intense Jewish cultural activity.[62] Ironically, perhaps, this proved to be true for the brief period before the radicalisation of Nazi policy in 1938 brought the curtain down on any illusions of a semi-autonomous Jewish existence within the Third Reich.

The spectacular extravaganza of the Berlin Olympics encouraged the hopes of German Jewry for a little while longer, bringing a toning down of the more vicious abuse and a halt to more blatant acts of anti-Semitic terror. The Nazis even soft-pedalled their own racist laws by permitting the token participation of a few Jewish athletes in their Olympic team to appease international criticism.[63] Germans were ordered to be on their best behaviour in order to radiate a positive image abroad of the new Reich as a law-abiding, peace-loving state. Significantly, Hitler postponed any act of vengeance against German Jewry for the assassination in February 1936 of the Swiss Nazi Party leader by David Frankfurter, a young Yugoslav Jew. But he was only biding his time. As he told an assembly of regional Nazi leaders on 29 April 1937, he had long ago made himself an 'expert' on the Jewish problem and in the next two to three years it would of course 'be settled one way or the other'.[64] Indeed, in a secret 1936 memorandum on the Four Year Plan, he made it clear that German Jewry would be expropriated in the event of the Reich going to war,

an eventuality for which he was already planning. Toward
the end of 1937, with full employment achieved, the drive t
completely eliminate Jews from the German economy was
noticeably accelerated. Not by accident this coincided with
the resignation of Schacht from the Economics Ministry,
followed in February 1938 by the removal of Von Neurath as
Foreign Minister as well as the sacking of War Minister Von
Blomberg and the chief of the Army High Command, Werner
Freiherr von Fritsch. At a stroke, the Chancellor had rid
himself of the last remaining representatives of aristocratic
conservatism in high positions, thereby gaining full control
over the armed forces and foreign policy.

A month later, Hitler annexed his former Austrian homeland
into what was henceforth called the Greater German Reich.
Vienna with its prosperous community of nearly 200,000 Jews
quickly became a model for the rapid forced emigration of Jewry
from the Reich. After a particularly violent and brutal campaign
of intimidation, Jews were forced by the SA to scrub the pave-
ments of Vienna with small brushes, watched by crowds of
jeering spectators, Jewish businesses were expropriated with
electrifying speed and Jewish homes shamelessly looted by Austrian Nazi thugs.[65] The Austrian tradition of anti-Semitism
(which had moulded the young Hitler thirty years earlier) flared
up again with an intensity that caught even the invading
Germans by surprise. The hysterical reception accorded to
Hitler on his triumphant return to Vienna in March 1938 provided the catalyst for this unprecedented outpouring of repressed hatred against the Jews.[66] The Austrian model of radicalised
anti-Jewish measures was immediately adopted in Germany
itself. A full scale 'Aryanisation' of the larger Jewish firms was
initiated by Hermann Goering, the overseer of the Four Year
Plan, as part of the broader policy of accelerated rearmament. A
decree of 26 April 1938 obliged all Jews to report their total
assets: in June 1938 drafts for the obligatory 'Aryanisation' of

Jewish businesses were already in place. The mood in Party circles and in the country was becoming more violently hostile to Jews. The *Times* correspondent noted that even in Berlin, hitherto 'the most tolerant German city in its treatment of Jews', slogans like 'Germans must not buy from Jews' or 'Out with the Jews' were visible in large characters across the street.[67] Storm troopers were seen picketing Jewish shops and rough handling their owners: a campaign of arrests led to about 1,000 Jews being taken off to concentration camps.

The flood of anti-Jewish legislation, the expropriations of businesses and the general aggression of the regime had inevitably produced a new wave of Jewish emigration from Nazi Germany, which began to alarm the democratic countries. At the initiative of the American President, Franklin D. Roosevelt, an international conference was convened at Evian, in France, ostensibly to address the plight of the Jewish refugees being ousted from Germany and Austria.[68] The organisers preferred, however, to emphasise that the talks covered political refugees from all countries. In attendance were representatives from thirty-two governments, including Great Britain and its dominions, most of the Latin American republics and European nations such as France, Belgium, Holland, Switzerland as well as three Scandinavian countries. The London *Daily Express* approvingly summarised some of the more characteristic responses to the challenge of the hour made by individual delegates. Thus the Australian Minister for Trade and Customs explained that his country could do nothing more for Jewish refugees. Australia wanted only British immigrants and they had no desire to import a 'racial problem' by 'encouraging any scheme of large-scale racial migration'. The Canadian representative, whose country's record on Jewish immigration was abysmal, evoked economic uncertainties and unemployment problems; Argentina indicated that it was looking mainly for 'experienced agriculturalists', which seemed to rule out most

Jews; Belgium would not assume any international obligations 'whose consequences she cannot foresee'.[69]

Most disappointing of all was the refusal by the United States and Great Britain to contemplate taking in any substantial number of Jewish refugees. Indeed, once America, the sponsoring nation, made plain its unwillingness to open its own doors, it had virtually doomed the Evian conference. In retrospect, it would appear that the whole exercise had been designed by the American State Department as a way to *divert* refugees from the United States and forestall any international pressure to liberalise the country's own immigration laws.[70] The British attitude was no less hypocritical. The Foreign Office successfully managed to keep Palestine off the agenda and blocked any denunciation of the Nazi government. The British delegation pleaded lack of resources to explain its own refusal to take any more Jews while vaguely promising to investigate whether a limited number of refugees could not be settled in its East African colonies. The London *Times*, in an editorial of 16 July 1938, praised this offer and commented: 'The refugee problem can be solved only by a mixture of mercy and cool calculation, both of which were shown in excellent proportion at Evian.'[71] Golda Meir, the future Prime Minister of Israel and at the time an observer at the Evian conference, took a very different view, writing in her autobiography: 'I don't think that anyone who didn't live through it can understand what I felt at Evian – a mixture of sorrow, rage, frustration and horror.'[72]

Most revealing of all as a response to this fiasco was Hitler's contemptuous reaction. Even before the results of the Evian conference were known, he mocked the humanitarian pretensions of the Western democracies (especially Britain and America) who claimed to be so solicitous for 'these criminals' (i.e. the Jews); later, in January 1939, he referred again to the charade: it was a 'shameful spectacle to see how the whole democratic world is oozing sympathy for the poor tormented

Jewish people, but remains hard-hearted and obdurate when it comes to helping them – which is surely, in view of its attitude, an obvious duty.'[73] Indeed, the Nazi leadership could only have felt bolstered in its increasingly brutal policy on the 'Jewish Question' by the results of the Evian conference. The whole miserable farce had demonstrated that Western nations were not at all willing to open their doors and accept Jewish refugees or to commit themselves to rescue actions where Jewish lives were concerned. Nor were they ready to publicly criticise Nazi anti-Semitic legislation – preferring instead to treat it as an *internal* German matter. Finally, there was another troubling implication, which was as yet only dimly visible on the horizon. If Nazi Germany could no longer expect to export, sell or expel its Jews to an indifferent world that plainly did not want them, then perhaps they would have to be removed altogether.

# III    *Persecution and Resistance*

All the Gestapo roads lead to Ponary and Ponary means death. Let us not be led like sheep to the slaughter. True we are weak and helpless, but the only response to the murders is self-defence. Brothers, it is better to die fighting like free men than to live at the mercy of the murderers.

**Abba Kovner**, Manifesto of Zionist Youth, Vilna, 31 December 1941

Why didn't we resist when they began to resettle 300,000 Jews from Warsaw? Why did we allow ourselves to be led like sheep to the slaughter?

**Emmanuel Ringelblum**, Diary, 15 October 1942

In exile the Jews had always been in a minority; they had always been in danger, but they had learned that they could avert danger and survive destruction by placating and appeasing their enemies ... A two thousand-year-old lesson could not be unlearned; the Jews could not make the switch [when their leadership realised] ... that the modern machine-like destruction process would engulf European Jewry.

**Raul Hilberg**, *The Destruction of the European Jews* (1973)

In October 1938 17,000 Jews of Polish origin hitherto residing in Germany found themselves brutally expelled en masse by the Nazi authorities. Dumped along the Polish-German frontier in appalling conditions, they were refused re-entry by the Polish government. Having previously rendered them stateless, Poland had already demonstrated its desire to rid itself of its Jewish citizens. Among the Polish Jews who suddenly found themselves abandoned in no-man's-land was the Grynszpan family. Their seventeen-year-old son, Herschel Grynszpan, then living alone as an illegal and stateless immigrant in Paris, was outraged by the treatment of his parents and of the Jews in general. (He later told French investigators: 'My people have a right to exist on this earth.')[1] In an act of anguished revenge, he shot the Third Secretary at the German Embassy in Paris, Ernst vom Rath. The German diplomat died of his wounds on 9 November 1938. Grynszpan's action was immediately denounced by the Nazi propaganda machine as a 'declaration of war' and part of a world-wide Judaeo-Masonic conspiracy. It would unleash an unprecedented orgy of ferocious anti-Jewish violence and terror across Germany, euphemistically referred to by the Nazis themselves as *Reichskristallnacht* (Crystal Night) after the crystal-like shards of broken glass from the shattered windows of Jewish shops across the land. All over Germany, more than 400 synagogues burned, while over 7,500 businesses and other properties owned by Jews were looted and ransacked. At least 100 Jews were murdered, many more injured, and 30,000 Jews were summarily packed off to concentration camps where they would suffer unspeakable indignities. Describing these events in Berlin on 10 November, the *Manchester Guardian* correspondent noted that the plundering and destruction of Jewish shops had already been going on for the better part of eighteen hours. 'There are streets in the business quarters whole sections of which this evening are literally paved with broken glass, while in the kerbs and on the road are lying smashed office furniture, typewriters, telephones, bales of papers and other wreckage which had been hurled out of the windows by the wrecking squads.'[2]

The British correspondent went on to recount how the wreckers 'entered the synagogues, throwing petrol over the pews and setting the interiors on fire. As far as could be observed the work of the fire brigades was largely to stand by and keep an expert watch that the fires did not spread from the synagogue interiors to neighbouring buildings ... the crowds watched the burning of the synagogues with apathy.'[3] The American Consul in Leipzig, David Buffum, who left one of the more graphic accounts of the pogrom, wrote that the barrage of Nazi ferocity 'had no equal hitherto in Germany, or very likely anywhere else in the world since savagery began.'[4] After describing the destruction and violation of property, he added: '... the most hideous phase of the so-called "spontaneous" action has been the wholesale arrest and transportation to concentration camps of male German Jews between the ages of sixteen and sixty, as well as Jewish men without citizenship. This has been taking place since the night of horror.'[5] Such was the scale of the damage that according to internal reports of the Security Services and other evidence, it would appear that a significant number of Germans were shocked and even disgusted at such vandalism of property and brazen violations of public law and order.[6] On the other hand, not only ideological fanatics took part. Among the mindless mobs of looters, there were many ordinary Germans incited to a fever pitch, who seized the opportunity to enrich themselves. Moreover, there was virtually no discernible public protest (not even from the churches) at this barbaric behaviour, though Jewish houses of worship had been a primary target of the destruction.

The pogrom had been incited and masterminded by Propaganda Minister Goebbels. It was he who had made the initial incendiary speech on 9 November in a Munich beer hall (commemorating the failed Nazi *putsch* of 1923) after news had come through of Vom Rath's murder. He called the diplomat's death the first shot in a new war between the Germans and Jews. His diaries reveal not only that the Führer was informed of every step but that Hitler explicitly wanted to make the Jews pay for the damage and expropriate their businesses.[7] Publicly, however, the Führer preferred to distance himself, preserving an attitude of aloof detachment. Hitler's immediate concern was that the pogrom should be given the appearance of being a 'spontaneous' expression of popular wrath against the Jews. The SS and SD leadership, which in principle rejected the methods of 'rowdy anti-Semitism', quickly recovered from its initial surprise and found new opportunities in the aftermath of the pogrom to pursue its own agenda and establish a firmer grip on all policy-making that related to the 'Jewish Question'.

Goebbels himself had been out of favour with Hitler since mid-1938 because of his messy affair with a Czech actress, a circumstance that may help to explain the particular zeal-ousness he exhibited in calling for vengeance against the Jews. He, too, was eager to re-establish his own *locus standi* in Jewish policy but would certainly not have incited the pogrom without Hitler's prior authorisation. Goering, on the other hand, who now supervised the 'Aryanisation' policy was determined to keep the 'Jewish Question' as far as possible out of radical Nazi hands. Like Himmler and Heydrich, who respectively controlled the German police and the security services (SD), he opposed methods of uncontrolled violence, preferring to tighten the net around German Jewry through administrative measures. Goering, in fact, considered actions like the *Kristallnacht* to be a serious public relations blunder and a deplorable lapse into 'wild Aryanisations'.[8] He wanted to expropriate Jewish property for the German state, not to see it destroyed by marauding mobs. Moreover, he was initially alarmed at the insurance claims (estimated at 225 million Reichsmarks) that could result. Himmler shared his disapproval, even writing in a memo that it was Goebbels' 'megalomania' and 'stupidity' that were pri-marily responsible for initiating an operation that could only exacerbate Germany's already difficult diplomatic situation. But whatever the policy differences and power struggles within the Nazi elite, there was no basic disagreement about the need for a 'reckoning with the Jews'.[9]

*Kristallnacht* was the most violent public display of anti-Semitism seen in German history since the Crusades. It also proved to be a significant turning-point on the road to the Holocaust. Undoubtedly, the lessons that the Nazi leadership drew in its aftermath marked a shift in its methods of persecution. At a marathon session in Goering's offices at the Reich Air Ministry on 12 November 1938, it was decided to levy a fine of one billion marks on German Jewry for what was styled its 'hostile attitude' to the German Reich and its people. After announcing the fine, Goering cynically added: 'Moreover, I have to say once again that I would not wish to be a Jew in Germany.'[10] The participants apparently felt that the public degradation they were inflicting on the innocent Jewish victims of the November pogrom in making them pay and even apologise for the huge damage caused by the Nazis was not enough. Goebbels, Goering and Heydrich took turns during the meeting in fantasising about or proposing additional humiliations: that Jews should wear personal insignia, that they should have isolated compartments in trains or be forced to give up their seats to Germans, that they should be placed in forests alongside animals they resembled etc.[11] Goebbels suggested expelling Jewish children still in German schools, banning Jews from all public places and imposing curfew restrictions. In the following month, the more concrete suggestions were promptly agreed to by Hitler, indicating that the momentum of the anti-Jewish campaign had indeed increased after *Kristallnacht*.[12]

The most practical outcome of the November 1938 meeting was to complete the process of eliminating the Jews from the economy and to co-ordinate the confiscation of all remaining Jewish factories and businesses. The department stores, major industrial concerns and merchant banks that had been spared longest were now asset-stripped, closed or taken over.[13] An additional decree was issued to exclude Jews from the retail trade, crafts and sales agencies, from managing firms or from membership of any co-operatives. In a highly significant sentence at the outset of his remarks, Goering invoked directly the

Führer's authority for these steps: 'Gentlemen! Today's meeting is of a decisive character. I have received a letter written on the Führer's orders by Bormann, the chief of staff of the Führer's deputy, requesting that the Jewish question be now, once and for all, co-ordinated and solved one way or the other ...' (so oder so).[14] So oder so was indeed a key Hitler phrase in relation to the Jews – one that intimated there would be no turning back from irrevocable decision. Nazi policy had clearly been radicalised sharply by Kristallnacht. In its wake, all Jewish business enterprise, freedom of movement and social intercourse with Germans was brought to a virtual end.[15] The scale and impunity of the violence had stigmatised the Jews, even more than before, as an unwanted pariah people, to be degraded at will, placed outside the ranks of society and the universe of moral obligation. Their existence on German soil was literally being torn up by the roots. Excluded from using public transport, from visiting concerts, theatres, cinemas, shopping centres, beaches and park benches or even owning a dog, German Jews were not merely outcasts at the end of 1939. They were already socially dead people. If they could lose their driving licences because their presence on the roads might offend the 'German traffic community', it could not be long before wearing the yellow star would definitively seal their pariah status.

Kristallnacht had dramatically accelerated Nazi measures against the Jews of the Third Reich. Its immediate effect was to increase the pressure for the emigration of German and Austrian Jews, which was still official Nazi policy. But it also encouraged attitudes that hinted at what would eventually climax in the 'Final Solution' a few years later. Thus, on 24 November 1938, the SS journal Das Schwarze Korps, under the heading 'Jews, what now?', prophesied that Germans could not tolerate the presence of hundreds of thousands of Jewish 'criminals' and 'sub-humans' much longer on Reich territory. Mocking the indifference and hypocrisy of the 'civilised nations' and 'the great screaming of world Jewry', it called for a solution that went beyond mere segregation. 'We would be faced with the hard necessity of exterminating the Jewish underworld in the same way as, under our government of Law and Order, we are wont to exterminate any other criminals, namely by fire and sword. The result would be the factual and final end of Jewry in Germany, its absolute annihilation.'[16] *Kristallnacht* and the blood-curdling verbal threats that followed suggested that the mood was ripe for the revival of an apocalyptic anti-Semitism that identified Jews with the criminal 'subhuman' underworld. The state pogrom intensified the strategy of demonisation that had accompanied the Nazi campaign against Jewry ever since 1919. But now, after twenty years, it seemed as if the fewer actual Jews still left in Germany, the more easily those that remained could be branded as total outcasts to fit the mould of existing propaganda stereotypes. Ian Kershaw has written that this process of depersonalisation accentuated the numbing indifference of German popular opinion, 'and formed a vital stage between the archaic violence of the pogrom and the rationalised "assembly line" annihilation of the death camps.'[17]

*Kristallnacht* also served another important function as a precursor for the dual war that Hitler was now feverishly planning. The conventional war of Nazi Germany against the great powers for territorial hegemony and *Lebensraum* in the east *and* the 'war against the Jews' entered a new phase of synchronisation. Ever since 9 November 1918, the two themes had been closely connected in Hitler's mind. As he told the Czech Foreign Minister in January 1939: 'With us the Jews would be destroyed (*vernichtet*); not for nothing had the Jews made 9 November 1918: this day will be avenged.'[18] Now, on 9 November 1938, twenty years after the German surrender, the pogrom against the Jews was a means to psychologically prepare the German nation for a new European war. It was Hitler's way to disabuse the Germans of any idea that the Munich peace

73

agreements two months earlier marked the end of the international political crisis.

Hitler's infamous Reichstag speech of 30 January 1939, delivered on the sixth anniversary of his accession to power, has to be seen in the context of a self-fulfilling prophecy and of a war that would have two faces.

> One thing I should like to say on this day that may be memorable for others as well as for us Germans: in the course of my life I have very often been a prophet, and have usually been ridiculed for it. During the time of my struggle for power it was in the first instance the Jewish race that only received my prophecies with laughter when I said that one day I would take over the leadership of the state, and with it that of the whole nation, and that I would then, among many other things, settle the Jewish problem. Their laughter was uproarious, but I think that for some time now they have been laughing on the other side of their face. Today I will once more be a prophet: if the international Jewish financiers in and outside Europe should succeed in plunging the nations once more into a world war, then the result will not be the Bolshevisation of the earth, and thus the victory of Jewry, but the annihilation of the Jewish race in Europe![19]

This was an extraordinary outburst from the leader of a great power and can hardly be reduced to a mere 'metaphor' or a piece of utopian rhetoric, as the German historian Hans Mommsen has tried to do.[20] Anyone viewing the film of the occasion and the vehemence with which Hitler delivered this particular section of his speech to the frenzied applause of the Reichstag delegates cannot doubt that it was a deadly serious threat. But it has to be analysed at several different levels. The most immediate target was world Jewry, whom Hitler typically held responsible for the mounting criticism of his regime after *Kristallnacht*. He was warning those who had 'laughed at him' or ridiculed his 'prophecies' and did not yet understand what he already knew with inner certainty because it lay at the very heart of his personality and mission – namely his *will to exterminate* the Jews. But it was also a threat against the Western democracies. Had he not repeatedly declared his willingness to collaborate with other states in seeking an 'international solution' to the 'Jewish Question'? In return he had heard only the sanctimonious hypocrisy of the liberal democracies, complaining of 'this barbaric expulsion from Germany of such an irreplaceable and culturally eminently valuable element.'[21]

Hitler knew that neither British nor American politicians had been willing to put their reproving speeches about Nazi Germany and the Jewish plight into practice. Did the Evian conference not conclusively demonstrate that in the wide empty expanses of the British Empire, the United States or Latin America, no room could be found for Jewish refugees? Hitler nevertheless dispatched his former Economics Minister Schacht on one last trip to England, to see if he could not reach an agreement with the American negotiator, Rublee, over ransoming German Jewry.[22] The Nazi plan was that world Jewry (and the democracies) would bankroll the emigration of their German co-religionists through a loan of one and a half billion Reichmarks, to be repaid in ten years' time through German exports. Acceding to this blackmail would in effect have meant financially rewarding the Nazis for their expropriation and expulsion of the Jews, though Hitler did not see it that way. Keeping the Jews in Germany alive had no more *raison d'être* for him except as a bargaining chip, as hostages in his cat-and-mouse game of war and peace with the West.

But there was yet another, more sinister level to this 'prophecy', which can be better understood in the light of his remarks to the South African Defence Minister Oswald Pirow, in Berlin on 24 November 1938. He had told his pro-German guest that 'world Jewry' (which in this case seemed to refer primarily to American Jews) regarded their European co-religionists as 'the advance troops for the Bolshevization of the world'; he had spoken heatedly of the Jewish 'invasion' from the east and declared that his mind was irrevocably made up: '... one day the Jews would disappear from Europe'. (*Die Juden würden ... aus Europa verschwinden*).[23]

In his Reichstag speech two months later, this prospect was more specifically linked to the outbreak of a *world* war. The prophecy of annihilation was impersonally couched but it clearly related to the *physical* destruction of European Jewry, especially if there should be any involvement of the United States and American Jewry (linked in Hitler's mind to the international Jewish financiers 'outside Europe'). The constant references back to his January 1939 prophecy during the war years, and especially *after* the 'Final Solution' had begun, cannot be accidental. Twice in 1942 and three more times in 1943 he recalled his words but each time he confused the date of his speech about 'annihilation' (30 January) with the outbreak of the Second World War in September 1939.[24] Such a compulsively repeated 'mistake' is in itself remarkable. My explanation would be that for Hitler the *world* war and the 'war against the Jews' were in fact *one and the same confrontation*. So, too, the 'prophet' and the *Realpolitiker* were one and the same person. The prophet was there to give periodic expression to the dark fantasies of *Sieg* or *Untergang*; the politician proceeded more pragmatically, with the requisite tactical flexibility adapting himself to the shifting international and diplomatic constellation, as he groped towards the self-fulfilling prophecy of *Vernichtung*.

Between 1933 and 1939, Nazi policies on the 'Jewish Question' had been influenced, as we have seen, by many contradictory currents within the German state and society as well as by forces beyond it. Although the Jews were perceived in unwavering terms by the Nazi leadership as a deadly 'enemy' to be isolated and removed from Germany, there was as yet no clear plan to exterminate them physically. In retrospect, one can see that between 1933 and 1938, the measures of economic boycott, legal exclusion and defamation had been carried out with some caution compared with the avalanche that followed. The Nuremberg Race Laws had marked an important advance in realising the Nazi Party programme and the traditional objectives of German anti-Semitism – namely racial separation and the removal of Jews from the economy, civil society and citizenship in the state. But they did not as yet shatter the institutions and will to live of German Jewry or the foundations of its economic existence. At the same time, despite their massively discriminatory character, the racial laws did not encounter any significant opposition from the conservative elites, the Churches, business circles, the intellectuals or the mass of the German population. Thus it would seem that at least until November 1938 (and possibly beyond) there was a public consensus on the 'Jewish Question' within which the Nazi regime still operated.

The increasingly visible movement in 1938/9 towards the radical policy of expelling Jews entirely from Germany's social and political space, was an important qualitative change in this situation. It could doubtless be rationalised as a logical step (in terms of bureaucratic logic) to the next stage of squeezing the Jews out of Germany, without any clear notion of what should follow. But while the central role of the bureaucracy and of internal power struggles over the right to influence the anti-Jewish policy is apparent, one can hardly ignore the crucial part played by Hitler in providing the dynamics and the momentum. As Goering tersely put it: 'In the last analysis, it is the Führer alone who decides.'[25] This was especially true with regard to grave decisions, such as those in favour of war and peace or concerning the when, where and how of unleashing the Holocaust. Only in Hitler's mind were war and genocide so closely related. It was his apocalyptic perspective that presupposed the widening and globalisation of the 'Jewish Question' as a pan-European issue in 1939, in the context of a coming world war. Once Germany was engaged, after September 1939, in a major European war against Poland, Great Britain and France that it seemed to be winning, the door would be open for a complete 'removal' of the Jews of Europe, though not yet their complete annihilation. The invasion of the USSR in June 1941 would bring in its wake a more violent and far-reaching extension towards a comprehensive 'solution', leading on to the beginnings of a streamlined annihilation of European Jews. Finally, with the entry in December 1941 of the United States into the war, the last remaining constraints on the organisational co-ordination of this plan were removed and it became fully operational.

What linked all these stages together was the fanatical Nazi commitment to the ideological fantasy that they were fighting a 'great racial war' in which *either* the 'German-Aryans' or the Jews must prevail and eventually rule the world. The overall Nazi project remained the racial 'purification' and reorganisation of Europe along ethnic lines, involving the resettlement and relocation of entire populations.[26] Within that overarching biological–political framework, the Jews were, however, a special case. For the 'Final Solution' did indeed suggest *finality* – it was a plan to hunt down and kill every single Jewish man, woman and child that could be seized on the continent of Europe from Paris to Bialystok, from Amsterdam to the island of Rhodes. The comprehensive *totality* of this genocidal project is what differentiated the Holocaust from massive Nazi violence inflicted on Poles, Russians, Ukrainians, Serbs and gypsies, not to mention the so-called 'mercy' killings of ethnic Germans, and the starvation of millions of Soviet prisoners of war, or the torture of Communists, the persecution of homosexuals or Jehovah's Witnesses.[27]

The implacable nature of the Nazi campaign against the Jews

derived from their special status as a *Weltfeind* (world enemy). Implicit in this ideological conception was the proposition that even successfully solving the problem of German Jewry (for example by complete emigration) could never bring the 'Jewish Question' to an end. For at the core of the conflict was the demonic Jewish world power that would always seek to destroy Germany, National Socialism and so-called 'Aryan' civilisation. The satanic quality of the adversary also meant that 'international Jewry' would constantly seek to widen the war and intensify the struggle in order to spill ever more precious German blood on the battlefield. Within this phantasmagoric logic of racial war, the most extreme measures could therefore be justified in advance as actions of imagined *self-defence*. Yet the simple truth remained that Jews as a group were weak, vulnerable, and had at no time harboured any aggressive designs against Germany.

There was, however, another empirical reality that the Nazis could not ignore. The invasion of Poland and its military occupation had at one stroke added more than two million Polish Jews to the Jewish population at Hitler's mercy. (As a result of the Nazi–Soviet pact, just over one million Jews in Eastern Poland would fall under Russian Communist rule from September 1939 until June 1941.) The dramatic increase in the numbers of Jews living in the German 'sphere of influence' underlined a dilemma that bedevilled the Nazis in their frantic efforts to create territories that were *judenrein* or 'free of Jews'. Each time they annexed or conquered an area, they acquired more Jews than they were managing to remove by encouraging emigration. Thus, after the *Anschluss* of March 1938, 200,000 Austrian Jews had entered the Greater German Reich. Following the rape of the Czech lands a year later, another 120,000 Jews came under Nazi control. After the collapse of Poland, further victories of the Wehrmacht in the west and then the conquest of the Baltic States, White Russia, the Ukraine, Galicia, the

Crimea and other lands to the east, hugely swelled the numbers of Jews in Nazi hands. What was to be done with them? In Warsaw alone, there were as many Jews in 1939 (about 330,000) as in the whole of the German Reich. As eastern Jews, they had long been objects of German fear and prejudice. Nazi propaganda now made sure that no German would ever forget that the *Ostjuden* were permanent sources of dirt, infectious disease, criminality, Bolshevism and the heart of the 'world Jewish problem'. Goebbels, after visiting the Lodz ghetto, on 2 November 1939, wrote in his diary: 'We travel through the ghetto. We get out and observe everything in detail. It's indescribable. These are not human beings any more, they are animals. Therefore, we have not a humanitarian task to perform, but a surgical one. One must cut here, in a radical way. Otherwise, one day, Europe will perish of the Jewish disease.'[28]

Goebbels, like many radical Nazi anti-Semites, regarded the eastern Jew as the quintessential animal-like 'other', symbolising pestilence and life-threatening disease. He had visited the ghetto to supervise the production of the violently anti-Semitic film *The Eternal Jew*, eventually screened in 1940. In an earlier diary entry of 17 October 1939, Goebbels was even more explicit: '... Pictures from the "Ghetto" film. Such a thing never existed before. Scenes so dreadful and brutal in their details that one's blood freezes. One pulls back in horror at so much brutality. This Jewry must be exterminated.'[29] It is almost as if Goebbels in viewing the first film tests of the *Judenfilm* made in Lodz (shortly after Wehrmacht units had occupied the city) was unconsciously offering us an X-ray preview of the mindset behind the decision to launch the Holocaust. On the same day Goebbels notes that he had mentioned the film to Hitler, who 'showed great interest'. *The Eternal Jew* as a finished product would in fact be a kind of tacit collaboration between Hitler, Goebbels and the film maker Dr Fritz Hippler.[30]

The German invasion of Poland immediately resulted in the

sadistic humiliation of Polish Jewry (orthodox Jews were often publicly degraded by having their beards and sidelocks ripped off) and the intermittent murder of some 7,000 Jews in the first three months of the campaign. On 21 September 1939, Heydrich set out the guidelines of SS policy in his instructions to the *Einsatzgruppen* of the Security Police. He distinguished between the 'final aim' and the stages leading towards it, beginning with 'the concentration of the Jews from the countryside into the larger cities'. The points of concentration were to be cities with rail junctions 'or at least located on railroad lines'. He also ordered the setting up of a Council of Jewish Elders in each Jewish community, an administrative body consisting of authoritative personalities and rabbis, who would be responsible 'for the exact and prompt implementation of directives already issued or to be issued in the future'.[31]

The Councils would also be held responsible for the evacuation of Jews from the countryside, for housing, transport, tax collection, labour allocation, hospitals, schools, orphanages, sewage disposal and other functions of the pre-war Jewish *kehilla* (community). The Councils (*Judenräte*) were to become a kind of horrible caricature of Jewish government, mediating between the fearfully oppressed Jewish population (who often resented their power) and the Nazi authorities to whom they were wholly subordinate. The Council leaders were under constant and tremendous stress in dealing with a ruthless Nazi officialdom, having to face daily pressures of extortion, reprisals, exactions and levies, as well as the desperate anguish of the starving Jewish population.[32] Their power derived from German masters but, knowingly or unknowingly, they presided over doomed communities. The composition of the Councils was usually middle class, selected from merchants, doctors, lawyers and other professionals who had been active in Jewish public life before the war. Sometimes they were selected on Nazi orders by prominent persons in the community, at other times the selection was quite arbitrary. Refusal to serve more often than not meant death. For the Nazis, the *Judenrat* was perceived as an instrument to dominate and rule the ghetto, as a valuable executor of their policies, saving them the task of policing and enforcing their own decrees.

By making the Councils responsible for life-and-death decisions, such as who would be handed over to the Germans for deportation to the death camps, the Nazi rulers managed to implicate the Jewish leadership in the bureaucratic process of destruction. In effect, according to Raul Hilberg's highly critical view of their role, Jews ended up providing the Germans with administrative personnel that enabled the machinery of annihilation to function more smoothly. In his view, the Jewish response pattern, fashioned by 2,000 years of ghetto history, was one of alleviation, evasion, paralysis and compliance.[33] The Jewish experience before the Holocaust had been that 'they could avert or survive destruction by placating or appeasing their enemies'.[34] Confronted by Nazi terror they could not make the switch and became part of the machinery of destruction. Under conditions of such degradation, some Jews even 'collaborated' with the enemy. For example, the much hated Jewish police force was directly responsible for physically rounding up deportees and pushing them on to trains, which made them accessories to the extermination of fellow Jews. They were part of a privileged power structure that was bound to lead to corruption, as well as severely undermining Jewish solidarity. But they, too, were coerced, often by means of the cruellest blackmail. Finally, Hilberg has argued that the Councils induced a fatally illusory feeling of 'normality' and submissive Jewish behaviour that greatly facilitated the work of the Nazis.

Hannah Arendt went even further and regarded such 'collaboration' as a symptom of the 'moral collapse' that Nazism caused throughout respectable European society, among persecutors, bystanders and victims alike. 'The whole truth was that if the Jewish people had been disorganized and leaderless, there would have been chaos and plenty of misery but the total number of dead would hardly have been six million.'[35] This was a highly simplistic verdict that ignores not only the circumstances and context but also the wide range of responses among Jewish Council leaders. Some were no doubt guilty of complicity or corrupted by their position of power, while others tried to protect Jewish interests as best they could. The head of the Warsaw *Judenrat*, the industrial engineer Adam Czerniakow, who committed suicide in 1942 (when the Nazis began to demand 10,000 'non-productive' Jews per day for 'resettlement', which invariably meant liquidation) was a good example of those council leaders who desperately sought salvation for Jews through building more ghetto industries and plants. A courageous man, constantly intervening with the Germans to alleviate their inhuman regulations, his diary conveys an overwhelming sense of powerlessness and failure.[36] By July 1942 over 100,000 Jews in the Warsaw ghetto had perished as a result of starvation and disease, especially typhoid and dysentery.

Czerniakow despised his counterpart in Lodz, the 'king' of the local *Judenrat*, Mordecai Rumkowski, as 'self-important', arrogant and stupid. A ghetto leader like Rumkowski who flamboyantly rode through his 'kingdom' in a horse-drawn carriage and issued banknotes with his portrait on them, had clearly developed megalomaniac tendencies. Yet Rumkowski pursued an identical strategy of 'rescue through work' in the hope that economic rationality might win out over Nazi ideological fanaticism. Increased productivity became a *goal in itself* despite the starvation. The head of the Lodz ghetto had organised the 180,000 strong ghetto population, (many of whom worked for the German army) efficiently and tyrannically – deciding who was to live and who to die. His reasoning summed up the horror of the Jewish predicament: 'I must cut off the limbs to save the body itself. I must take the children because if not, others will be taken, as well.'[37] Like the chairman of the Vilna *Judenrat*, Jacob Gens, he believed in the bargaining process, in providing the Germans with all the Jews they demanded, in the vain hope of thereby protecting and saving those who remained. Gens was no less authoritarian in his leadership style than Rumkowski and equally convinced that only his methods offered any hope for the constantly squabbling and fractious Jewish community. Opinions about his role remain divided but the charge of collaboration is hard to refute. Gens was shot by the Gestapo a few days before the liquidation of the Vilna ghetto, while Rumkowski went to the gas chambers along with most of the inhabitants of the Lodz ghetto in 1944.

Ghettos had been established throughout Poland from the end of 1939. The largest of them all was the Warsaw ghetto, which suffered from obscene overcrowding, holding as many as half a million Jews at its peak. Sealed off in November 1940 by barbed wire from the rest of the city (though there was an active smuggling route), the ghetto population was packed into 1.3 square miles compared to the area of 53.3 square miles inhabited by Polish Christians. The gates to the ghetto were guarded by German, Polish and Jewish police. Inside this living hell, Jews were forbidden to keep cash or merchandise. They lived in complete economic isolation from the outside world. When pressed into forced labour the Jews were paid nothing or else a tiny sum of money, usually insufficient to buy even a loaf of stale bread. In the largest ghettos, Warsaw and Lodz, about a quarter of the Jews died from disease, starvation and the inhumanly harsh conditions. The Nazis spuriously claimed that they had created the ghettos to prevent the spread of epidemics, but their insidious propaganda goal was to mark off the Jews as people who were not only different but physically degenerate. By starving them, they could ensure that reality resembled the stereotype, even as they decimated their numbers. The contemporary chronicler of the Warsaw ghetto, Chaim Kaplan, who wrote poignantly about 'the gigantic catastrophe' that had descended upon Polish Jewry, commented in his diary on 10 March 1940 that the depth of Nazi anti-Semitic hatred went far beyond political ideology.[38] His remarks are worth quoting at some length:

> It is a hatred of emotion, whose source is some psychopathic disease. In its outward manifestation it appears as physiological hatred, which sees the object of its hatred as tainted in body, as lepers who have no place in society ... But the founders of Nazism and the party leaders created a theoretical ideology with deeper foundations. They have a complete doctrine which represents the Jewish spirit inside out. Judaism and Nazism are two attributes to the world that are incompatible, and for this reason they cannot co-exist side by side. For 2,000 years Judaism has left its imprint, culturally and spiritually, on the nations of the world. It stood fast, blocking the spread of German paganism ... Two kings cannot wear one crown. Either humanity would be Judaic or it would be pagan-German. Up until now it was Judaic. Even Catholicism is a child of Judaism, and the fruit of its spirit ... The new world which Nazism would fashion, would be pagan, primordial, in all its attitudes. It is therefore ready to fight Judaism to the finish...[39]

In the abyss of the Warsaw ghetto, Kaplan had grasped something of the violently pagan essence of Nazism while insisting on the extraordinary vitality of Judaism even in the midst of the inferno.

Though Polish Jewry outwardly lay crushed and broken amidst the terrible suffering inflicted upon it by its Nazi conquerors, it had not lost its vibrant will to live, its love of life or its indomitable spirit. Kaplan records the extraordinary atmosphere a few months after the Warsaw ghetto was sealed: 'In the daytime, when the sun is shining, the ghetto groans. But at night everyone is dancing even though his stomach is empty.

Quiet, discreet evening music accompanies the dancing. It is almost a *mitzvah* to dance. The more one dances, the more it is a sign of his belief in the "eternity of Israel". Every dance is a protest against our oppressors.'[40]

Despite their desperate situation Jews managed to set up study groups, lending libraries and underground schools in the ghettos. There were committees that provided child care and charity for the needy as well as maintaining a wide variety of cultural activities. Ghetto dwellers sought, despite the tragic circumstances, to preserve (as best they could) their fidelity to tradition and Jewish religious values. The salvaging of Torah scrolls, Talmud study, prayer and bar mitzvah celebrations, along with Hebrew language classes, continued. To quote Chaim Kaplan, writing in his diary on 2 October 1940, on the eve of the High Holy Days:

> Again: everything is forbidden to us; and yet we do everything! We make our 'living' in ways that are forbidden ... It is the same with community prayers: secret *minyanim* in their hundreds all over Warsaw hold prayers together and do not leave out even the most difficult hymns. Neither preachers nor sermons are missing; everything is in accordance with the ancient traditions of Israel.[41]

This was a spiritual self-affirmation no less significant than more obviously political and military forms of resistance. Despite the gnawing hunger and recurring outbreaks of typhus, the tenacity with which the intelligentsia in the Warsaw ghetto fought to keep alive the cultural heritage of such a highly diverse community was truly remarkable.[42] Concerts, seminars, literary evenings and discussions were regularly held at the Judaic Library. There were festivals of Jewish culture and music. Poets and prose writers recited from their works, chamber music was played, plays were performed. The classics and more recent works of world literature were avidly read. Orphanages, too – like that of Janusz Korczak – ran cultural programmes for the general public, reaching members of the Jewish community who had never previously attended such events.[43] There were so-called 'children's corners', where, apart from food, children were offered some form of education and entertainment.

Such intense cultural activities eloquently testified to the refusal of Polish Jewry to accept their degradation to the level of beasts, which the Germans tried by every conceivable means to impose upon them. Notwithstanding their awareness of impending catastrophe, they were determined to fight for their individual and collective Jewish identity, for their human dignity and some form of national survival, however remote the prospects might seem.[44] The common cliché that Jews did not resist their persecutors and simply went 'like sheep to the slaughter' is neither an accurate nor a fair description, though in its original context it was intended by the Jewish Resistance more as a call to arms. When presented as a blanket criticism, it overlooks the extraordinary lengths to which the Nazis went in disguising the genocidal intent of their policy toward the Jews. The perpetrators deliberately encouraged false hopes and the illusion that compliance and work might be the salvation of Jewry.

The slogan of 'sheep to the slaughter' also overlooks the fact that the notion of total physical extermination was not only unprecedented but must have seemed to most Jews (and Gentiles) like the product of a diseased imagination. It under-estimates the state of sheer exhaustion and demoralisation in which the ghettoised Jews found themselves and the degree to which they were isolated and cut off from the outside world. It ignores the intimidating effects of collective punishment as practised by the Nazis whenever they were faced with even the most trivial and minor acts of defiance. The knowledge that the Germans would exact terrible reprisals was a serious dis-incentive all over Europe to any attempt at armed resistance. There were relatively few efforts at revolt, for example, by the many well-trained Allied soldiers and the hundreds of thousands of Russian prisoners of war in German camps, though they were watched over by a fairly small number of guards. Charges of passivity have rarely been made against them. Yet Western prisoners were not subjected to the unrelenting dehumanisation that was the common fate of the Jews in the ghettos and the Nazi camps.

The Jewish population, to a much greater extent than any other, had the terrifying experience of being hunted down like wild animals. To make matters worse, they found themselves – at least in eastern Europe – in a generally hostile and anti-Semitic environment. Even in the event of escape, Jewish men were still marked by circumcision, often easily identified by their beards and facial features or else by their distinctive garb. Despite these great obstacles, Jews did subsequently rebel in the ghettos of Warsaw and Bialystok, in the death camps of Treblinka, Sobibor and Auschwitz and took up arms with the partisans wherever they succeeded in escaping their tormentors. Probably, it was no accident that the progenitors of militant resistance came from Lithuanian Jewry, the first to be subjected to savage and massive killing conducted by the Germans with enthusiastic participation from the local population.[45] It was as if they sensed that Lithuania was a kind of experimental laboratory for the 'Final Solution'. This realisation gave birth to the armed struggle in the Vilna ghetto in January 1942. It was based on the prophetic insight of the Zionist Pioneer Youth Group (*Hashomer Ha-Tsair*) that 'Hitler aims to destroy all the Jews of Europe' (this was three weeks before the Wannsee Conference) and that the Lithuanian Jews were 'fated to be the first in line'.[46]

In his manifesto of 31 December 1941, Abba Kovner, the leader of the group, warned that only a quarter of the 80,000 Jews of Vilna remained and that those taken from the ghetto would never return. It was in this context that he added: 'Let us not be led like sheep to the slaughter. True we are weak and helpless, but the only response to the murders is self-defence.'[47] The revolt was a desperate gesture of defiance that led to the formation of a United Partisan organisation, drawn from all groups in Jewish political life but principally including Zionists, Bundists and Communists. The Jewish youth groups were unburdened by family responsibilities and more receptive to revolutionary action. They instinctively opposed the position of those *Judenräte* that advocated obedience and passivity, in the vain hope of warding off greater evils. In the summer of 1943 some of the young Jewish fighters managed to escape from the Vilna ghetto, forming partisan units and contributing to the eventual liberation of their city.

Armed revolts also broke out elsewhere in at least twenty ghettos in eastern Europe, the best known of them being the uprising in the Warsaw ghetto, which continued for almost a month from 19 April until 15 May, 1943.[48] It was indeed the first armed rebellion by civilians anywhere in Nazi-occupied Europe, taking the Germans completely by surprise. The ghetto fighters consisted initially of the 600-member Jewish Fighting organisation led by twenty-four-year-old Mordechai Ani-elewicz, and the National Military organisation, which had 400 men and women in its force. Armed with only a few machine guns and rifles and a larger number of grenades and Molotov cocktails, the ghetto fighters had little training and minimal help from the local Polish Resistance. They had witnessed the disappearance of the bulk of the ghetto inhabitants whether through deportations to the death camps or through death by starvation and disease. The remaining 60,000 Jews in the Warsaw ghetto, many of them teenagers, were the most able-bodied survivors, who had been left for last. When the SS entered the ghetto to round up more Jews for deportation, to their great astonishment they were met by bombs, shooting and mine explosions. It would eventually take 3,000 troops under the command of SS General Jürgen Stroop, equipped with heavy machine guns, howitzers, artillery and armoured vehicles – subsequently reinforced by bombers and tanks – to overcome the hopelessly outgunned Jewish resistance. The Jews held on in the sewers underneath the city, until the ghetto had been totally razed by German forces, some of the fighters jumping from the burning buildings rather than surrendering to their oppressors. They knew from the outset that they were engaged in a hopeless battle, but they were determined to die with honour and dignity. In his last letter from the ghetto on 23 April 1943, Mordechai Anielewicz observed that 'what happened exceeded our boldest dreams' and that 'what we dared do is of great, enormous importance . . .'[49] He had no illusions about his own fate or that of his comrades. What mattered most was that self-defence in the ghetto and Jewish armed resistance had finally become a reality. Over 15,000 Jews died in battle and more than 50,000 were captured and sent to death camps.

It is important to note that there were also revolts in the death camps themselves, including one in Auschwitz, where prisoners blew up one of the crematoria, killing several SS guards, as well as a much bigger rising in Treblinka (August 1943). At Sobibor, on 14 October 1943, several hundred prisoners stormed the gates in a rebellion that led to the shutting down of the camp two days later. Though a majority of the prisoners perished in the break-out attempt, over a hundred managed to escape, many joining partisan units in the forests. Tens of thousands of Jews across Nazi-occupied Europe took part in the various partisan or resistance movements, some to seek revenge on their murderous enemy, others to save their own lives and where possible those of their fellow Jews. Jewish partisans fought bravely in the forests of the Ukraine, and Poland, in the Carpathian mountains, White Russia and Lithuania.[50] In eastern Europe, the partisan activity usually took place in separate Jewish units because of the open hostility from the local populations. Sometimes this antagonism extended to the anti-Nazi partisan groups, which in Poland and elsewhere were not infrequently riddled with anti-Semitism. The fighting Jewish Brigade formed in the forests near Vilna under Abba Kovner was the most celebrated of all the Jewish partisan groups. Other focal points of Jewish resistance were in the areas of Bialystok, Kovno and Minsk, where Jews were prominent from 1943 in the multinational partisan units under Soviet control. The Soviet High Command, as a matter of principle, did not approve or permit the existence of separate Jewish partisan units.[51] In southern and western Europe, Jews faced a less overt form of hostility from the indigenous population and found it easier to operate as part of the national resistance movements in countries such as France, Belgium, Holland, Italy, Greece and Yugoslavia (where about 2,000 Jews fought in the ranks of Tito's guerrilla movement).[52] Despite the adverse conditions, Jews were also prominent among the founders of the partisan movement in Slovakia, with at least 2,500 Jews fighting in the Slovak national rebellion in the summer of 1944.

In France, Jews at one stage represented over fifteen per cent of the Resistance forces, more than twenty times their proportion of the total population. Their role in positions of leadership and command as well as in the rank and file of the Resistance was outstanding. Half of the founders of *Libération* were Jews and they composed almost 20 per cent of the National Committee members, the highest institution of the French underground. The founder of the Franc Tireurs in the Paris region in 1942–3 was a Jew, as were a disproportionate number of those who rallied to De Gaulle's Free French forces in London. Often enough, the Jewish resistance fighters in France and western Europe suppressed the fact of their Jewishness. Sometimes this was for security reasons. Others may have believed that it would not help the Allied cause, either because the Germans and their French collaborators at Vichy would exploit the fact, or out of fear that it might arouse latent anti-Jewish feelings in the Resistance.[53] No doubt many also felt their French identity to be more important than their Jewish loyalties or origins. The relatively high number of Jews in the French Communist resistance was also downplayed, both by Jews themselves and by the Communist Party. Mostly this was for political and ideological reasons not dissimilar from those prevailing in the wartime Soviet Union and eastern Europe. One result of this discretion has been that the story of Jewish resistance in the Holocaust period is less known than it should be, except in Israel, where it assumed overriding importance. But the dominant narratives are often distinctly selective. If we also consider the heroism and skill of the more than half a million Jewish soldiers in the ranks of the Red army, as well as the distinguished service of more than 700,000 Jews in the British and American armies (not to mention other Allied forces) then the military contribution of Jews serving in regular armies to the defeat of Nazi Germany was by no means negligible. Approximately 10 per cent of world Jewry (1.6 out of 16 million Jews in the world in 1939) actually fought in the war, including the 35,000 Palestinian Jews who volunteered for the Jewish Brigade in the British army.

Within Germany itself, there was virtually no armed resistance of any sort, and thus no armed Jewish resistance either. But a significantly high proportion of German (and Austrian) Jews who emigrated from the Reich before 1939 did become involved in Belgian, Dutch, Italian and French resistance to fascism and in efforts to sabotage the German occupation. Those Jews who remained in Germany under the prevailing conditions of ruthless *Gleichschaltung* (the forcing into line of institutions) had no possibility of direct political resistance. But this did not deter either the rabbis or the official representatives of the German Jewish community, from making dignified protests against the persecutions and the first deportations to the east.[54]

Moreover, the Jewish press in the Third Reich, for as long as it survived, was without doubt the last enclave of liberal and humanist values still permitted in Nazi Germany. Between the lines, one can read many instances in its pages of veiled protest against the state-sponsored propaganda that mercilessly degraded Jews to the level of subhumans.[55]

Despite the totally isolated and vulnerable position of German Jewry in the Third Reich, there were probably 2–3,000 Jews, mainly young people, directly active in the German anti-Nazi underground.[56] This is a remarkably high number given that there were only 200,000 Jews left in Germany at the outbreak of war in September 1939. (The proportional equivalent of such a figure for the German population would have been about 700,000 anti-fascist militants, of which there is certainly no evidence.) However, it needs to be remembered that the Jewish anti-fascists (mainly socialists and communists) generally felt that their affinities and first loyalties were to the German workers' movement. Jews were especially numerous in the German communist resistance, which included the wholly Jewish underground group led by Herbert Baum, responsible for the courageous, though ill-conceived and disastrous attack on the Nazi propaganda exhibition 'Das Sowjetparadies' in the Berlin Lustgarten. The boys and girls of the Baum group were atheists who stood completely outside the Jewish community.[57] Their alienation from Jewry was fully reciprocated by Jewish communal feelings about Communist agitation. It did not help that the Communists periodically indulged in crude propaganda against 'Jewish capitalists', even after such a group had ceased to exist in Germany. On the other hand, following the *Kristallnacht* pogrom of 1938, the Communist underground press did display some real signs of solidarity with the persecuted Jewish population.[58] Despite the non-democratic, totalitarian character of their organisation and ideology, the Communists were particularly prominent among those who made the greatest sacrifices within the limited German resistance.

The Jewish youth movement in Nazi Germany (which reflected a diversity of cultural and political trends within German Jewry) was also a favourable seedbed for anti-fascist activity. This partly derived from the strong socialist orientation of many of the Zionist youth groups, dating back to the days of the Weimar Republic. The movement led a unique existence under the Third Reich, preserving under the noses of the Gestapo the more humanistic aspects of the pre-1933 German culture that were fast disappearing in society as a whole. For a number of years until it was banned, it could even be said that the Jewish youth movement provided what Arnold Paucker has called 'an oasis of free thinking in a totalitarian Germany' that continued to flourish and stimulate anti-Nazi activity.[59] Later, during the war years, anti-fascist Jews in Germany and outside carried on more dangerous illegal actions ranging from sabotage, assassination attempts and pacifist propaganda to helping Allied prisoners of war to escape. These activities, like those of Jews in other areas of the resistance, had many motivations and were not always inspired by the 'Jewishness' of the individual participants. Nevertheless the prominence of many Jews in the resistance was not unconnected to their principled and strong emotional identification with the goals of the anti-Nazi coalition, as members of a specially persecuted minority group.

# IV    The 'Final Solution'

If just once, at the beginning or during the course of the war, we
had exposed twelve or fifteen thousand of those Hebrew corrupters
of the people to poison gas ... the sacrifice of millions of men
would not have been in vain. On the contrary, if we had rid
ourselves of those twelve or fifteen thousand fiends, we might
perhaps have saved the lives of a million good brave Germans.

**Adolf Hitler**, *Mein Kampf* (1925)

We travel through the ghetto. We get out and observe everything
in detail. It's indescribable. These are not human beings any more,
they are animals. Therefore, we have not a humanitarian task to
perform, but a surgical one. One must cut here, in a radical way.
Otherwise, one day, Europe will perish of the Jewish disease.

**Joseph Goebbels**, Diary, 2 November 1939, Lodz (Poland)

And then they all come, those worthy 80 million Germans, and
each one has his own decent Jew. Of all who talk that way, none
of them has watched, none of them has gone through it. Most of
you know what it means to see 100 bodies lying there, 500 lying
there or 1000 lying there. To have gone through this and, aside
from exceptions due to human weakness, to have remained decent,
that has made us tough.

**Heinrich Himmler**, Speech to Higher SS and Police Leaders,
Poznan, October 1943

It is sometimes forgotten that Jews were not the primary target
of the Nazis during the first eighteen months after the invasion
of Poland in September 1939. The Germans, having decided in
agreement with the Soviet Union on the destruction of the
Polish state, proceeded to decapitate its elites, to 'transfer'
parts of the Polish population eastwards, to extinguish any

manifestation of their national identity and to reduce the mass of its people to helotry. In 1939–40, for example, close to 10,000 Polish intellectuals, members of the nobility and clergy were killed by the *Einsatzgruppen* in a deliberate effort to crush Polish national resistance. In the wake of the killers, came German economists, technical experts and academic planners who calculated that much of Poland's rural population was 'nothing more than dead weight', superfluous people whose continued presence was an obstacle to industrial 'development' and to Germany's economic interests. 'Negative demographic policy' – a technocratic concept emanating from Goering's Four Year Plan Agency – envisaged organising the deaths of millions of Poles and Russians (after June 1941) as a solution to problems of food supply as the war was extended.[1] It was no accident that two million Soviet prisoners of war were allowed to die of starvation in German camps before the end of 1941. Goering himself predicted in November 1941 that 'twenty to thirty million people will starve in Russia'. Perhaps, he cynically added, that was a good thing 'since certain people will have to be decimated'. New strategies of racial reordering, in the name of 'Germanisation' and a settlement policy for the conquered territories were being devised in the framework of Himmler's *Generalplan Ost*, which covered the whole area between Leningrad and the Crimea.[2]

During the 1939–41 period, the Nazis had still not worked out a clear, consistent policy with regard to Jews, Poles or even the half-million ethnic Germans they had 'repatriated' to German-annexed territory. On 25 May 1940, Himmler had submitted a secret memorandum, entitled 'Reflections on the treatment of the Peoples of Alien Race in the East' to Hitler. With regard to the non-German population as a whole he made it clear that the sole aim of schooling the 'subhuman people of the East' must be to teach them simple arithmetic, learning to write their own names and 'to obey the Germans'.[3] The Poles were to be treated as 'a people of labourers without leaders' whose main task was to provide the Reich with migrant workers. Without any qualms Himmler also advocated kidnapping 'racially' valuable Polish 'children of good blood' (blonde, blue-eyed and Nordic-looking) and sending them to the Reich to be brought up as German 'Aryans'. At this early stage, Himmler explicitly rejected 'as un-German and impossible the Bolshevist method of physical extermination of a people'. Instead, he appeared to be relying on a mixture of 'racial sifting', resettlement and splitting up the different ethnic groups in Eastern Europe 'into as many parts and fragments as possible'. He also hoped that 'the concept of Jews will be completely extinguished through the possibility of a large emigration of all Jews to Africa or some other colony.'[4]

Himmler was probably alluding to the idea still being seriously considered in leading Nazi circles of deporting Jews en masse to the East African tropical island of Madagascar, then a French colony. In 1937 the Polish government had approached the French and British about sending a million Polish Jews either there or to southern Africa. Now, following the defeat of France, Franz Rademacher (the official responsible for Jewish affairs at the German Foreign Office) had drawn up a memorandum envisaging the mass deportation of 4 million Jews from Europe and their resettlement in Madagascar, once the island was transferred from French to German control. The funds for this population transfer would naturally be provided by the despoiled Jews. They would supposedly enjoy nominal self-government in the administration of the law courts, culture and economic life but would ultimately be under the 'expert' control of the SS. Of course, the deported Jews would be stripped of German or any other European citizenships, becoming instead citizens of the 'great ghetto' henceforth to be known as the Madagascar Mandate.[5] Rademacher even saw this project as a useful Nazi response to Zionist ambitions in Palestine: 'This arrangement will prevent the possible establishment of a Vatican State of their own, in Palestine by the Jews, thus preventing them from using for their own purposes the symbolic value which Jerusalem has for the Christian and Mohammedan portions of the world.'[6] More ominously, Rademacher added that 'the Jews will remain in German hands as a pledge for the future good conduct of the members of their race in America'.

The Rademacher plan had the approval of Foreign Minister Von Ribbentrop and was taken seriously (with some modifications) by Heydrich and his SS bureaucrats, as long as their domination of the project could be assured. But the German failure to defeat Great Britain in 1940 meant that control of the sea traffic in the Atlantic, which was essential to the success of the plan, could not be assured. Although the plan would still sometimes be referred to by Hitler in conversations with Mussolini and other foreign leaders, the African solution would soon be quietly shelved. Formally, however, it was only on 10 February 1942 that Foreign Office departments finally received an official confirmation from Rademacher of what Hitler had decided several months earlier: 'The war with the Soviet Union has in the meantime created the possibility of disposing of other territories for the Final Solution. In consequence, the Führer has decided the Jews should be evacuated not to Madagascar, but to the East. Madagascar need no longer therefore be considered in connection with the Final Solution.'[7]

The German invasion of the Soviet Union in June 1941, codenamed 'Operation Barbarossa' was indeed to be inextricably linked with the decision to implement a genocidal war against all the Jews of Europe. It would also cost the lives of 20 million Soviet citizens (more than half of whom were civilians) including 3 million Red army prisoners of war, starved to death by the Germans. In this gigantic confrontation, which has been rightly called 'the most savage military campaign in modern history', all traditional conventions of behaviour, let alone ethical or legal restraints were wholly abandoned.[8] In the so-called 'Commissar Order' of 6 June 1941 the German army was specifically told by its commanders not to show any mercy or 'respect for international law' in the fight against Bolshevism and specially against 'the political commissars of all kinds'. This communist enemy allegedly employed 'barbaric, Asiatic fighting methods', which therefore necessitated the immediate execution of all Red army political officers. Some 600,000 of these officers were summarily shot by the Wehrmacht in the first few months of fighting. Ruthless punitive action was also stipulated against partisans and anyone assisting them, as well as against Jews and members of the Communist Party. The Wehrmacht or regular German army was ordered to provide close military and logistical assistance to the *Einsatzgruppen* (mobile killing units) of the SS who would follow in their footsteps and whose task was the murder of Jews and other Soviet citizens designated for elimination.

The four *Einsatzgruppen* battalions that operated on the vast Russian front from the Baltic to the Black Sea would, with the help of the Wehrmacht and Nazi police units, murder more than one million Jewish men, women and children in the first eighteen months of the Russian campaign. In the Ukraine, beginning in Lvov, they found willing collaborators in the massacre of Jews among Ukrainian nationalists. A report by the *Einsatzgruppen* for the period of 1–31 October 1941 dealt with the extermination in the Ukraine, including the notorious Babi Yar massacres of Jews just outside the Ukrainian capital city of Kiev.[9] The report cryptically noted:

> The bitter hostility of the Ukrainian population against the Jews is extremely great, because it is thought that they were responsible for the explosions in Kiev. They are also seen as NKVD [Soviet secret police] informers and agents, who unleashed the terror against the Ukrainian people. All Jews were arrested in

retaliation for the arson in Kiev and altogether 33,771 Jews were executed on September 29th and 30th. Gold, valuables and clothing were collected and put at the disposal of the National Socialist Welfare Association, for the equipment of the *Volksdeutsche*, and in part given to the appointed city administration for distribution to the needy population.[10]

The indescribable horror of this bloodbath against defenceless and innocent men, women and children is never of course, remotely glimpsed in such sterilised accounting or in other German documents.

Some of the earliest massacres took place in the Baltic states where the *Einsatzgruppen* were enthusiastically aided, especially by Lithuanians. Here is a typical extract from a report by Karl Jäger, Commander of *Einsatzgruppe 3*, on the extermination of Lithuanian Jews, a document which was dated Kovno, 1 December 1941. It too is written in the stone-cold language characteristic of such reports, which usually include a precise statistical breakdown of the numbers of victims:

... I can confirm today that *Einsatz Kommando 3* has achieved the goal of solving the Jewish problem in Lithuania. There are no more Jews in Lithuania, apart from working Jews and their families. These number: in Shavli, about 4,500, in Kovno about 15,000, in Vilna, about 15,000.

I want to eliminate the working Jews and their families as well, but the Civil Administration (*Reichskommissar*) and the Wehrmacht attacked me most sharply and issued a prohibition against having these Jews and their families shot. The goal of clearing Lithuania of Jews could be achieved only through the establishment of a specially selected Mobile Commando under the command of SS *Obersturmführer* Hamann, who adopted my aims fully and who was able to ensure the co-operation of the Lithuanian partisans and the civil authorities concerned. The carrying out of such *Aktionen* is first of all an organisational problem. The decision to clear each sub-district systematically of Jews called for a thorough preparation for each *Aktion* and the study of local conditions. The Jews had to be concentrated in one or more localities and, in accordance with their numbers, a site had to be selected and pits dug ... The Jews are brought to the place of execution in groups of 500, with at least 2 kms distance between groups ... All the officers and men of my command in Kovno took active part in the *Grossaktionen* in Kovno. Only one official of the intelligence corps was released from participation on account of illness.

I consider the *Aktionen* against the Jews to be virtually completed. The remaining working Jews and Jewesses are urgently needed, and I can imagine that this manpower will continue to be needed urgently after the winter has ended. I am of the opinion that the male working Jews should be sterilised immediately to prevent reproduction. Should any Jewess nevertheless become pregnant, she is to be liquidated..."

The pattern of killing by the murder squads as it is described here, was typical enough for the Eastern Front and a faithful reflection of the 'ideological war' of extermination and enslavement that Hitler had ordered. The Wehrmacht (which objected in Poland and Lithuania to murdering valuable Jewish workers) did, however, actively participate in the killings of Jews in the Soviet Union. The commander of the Sixth Army, Field Marshal Von Reichenau, explained to his troops in an order of the day, issued on 10 October 1941, what the rationale for their conduct in the war against Bolshevism had to be:

The essential goal of the campaign against the Jewish-Bolshevik system is the complete destruction of its power instruments and the eradication of the Asiatic influence on the European cultural sphere ... In the East the soldier is not only a fighter according to the rules of warfare, but also a carrier of an inexorable racial concept (*völkischen Idee*) and the avenger of all the bestialities which have been committed against the Germans and related races.

Therefore the soldier must have *complete* understanding for the necessity of the harsh, but just atonement of Jewish sub-humanity. This has the further goal of nipping in the bud rebellions in the rear of the Wehrmacht which, as experience shows, are always plotted by the Jews.[12]

On 20 November 1941, General Erich von Manstein, commander of the Eleventh Army and one of Germany's most brilliant generals, elaborated on this theme.

Since 22 June the German *Volk* is in the midst of a battle for life and death against the Bolshevik system. This battle is conducted against the Soviet army not only in a conventional manner according to the rules of European warfare ... Jewry constitutes the mediator between the enemy in the rear and the still fighting remnants of the Red army and the Red leadership. It has a stronger hold than in Europe on all key positions of the political leadership and administration, it occupies commerce and trade and further forms cells for all disturbances and possible rebellions.

The Jewish-Bolshevik system must be eradicated once and for all. Never again may it interfere in our European living space. The German soldier is therefore not only charged with the task of destroying the power instrument of this system. He marches forth also as a carrier of a racial conception and as an avenger of all the atrocities which have been committed against him and the German people.

The soldier must show understanding for the harsh atonement of Judaism, the spiritual carrier of the Bolshevik terror ...[13]

Such ideological statements by top German field commanders exhorting their troops to ever greater ferocity against the 'racial' and political enemies of the Reich, were becoming commonplace. The military leaders spoke, like Colonel General

Hoth, commander of the Seventeenth Army on 25 November 1941, of 'our mission to save European culture from the advancing Asiatic barbarism'; of the German sense of 'honour' and race when confronting the Jewish-Bolshevik 'disregard of moral values'. Not only the commanders but also the combat troops accepted this Nazified view of the war as an ideological struggle for survival against demonic Jewish-Bolshevik enemies. As Omer Bartov has pointed out, Wehrmacht soldiers serving on the Russian front were young men 'who had spent their formative years under the Third Reich and were exposed to large doses of indoctrination in Nazified schools and especially in the Hitler Youth and the Reich labour service.'[14] Their education and socialisation had instilled in them the mindset requisite for a genocidal task.

More specifically, the *Vernichtungskrieg* (war of destruction) that the army waged against the Soviet Union, against 'Judaeo-Bolshevism' and the 'Asiatic hordes' in the east, provided the precondition for the 'Final Solution of the Jewish Question' in Europe. On this issue, Hitler knew that his conservative, anti-Bolshevik generals were in broad agreement with his views, just as they had no difficulties with the idea of starving or working to death Slav *Untermenschen*, or reducing them to a reservoir of slave labour for the German *Herrenvolk* (master-race). 'Operation Barbarossa' had opened up new vistas for the Nazi elite in terms of 'solutions' to a series of long-range problems they had hitherto postponed or held on ice. Ever since the 1920s Hitler had dreamed of a war against the Soviet Union, to establish *Lebensraum* (living space) to the east in a Greater German Empire. But this would have to be a *Weltanschauungskrieg* (war of ideologies) to destroy international Communism which was itself regarded by the Nazis as the main political arm of Jewry – the expression of its will to dominate the world.[15]

As the gigantic battle with the USSR approached, it is striking how Hitler began to return to the language of *Mein Kampf* and the anti-Semitic racial eschatology of his early days as an agitator in Munich. At a preparatory conference on 30 March 1941 Hitler had emphatically informed his military commanders that war with the Soviet Union would be 'a struggle between two opposing world outlooks' (*Kampf zweier Weltanschauungen gegeneinander*) – a race war totally different from the confrontation in the West.[16] The guidelines he laid down for the ruthless elimination of Bolshevik commissars, partisans and Jews, were carried out to the letter – as we have seen – by his generals and troops in the field.

It is important to grasp the qualitative leap which was now taking place along the continuum of murderous actions that taken together comprise the Holocaust. The period from the conquest of Poland until June 1941 can in retrospect be seen as a 'testing laboratory' for Hitler's racial and imperial ambitions. In Poland, the racial policies designed to expel Poles and Jews from areas annexed to the Reich and replace them with 'racially pure' Germans and *Volksdeutsche*, none the less enjoyed only limited success. The civilian Governor-General of the General Government in conquered Poland, Hans Frank was constantly complaining that his fiefdom had become a vast dumping ground for Jews from Germany, Austria and the other annexed Polish territories, in circumstances that were a burden on his overstretched administration. In the ghettos, as a result of deliberate German cruelty, there were acute overcrowding, chronic shortages of food and a complete absence of sanitation, leading to outbreaks of typhus and other infectious diseases. Though hundreds of thousands died in these appalling conditions or in the labour camps, and Jews were brutally and randomly killed, systematic mass murder was not yet German policy in the spring of 1941. Soviet Russia, on the other hand, became the arena for the final struggle, 'the prelude to the millennium' to borrow Lucy Dawidowicz's pregnant phrase for the Nazi apocalypse.[17]

On 31 July 1941 (almost six weeks after the invasion of the USSR began) Heydrich received an order from Goering 'to carry out all preparations with regard to the organisation, the material side and financial viewpoints for a total solution (*Gesamtlösung*) of the Jewish question in those territories of Europe which are under German influence'. He was further instructed to submit a draft 'showing the administrative, material and financial measures already taken for the execution of the intended final solution (*Endlösung*) of the Jewish question'.[18] It is also well established that in mid-June 1941 Heydrich had given the higher SS and police leaders in the east open-ended orders about killing Jews, saboteurs, subversives and Comintern officials. His instructions did not, however, go much beyond the Commissar Order that had preceded the invasion. Under the cover of protective security measures against partisans in the occupied territories, it was however easier – as Hitler himself pointed out in a planning conference on 16 July 1941 – 'to wipe out anyone who gets in our way'.[19] Eichmann himself during his interrogation by the Israeli police in 1960 affirmed categorically that sometime in August 1941 he had heard point-blank from Heydrich: 'The Führer has ordered physical extermination.'[20] He assumed that the order must have come down through Himmler and would never have been put into writing, on which point he was probably correct.

In September 1941, as German forces became increasingly bogged down in their military campaign, the killing of Soviet Jews greatly increased. Significantly, Hitler had indicated on the evening of 2 October 1941 that these accelerating massacres in the east enjoyed his full approval. Recalling yet again his Reichstag prophecy of January 1939 that 'the Jew would disappear from Europe', he cynically told Himmler and Heydrich: 'It's not a bad idea, by the way, that public rumour attributes to us a plan to exterminate the Jews. Terror is a salutary thing.'[21] This statement occurred just over a month after Himmler had informed the *Gauleiter* of the Wartheland, Arthur Greiser, (on 18 September 1941), that it was 'the Führer's wish that the Altreich and the Protectorates (Bohemia and Moravia) should be cleared of Jews from west to east. I am therefore doing all I can to see that the deportation of the Jews out of the Alt-Reich and the Protectorates into the territories assimilated into the Reich during the past two years is completed during this year as a first stage, preparatory to their being sent further east early in the new year.'[22]

Hitler's September 1941 order for the 'removal' of Jews from the Reich to the east was highly suggestive because it went beyond the more geographically limited killing of Soviet Jews towards a pan-European solution of the 'Jewish Question'. Heydrich, at a conference in Prague on 10 October 1941, also spoke of the Führer's wish 'that German Jews be deported to Lodz, Riga and Minsk by the end of the year, if possible'.[23] This formula of 'the Führer's wish' (*des Führers Wunsch*) evoked by both Himmler and Heydrich, would come to assume a life of its own during the Holocaust, as one of those key code words (like 'evacuation', 'resettlement', 'transport to the East') that covered or disguised the horrible reality of mass murder. The circular of 23 October 1941 from Gestapo chief Heinrich Müller (issued in Himmler's name) banning 'all further Jewish emigration, with immediate effect', was one more decisive pointer to the emergence of a new phase.[24] For where would the Jews go if they could no longer emigrate, or stay where they were? This question was all the more acute as the Russian winter set in and heavy German losses were for the first time being sustained at the hands of the 'Jewish-Bolshevik' enemy.

There were also other significant indicators regarding a decision for genocide around September/October 1941. The brutality of face-to-face mass shootings on the Eastern Front were beginning to take their psychological toll on the *Einsatzgruppen* and Himmler (after witnessing one such execution) had become more 'sensitised' to the needs of his troops and the desirability of a so-called 'humane' method of killing. By September 1941 *Einsatzgruppe C* was in possession of a truck that used exhaust gases to kill the trapped Jewish victims. In October 1941 plans for the construction of gassing apparatus had been discussed between Adolf Eichmann, Alfred Wetzel (the Jewish expert of the *Ostministerium*), and Viktor Brack, the supervisor of the euthanasia programme in the Führer's Chancellery.[25] It was agreed that 'there is no reason why those Jews who are not fit for work should not be removed by the Brack method (i.e. gassing) ... the workworthy on the other hand will be transported to the east for labour.'[26]

Riga and Minsk were mentioned as destinations for deported German Jews from the Alt-Reich who would be handed over to the *Einsatzgruppen* commanders on arrival. The Germans had, of course, no intention of feeding the new mass influx of deported Jews that they were deliberately organising. Incapable of hard labour, what prospect did these Jews have of survival? Moreover, now that a better, though still primitive, technology (mobile 'gas vans' emitting carbon monoxide) was decided upon, it remained only to find the sites and construct the 'annihilation camps' (*Vernichtungslager*). The first death camp was built at Chelmno (Kulmhof) in Poland, where the gassing of Jews (using exhaust gas from vans) began on 8 December 1941.[27] It appears that Himmler had been given a special authorisation to have 100,000 Jews killed there. (About this time, gas trucks were also being used by the Germans to kill Jews in Semlin, Serbia).[28] This was followed by the building of Belzec in eastern Poland (near the former Soviet border), the first extermination camp to be equipped with permanent gas chambers, which was established in March 1942. By then, Auschwitz-Birkenau in Silesia, which became the biggest of all the death camps (though it was a concentration and industrial labour camp as well) was also operational though the gassing of Jews only began two months later.[29] Sitting astride the major railway artery from Vienna to Cracow, this huge complex of camps – known more simply if misleadingly as Auschwitz (Oswiecim in Polish) ultimately became the most notorious symbol of the Holocaust as an assembly-line process of mass murder. It is estimated that approximately 1.2 million Jews died in the gas chambers of Auschwitz-Birkenau, along with a much smaller number of Poles, gypsies and Soviet prisoners of war. Similar killing facilities were constructed at other death camps in Poland, such as Sobibor (May 1942), Treblinka (July 1942) and Majdanek (autumn 1942), whose sole purpose and product was mass murder.

Towards the end of 1941, pressures for the physical elimination of the Jews were building up from many sides, especially in that strange no-man's-land known as the General Government. Its Governor-General, the former lawyer Hans Frank, in a notorious speech of 16 December 1941 in Cracow, could not have been more explicit about his intentions. '... One way or another – I will tell you that quite openly – we must finish off the Jews. The Führer put it into words once: should united Jewry again succeed in setting off a world war, then a blood sacrifice shall not be made only by the peoples driven into war, but then the Jew of Europe will have met his end.'[30] The Governor-General's mimicking of Hitler's *so oder so* (one way or the other) was becoming the Nazi signature tune for the Holocaust.

Frank then referred dismissively to 'criticism' of the cruelty and harshness of measures 'now applied to Jews in the Reich' (the deportations etc.). In language that was again unmistakably reminiscent of Hitler, he ranted that one could have pity 'only for the German people and for nobody else in the world'. If European Jewry survived the war, he declared, while Germans had sacrificed 'the best of our blood' for Europe, this would be at most a half-success. His confident expectation was however that 'the Jews will disappear' and hence he intended to send a representative to Reinhard Heydrich's planned January 1942 conference in Berlin (an allusion to the forthcoming Wannsee meeting). Speaking as an old Party man, Frank then reported to his audience about what he had been told on a recent visit to Berlin: that instead of making trouble by refusing to have more Jews thrown into his territory, he would do better to 'liquidate' them himself. There was no room for sentimentality or compassion, he concluded.

> We must destroy the Jews wherever we meet them and whenever the opportunity offers so that we can maintain the whole structure of the Reich here ... The Jews batten on to us to an exceptionally damaging extent. At a rough estimate we have in the Generalgouvernement about 2.5 million people (Jews) – now perhaps 3.5 million who have Jewish connections and so on. We cannot shoot these 3.5 million Jews, we cannot poison them, but we can take measures that will, one way or another [so oder so], lead to extermination, in conjunction with the large-scale measures under discussion in the Reich.[31]

The planned measures in the Reich to which Hans Frank vilely alluded, were to be spelled out in some detail at t notorious ninety-minute Wannsee Conference of 20 January 1942, held in the serenity of an elegant suburban villa in Berlin. It was organised by Reinhard Heydrich in his capacity as Chief of the Security Police and the SD, but more importantly as the designated 'Plenipotentiary for the Preparation of the Final Solution (Endlösung) of the Jewish Question'. Heydrich, the most 'Aryan-looking' of the Nazi leadership and a fanatical anti-Semite (despite misleading rumours of his partly Jewish ancestry), was determined to push the meeting forward in brisk and businesslike fashion.[32] The conference, which was to have been held originally on 8 December 1941, had already been delayed for six weeks. Its ostensible purpose was to co-ordinate and agree the guidelines of a general plan with the various Reich ministries and service chiefs to exterminate (though the word was naturally avoided) *all* of European Jewry. There were five representatives of the SS and police present, including Gestapo Chief Heinrich Müller and the conscientious Adolf Eichmann (from the Reich Main Security Office), who took the minutes. The nine civilians represented respectively the Ministry of the Interior (Dr Stuckhart), the Ministry of Justice (Dr Freisler), the Reich Chancellery (Kritzinger), the Ministry of the Occupied Eastern Territories (Drs Meyer and Liebbrandt), the office of the Four Year Plan (Neumann), the office of the Governor-General (Dr Bühler), the Party Chancellery (Klopfer) and the Foreign Ministry (Dr Luther).

Heydrich opened the meeting by referring back to earlier commissions he had received from Goering in September 1939 and July 1941 to prepare a practical and organisational plan for 'the final solution of the European Jewish Question'. This task demanded 'prior joint consideration by all central agencies directly involved in these questions with a view to maintaining parallel policy lines'. With evident relish, he emphasised that the responsibility for handling the 'Final Solution' would be centralised in the hands of the Reichsführer SS (Himmler) and himself as Chief of the Security Police and the SD. Heydrich then briefly reiterated two key elements in the struggle hitherto waged by the Reich against the enemy, namely the 'forcing of the Jews out of the living space (*Lebensraum*) of the German people' and out of the various areas of its life (*Lebensgebiete*).[33] Accelerated emigration of the Jews had until recently been vigorously pursued 'as the only possible provisional solution'. Heydrich recalled some of the difficulties encountered along this road, including restriction or cancelling of entry permits by foreign governments, lack of shipping space and financial obstacles. Nonetheless, in eight years of Nazi rule – from 30 January 1933 until 31 October 1941 – when Himmler had banned emigration (because of wartime conditions and new 'possibilities in the East'), 537,000 Jews had been 'sent out of the country'. They comprised 360,000 from Germany proper, 147,000 from Austria (after March 1938) and about 30,000 from Bohemia and Moravia. The wealthy Jews and major foreign Jewish organisations had been made to finance this emigration. But this was past history, a mere prelude to the great tasks ahead.

In place of emigration, there was now a new prospect, namely 'the evacuation of the Jews to the East in accordance with the prior approval of the Führer' (*nach entsprechender vorheriger Genehmigung durch den Führer*). This 'evacuation' or deportation to the east was only a temporary expedient on the road to 'the coming final solution of the Jewish Question' (*die kommende Endlösung der Judenfrage*). But to use Heydrich's technocratic jargon, 'practical experience of the greatest importance' had already been acquired. Presumably, Heydrich was elliptically referring both to organisational experience in deportations and the lessons learned in shooting, gassing and other killing techniques that had been tried out in the east during the preceding six months.

According to the overblown estimates of the Reich Main Security Office, the 'Final Solution' of the European Jewish Question would encompass no less than 11 million Jews. (Heydrich implied that even this calculation might be on the low side, since foreign countries that only partially applied racial principles, usually underestimated the true number of Jews). His population table included on its target list the 330,000 English Jews, 4,000 Jews from Ireland and Jews from neutral countries such as Sweden (8,000), Switzerland (18,000), Spain (6,000) and Turkey in Europe (55,500), none of whom would suffer German occupation. Estonia was the one country already listed as 'free of Jews' (*Judenfrei*). Particularly high Jewish population estimates were quoted for the USSR (5 million Jews),

Ukraine (2.99 million) and unoccupied France (700,000). According to Heydrich, Europe was 'to be combed from west to east' while implementing 'the Final Solution', with the area of the Reich (Germany, Austria, Bohemia and Moravia) receiving priority 'because of the housing problem and the socio-political needs'. In reality, the Holocaust would proceed somewhat differently.

Heydrich envisaged some difficulties in countries like Hungary and Romania that he regarded as corrupt, even asserting that 'in Hungary it is imperative that an adviser in Jewish questions be pressed upon the Hungarian government without too much delay'. On the other hand, in Slovakia and Croatia, he believed that 'the most essential problems in this field have already been brought near to a solution.' Heydrich did not expect too many difficulties 'in registering Jews for evacuation' in occupied or unoccupied France; however, he spoke only of 'preparatory steps to settle the question in Italy'. Chillingly deceptive was his casual mention of the 'five million Jews in European Russia', without so much as a hint that Soviet Jews in their hundreds of thousands had already been massacred. Instead, he gave a distorted occupational breakdown of Russian Jewry, cynically adding: 'The influence of the Jews in all walks of life in the USSR is well known.'

The timing of each 'evacuation' project would, he claimed, be 'determined chiefly by the military developments'. In territories or areas influenced by the Reich, competent Foreign Office people were expected to confer on the 'Jewish Question' with the relevant SD officials. The zealous Foreign Office representative, Martin Luther, a relentless bloodhound in 'Jewish affairs', drew attention to likely problems with the Scandinavian countries, but given the small number of resident Jews there, he suggested that a deferment of the 'evacuations' might be in order.[34]

Heydrich then briefly detailed the 'special administrative and executive measures' that were to apply to the conscription of Jews for labour (*Arbeitseinsatz*) in the eastern territories. Despite his laborious euphemisms it must have been clear to all the officials present that most of the deported Jews would certainly be 'unfit for labour' and therefore could expect to be disposed of immediately. For those who were fit, he envisaged large labour gangs (with the sexes separated), which would be formed for road-building 'in which task a large part of them will undoubtedly fall out through natural elimination (*durch natürliche Verminderung ausfallen wird*)'. These work projects, reminiscent of the Stalinist Gulags, never came to fruition, apparently vetoed by Hitler, who temporarily preferred at this point to use the available manpower for other ends. Those Jews who survived this nightmare scenario could not, of course, be allowed to go free. They would have to receive 'special treatment' (*Sonderbehandlung*) since they represented the most physically resistant, 'a natural selection of the fittest', a 'germ-cell (*Keimzelle*) of a new Jewish revival'. This, according to Heydrich's way of thinking, was proven by 'the experience of history'.[35]

Finally, the protocols of the Wannsee conference devoted considerable space to the question of *Mischlinge* (half-Jews or mixed breeds) and mixed marriages, a fact that has puzzled some historians – especially since the lengthy and abstruse discussions did not seem to produce any conclusive result. For the Nazis this was not merely a smokescreen but an issue of real importance and conceptual difficulty.[36] No less than 75,000 persons had been defined as first-degree *Mischlinge* (two Jewish grandparents) and 125–130,000 as second-degree (one Jewish grandparent). It had been crucial for German officials to know who should be treated as a Jew ever since the Nuremberg Laws of 1935, which in principle remained valid for the implementation of the 'Final Solution'. *Mischlinge* of the first degree were, as before, to be treated as Jews and those of the second degree, as Germans. But there were some exemptions. For instance, the children of a first-degree 'mixed blood' in a marriage with 'person of German blood' were regarded 'essentially as Germans'. Their 'mixed blood' parent would also be exempt from 'evacuation'. Similarly privileged would be those cases of 'personal merit' involving a first-degree Mischling previously exempted by the highest party or state authorities. But even the exceptions would have to undergo 'voluntary' sterilisation, if they wished to stay in the Reich. It looked like and was indeed a hopelessly entangled bureaucratic thicket of racist insanity, but for the Nazis these were deadly serious issues. Heydrich and the Reich Main Security Office could be well satisfied with their results in most areas. They failed, however, in their desire to stiffen and unify the convoluted legislation on half- and quarter-Jews. Partly they were blocked by bureaucrats like Stuckart, by the Führer's Chancellery and possibly by Hitler himself until he reversed his position in 1944.

In the concluding session of the Wannsee Conference, it was notable that Under-Secretary of State Dr Buehler insisted that the 'Final Solution' should first of all be implemented in the Government General where he claimed that 'the Jews represented an immense danger as carriers of epidemics' and were permanently undermining the economic system through black-market operations. Echoing the demands of the absent Hans Frank, he declared that the majority of the 2.5 million Jews were 'unfit for work' – tantamount to passing a collective death sentence on them in the context of such murderous deliberations. The protocol laconically states: 'He had this one request only, namely that the Jewish question in this territory be solved as quickly as possible.' In fact, with the exception of Galicia, where German massacres of Jews had already started in October 1941, no systematic extermination in the Government General began until the spring of 1942.[37]

What then was the historic significance of the Wannsee conference? Clearly, despite its sanitised language, it does lay out a general and centrally organised plan for the massacre of *European* Jewry (in its entirety) and it is the only official document that has survived, that does so in such detail. It is the first text that definitively reveals the fates of *western* and *central European* Jews, as well as those of the millions of Polish and Russian Jews, whose murder was already under way. That latter reality is typically glossed over in the document. The Wannsee conference also demonstrated that the German state bureaucracy had no serious objections to the genocidal plans to be implemented by Heydrich's Reich Main Security Office, with the exception of some anticipated difficulties and reservations concerning *Mischlinge*. By implication, it was also evident that the vast majority of German Jews (except again for certain carefully defined categories who were protected by mixed marriage) were doomed to suffer the rigours of the 'Final Solution'.

The first deportations of German Jews in mid-October 1941 had not always resulted in instant death. An element of uncertainty about how to deal with them is suggested by a letter in December 1941 from Wilhelm Kube (General Kommissar of Belorussia and an old Party member) to Heinrich Lohse, describing the condition of German Jews in Minsk, and asking for clear directives. Kube observed that these Jews deported from Germany to the Minsk ghetto included First World War heroes decorated with the Iron Cross, war invalids, half- and even three-quarter 'Aryans'. He asserted that they differed sharply from Russian Jews in their skills, productivity and 'personal cleanliness'. These German Jews were 'people who came from our own cultural sphere', not at all like 'the brutish hordes in this place'. Kube asked if the proposed slaughter was to be carried out by Lithuanians and Letts, 'themselves rejected by the population here' and respectfully requested that 'the necessary action be taken in the most humane manner'.[38] He did not want, however, to give an order for liquidation on his own responsibility.

Kube's misgivings remind one that the application of the genocidal plan to German Jews was not immediately self-evident, even for some hardened and convinced Party members. This fact was reflected in the delay – until late 1941 – in applying a measure like wearing the yellow star to Jews of the Reich (Germany, Austrian and the Czech Protecktorat) or in finally completing the deportations from Germany. Indeed, the German Reich was not declared *judenrein* until June 1943. The Nazi regime proceeded more cautiously in this area since the forcible removal of German Jews could not be concealed from the population and might provoke uncomfortable questions about their final destination.

An even more serious potential obstacle to a speedy and comprehensive elimination of the Jews arose from the usefulness to the German military machine of industrious Jewish workers in the eastern territories. The SS were determined to overrule, wherever possible, such pragmatic considerations. This would be made crystal clear in reply to the important query raised on 15 November 1941 by Heinrich Lohse (Reich Commissar for Ostland), who had written to the Ministry for the Eastern Territories, concerning Jewish workers. He wished to know if there was 'a directive to liquidate all the Jews in *Ostland*?'[39] Was this to be done 'regardless of age, sex, and economic requirements (for instance, the Wehrmacht's demand for skilled workers in the armament industry)?' Lohse was all in favour of 'the cleansing of *Ostland* of Jews' but he was also sensitive to the needs of the armament plants and repair workshops. In the Baltic states, as in Poland and the west, but unlike the Soviet Union or Yugoslavia, the army did not see itself as engaged in the murder of Jews. To deprive the factories working for the German army of Jewish workers 'through their liquidation', when they could not yet be replaced by local personnel, did not seem sensible to Lohse. The reply he received from the Reich Ministry for the Occupied Eastern Territories (signed by liaison officer Otto Bräutigam) was significant: 'The Jewish question has presumably been clarified meanwhile by means of verbal discussion. In principle, economic considerations are not to be taken into account in the settlement of the problem. It is further requested that any questions that arise be settled directly with the Higher SS and Police Leader' (*Höherer SS-und Polizeiführer*).[40]

It is evident from such correspondence that the implications of the 'Final Solution' were not always apparent to those in the field who were expected to implement orders from Berlin. No doubt there was much chaos, administrative confusion, clashing interests and logistical problems that needed *ad hoc* or improvised solutions. But that does not mean that the mass murder of European Jewry was something that the Nazis simply stumbled into, without any centralised control or ideological guidelines. Unfortunately, for Hitler, the *Endlösung* was a matter of grand policy though he left the execution of its details to trusted subordinates such as Himmler and Heydrich.

An illuminating example of Hitler's vision of the 'Final Solution', not long before the Wannsee conference, is revealed in his conversation of 28 November 1941 with the Grand Mufti of Jerusalem, Haj Amin el-Husseini – the exiled leader of the Palestinian Arabs then living in Berlin. Ever since 1933, Haj Amin had eagerly sought to win Nazi support for his Palestinian nationalist and pan-Arab aims, with somewhat mixed results. Like many Arab nationalists in the 1930s he ardently admired the order and discipline of the new German Reich, looking to Hitler to overthrow British imperialism in the Middle East and help him to destroy the 'Jewish National Home' in Palestine.[41] At their meeting in Berlin, the Mufti emphasised that the Arabs had the same enemies as Nazi Germany, 'namely the English, the Jews, and the Communists'. The Arab world, he declared, was ready to co-operate with the German Reich by acts of sabotage and revolt against the British as well as raising a Muslim Arab legion to fight in the Balkans. In exchange, the Mufti desired a public declaration by Hitler in favour of Arab national goals and the liberation of Palestine from the Zionist Jews.

Hitler was cautious regarding such a commitment. He reminded the Mufti that he was speaking 'as a rational man, and primarily as a soldier', who believed that the fate of the Arab world would be ultimately decided by the 'very severe battles going on in the Soviet Union'. On the other hand, he was positively effusive in explaining to the Palestinian leader the rationale for the anti-Jewish crusade that he was conducting. He told the Mufti that 'Germany stood for uncompromising war against the Jews' (*Deutschland trete für einem kompromisslosen Kampf gegen die Juden ein*). He was resolved, 'step by step, to ask one European nation after the other to solve its Jewish problem, and at the proper time to direct a similar appeal to non-European nations as well'.[42] At the same time, he spelled out the *ideological* meaning of the Second World War in terms more sharply formulated than in any other single German diplomatic document. 'Germany is at the present time engaged in a life-and-death struggle with two citadels of Jewish power: Great Britain and Soviet Russia.' Hitler conceded that 'theoretically there was a difference' between English capitalism and Soviet Russian Communism. But in practice, he observed, 'the Jews in both countries were pursuing a common goal'.[43] However, the hour of 'reckoning with the Jews' was now fast approaching. 'This was the decisive struggle' (i.e. against the Jews), Hitler informed his Arab guest. Politically, the war was mainly 'a conflict between Germany and England', but ideologically 'it was a battle between National Socialism and the Jews' (*weltanschaulich sei es ein Kampf zwischen den Nationalsozialismus und dem Judentum*).[44]

Hitler also asked the Mufti to lock 'in the uttermost depths of his heart' the information that 'he would carry on the battle to the total destruction (*Zerstörung*) of the Judaeo-Communist empire in Europe'.[45] This was a decidedly thick hint of the massive annihilation of Jewry that was already under way and would soon be greatly accelerated. Moreover, the war against the Jews would not to be confined to the European continent, once the German armies had reached the exit of the Caucasus and stood poised on the northern edge of the Middle East. Hitler also reassured the Palestinian leader that he was actively opposed to the Jewish National Home as 'a state centre' (*ein Staatlicher Mittelpunkt*) whose influence could only be destructive. More important still, he promised that when the hour of Arab liberation struck, the sole German objective in the Middle East would be 'the destruction of the Jewish element residing in the Arab sphere under the protection of British power' (... *die Vernichtung des in arabischen Raum unter der Protektion der britischen Macht lebenden Judentums sein*).[46]

Hitler's reply revealed the global vision behind his genocidal project, encompassing even the Middle East and 'extra-European' peoples. It is not confined to European Ashkenazi Jews but also includes 'the Jewish element residing in the Arab sphere'.[47] It is directed against 'Jewish' capitalism (Great Britain) no less than Judaeo-Communism (in the USSR). The imminent entry of the United States into the war (within less than two weeks) would highlight even more the globalisation of the conflict and by definition its 'Judaisation'.

The German historian Christian Gerlach recently argued Hitler's decision to irrevocably destroy the Jews of Europe was formally taken as late as 12 December 1941, one day after his declaration of war on the United States. His most important evidence (from Goebbels' notes) consists of remarks made by Hitler in his private residence that very afternoon, before the assembled Nazi Party *Gauleiter* and Reich leaders.[48] As he would do before and after December 1941, Hitler returned once more to the famous prophecy of destruction, uttered nearly three years earlier, about what would happen 'if the Jews again provoked a world war'. He solemnly warned that these were not 'vain words', since the 'world war' had now arrived and, 'the destruction of the Jews must be the necessary result'. There was no room for sentimentality regarding the Jews since the German people had 'already sacrificed 160,000 dead on the Eastern Front'. Hence those who were 'truly responsible for this bloody war' (i.e. the Jews) should pay for it with their own lives.[49]

This was open incitement to mass murder, all the more significant in view of the forum before which it was made. Almost all the top Party leadership and most of the decision-makers who would have to implement the 'Final Solution' in their fiefdoms were present. Moreover, with American entry into the war, the Jews of Europe had lost whatever role they might still have had (in Nazi minds) as bargaining chips with which to restrain or control the behaviour of the United States. Nazi Germany would henceforth be at war with three extra-European global powers (the USA, the USSR and the British Empire) – a fact that strengthened the Nazi vision of Germany as the protectionist guardian of the European continent. Jews, in this context, could be all the more easily demonised as the threatening 'fifth column', the revolutionary subversives and plotters against whom European nations had to unite under Nazi leadership.

However, there are solid grounds to believe that the 'Final Solution' was decided upon well before December 1941. Plans for gassing Polish Jews were already under way by then and earlier statements by Goebbels, Rosenberg and Heydrich as well as Hitler himself had clearly pointed in the direction of genocide. For instance, in a letter of 6 November 1941, Heydrich had written to the German High Command in Paris explaining why he had authorised the bombings of seven Parisian synagogues, an action that had taken place on 2 October 1941.[50] The terrorist bombings had been carried out by a group of collaborationist French anti-Semites with German SD assistance. Heydrich informed the German military commander, Otto von Stülp-nagel, that he had only acted 'from the moment when, at the highest level, Jewry had been forcefully designated as the culp-able incendiary in Europe, one which must definitely disappear from Europe'.[51] Presumably the explosions of 2 October must have already been organised in September 1941. Since only the Führer could have been meant by Heydrich as the authority 'at the highest level' who had branded Jews as 'incendiaries' and as 'guilty' (of the war), this statement implies that the decision to exterminate the Jews was already known to Heydrich in September 1941, if not earlier.

On 30 January 1942 at the Berlin *Sportpalast*, Hitler wrapped up his prophecy of 'complete annihilation' in Old Testament language, declaring that henceforth the philosophy of 'an eye for an eye, a tooth for a tooth' would be applied to 'the most evil world enemy of all times'.[52] It is significant that Hitler's rambling table-talks from the end of January 1942 were now increasingly fixated on the responsibility of the Jews for the world war, and their role as a 'perpetual ferment'. The need for a 'radical solution' and for comprehensive measures at a *European* level were asserted as if the process were not yet in full swing but somehow still imminent. Yet we know from various sources, including Goebbels' diaries, that Hitler was indeed the driving force of the genocide and followed it closely. On 6 March 1942, Goebbels noted the Führer's conviction that 'the greater the number of Jews liquidated, the more con-solidated will be the situation in Europe after this war'.[53] Two weeks later, the Propaganda Minister wrote with obvious sat-isfaction that 'the Führer is as uncompromising as ever' about ridding Europe of the Jews, 'if necessary by applying the most brutal methods'.[54] On 27 March 1942 he describes the deport-ation of Jews from the Government General to the east as 'a pretty barbarous business'.[55] Goebbels estimated that about 60 per cent of these Jews had already been liquidated and another 40 per cent were being taken for forced labour: 'The former *Gauleiter* of Vienna (Globocnik), who is in charge of the operation, is carrying it out with a good deal of circumspection, and his methods do not seem to be attracting much publicity. The Führer is the moving spirit of this radical solution both in word and deed ...'[56]

For Hitler, the struggle against the Jews was indeed far more than a mere instrument of propaganda or political means to achieve other ends. In his vocabulary, the Jews were constantly likened to vermin, to 'propagators of infection', to the germs of a deadly plague, to bacteria, or malignant disease – or, as he had called them back in 1919, a 'racial tuberculosis of the peoples' (*Rassentuberkulose der Völker*). At dinner on the evening of 22 February 1942 Hitler exclaimed: 'How many diseases must owe their origins to the Jewish virus! Only when we have eliminated the Jews will we regain our health.' This obsessive linkage between Jews and deadly disease was one that he was constantly seeking to impress upon visiting foreign statesmen, allies and collaborators. On 21 July 1941 he told the Croatian Foreign Minister that because of the Jews Russia had become 'a plague centre (*Pestherd*) for humanity'.[57] During his meeting with the Hungarian ruler Admiral Horthy at Klessheim Castle on 17 April 1943, he warned his unreliable ally that nations 'which did not rid themselves of the Jews perished'. Referring to the Jews of Poland, Hitler denied that the mass killings were cruel. 'If they could not work, they had to succumb. They had to be treated like tuberculosis bacilli with which a healthy body may become infected.'[58]

Heinrich Himmler, the architect and organiser of the 'Final Solution' as an administrative task certainly shared this view that the Jews were deadly bacteria that had to be ruthlessly eradicated. In his speech before senior SS officers in Poznan on 4 October 1943, Himmler spoke openly of the 'Final Solution' as a *hygienic* measure (*eine Reinlichkeitsangelegenheit*). 'We have exterminated a bacterium because we do not want in the end to be infected by the bacterium and die of it ... Wherever it may form, we will cauterise it.'[59] Himmler's concern for Jewish 'contagion' extended to women and children. 'I did not consider that I should be justified in getting rid of the men – in having them put to death, in other words – only to allow their children to grow up to avenge themselves on our sons and grandsons. We have to make up our minds, hard though it may be, that this race must be wiped off the face of the earth.'[60]

The pedantic and methodical Himmler also made much of the imagined 'security threat' in justifying the Holocaust to the assembled audience of eminent SS and police officials, as a necessary preventive measure: '... for we know how difficult we should have made it for ourselves if, with the bombing raids, the burdens and deprivations of war, we still had the Jews today in every town as secret saboteurs, agitators and troublemakers. We would probably have reached the 1916–17 stage when the Jews were still part of the body of the German nation.'[61]

The Reichsführer SS and Chief of the German Police also addressed the 'ethical' dilemmas and 'idealism' required for carrying out such a gigantic task as the 'Final Solution'. His Poznan speech was full of memorable clichés about 'honour', 'loyalty' and 'decency' in the face of mountains of corpses. 'To have stuck it out and at the same time – apart from exceptions caused by human weakness – to have remained decent men (anständig geblieben zu sein), that is what has made us hard. This is a page of glory in our history, which has never been written and never is to be written.'[62] Himmler did not hide the fact that the 'Final Solution' was a 'grave matter'. He was even frank enough to speak about it publicly as 'the extermination (Ausrottung) of the Jewish race' and to admit that this was one of 'the most frightening orders an organisation could ever receive'.[63] In his quietly sinister way he managed to convey to his men the sense that they were engaged not so much in murder as in a sacred mission through which the SS elite would forge a new race of blond, blue-eyed Germanic heroes. Precisely because they were a *Herrenvolk*, however, the Germans had to be pure and 'decent', incapable of theft or graft. Mass murder was permissible and even admirable in an 'idealistic' cause like National Socialism, but small misdemeanours that infringed Himmler's petit-bourgeois moral code were not tolerable. This did not prevent the Reichsführer SS at the end of the war from proposing deals to the West that involved trading or selling Jews for military, monetary or political advantage. In November 1944, on his own initiative, Himmler ordered a halt to the gassing of Jews, in the vain hope that he could thereby achieve a secret arrangement with the Western Allies to join forces against the Soviet Union.[64]

On the other hand, Hitler remained totally uncompromising to the bitter end, convinced that he had rendered a great service to humanity by opening the eyes of the whole world to the 'Jewish peril'. On 13 February 1945 he boasted that National Socialism had truly 'lanced the Jewish abscess', predicting that 'the world of the future will be eternally grateful to us'.[65] Hitler's so-called 'Political Testament' was dictated on the morning of 29 April 1945 (the day before his suicide) as Soviet artillery fire bombarded the Reich Chancellery in Berlin. The document recorded his 'love and loyalty' to the German people, who had given him the strength to make decisions of unprecedented difficulty. Not for the first time, he affirmed that he had never sought war against England and America. He held the Jews exclusively responsible 'for this murderous struggle' and especially for the many victims of massive aerial bombing, prophesying that, 'out of the ruins of our towns and monuments', the hatred against 'International Jewry and its helpers' would inexorably grow.[66] He had fairly warned the Jews ('these international conspirators in money and finance') that they would have to pay the price for initiating the world war. This time, however, it was not only to be the 'millions of Europe's Aryan people' who would starve or 'be burned and bombed to death in the cities'. The Jewish warmongers would also 'atone for their crime, even if by more *humane* means ...'[67]

Hitler's last testament was both a justification for mass murder and the first act of Holocaust denial. His war against the Jews had by his own reckoning been an act of self-defence 'against the poisoners of all the peoples of the world'. He always sought nothing but peace. It was the 'international financiers' who had forced him into war. Gassing and shooting the Jews had been his 'humane' response to the Allied bombing raids on Germany, which according to the Nazi world-view were an act of 'Jewish' aggression against 'Aryan' humanity. This was the strange, shadowy world that the Führer inhabited. The Holocaust was indeed a logical culmination of Hitler's messianic megalomania and the perverted religiosity that had animated his politics. In its self-enclosed 'finality' it resonated with sinister echoes of the Last Judgement, the final destruction of the Jews heralding the dawn of a new millennium, the redemption of the End of Days. Hitler's apocalyptic perspective cannibalised and radicalised a long tradition of Christian and anti-Christian Juda-eophobia in the West even as it destroyed the moral foundations of the European civilisation that it so falsely claimed to defend. As Lucy Dawidowicz eloquently pointed out a quarter of a century ago, the Holocaust was not just another anti-Semitic undertaking. 'It was part of a salvational ideology that envisaged the attainment of Heaven by bringing Hell on earth.'[68]

# V    *Between the Cross and the Swastika*

It is a Christian action to expel the Jews, because it is for the good of the people, which is thus getting rid of its pests.

**Father Jozef Tiso**, President of Slovakia, speech of August 1942

I must make heard the indignant protest of the Christian conscience and I proclaim that all men, Aryan or non-Aryan, are brothers, because they are created by the same God ... the current anti-Semitic measures are in contempt of human dignity, a violation of the most sacred rights of the individual and the family...

**Bishop Pierre-Marie Théas** (Montauban), protesting the deportation of French Jews, September 1942

Christianity in Germany bears a greater responsibility before God than the National Socialists, the SS and the Gestapo. We ought to have recognised the Lord Jesus in the brother who suffered and was persecuted despite his being a communist or a Jew.

**Pastor Martin Niemöller**, lecture in Zurich, March 1946

The resurgence of Germany ('*Deutschland Erwache*') and the destruction of the Jews ('*Judah Verrecke*') had been organically related processes in Hitler's mind ever since the 'catastrophe' of November 1918. They had been framed in eschatological terms as a kind of cosmic war of the forces of Light against the fiendish powers of Darkness. 'There is no making pacts with Jews', Hitler had declared in *Mein Kampf*, 'there can only be the hard either-or'.[1] Pointedly, he warned his audience in the Munich beer-cellars on 27 February 1925: 'Either the enemy will walk over our corpses, or we will walk over his.'[2] In this life-and-death fight against the satanic forces of evil, Hitler liked to pose as the chosen Redeemer of the Germanic *Volk* (and of the entire non-Jewish world), conducting a millenarian struggle for salvation. This militant style of salvationist politics frequently borrowed from Christian language and imagery while adapting them to widely prevalent obsessions about impending German national doom or 'Aryan' racial extinction. The extremity of the German plight was used to justify in advance the inversion of all humanitarian values. 'We want to prevent our Germany from being crucified too! Let us be inhuman! But if we save Germany, we have eliminated the greatest injustice in the world. Let us be unethical! But if we save our *Volk*, we have broken a path for morality again!'[3]

When Hitler spoke of rescuing Germany, the 'Aryan' nations and European civilisation from crucifixion by a 'diabolical Jewish world enemy', he did not flinch from comparing himself to the Christian saviour, blasphemous though such an allusion must appear in retrospect. In his early speeches in Catholic Bavaria he regularly evoked New Testament passages recalling that Christ 'took to the whip to drive from the temple of the Lord this [Jewish] adversary of all humanity'.[4] Jesus, too, he reminded his predominantly Catholic audiences, had lived in a 'materialistic world contaminated by Jews', where the state power was corrupt and incompetent.[5] In Hitler's imaginary self-projection, Christ seemed more like Siegfried, a Germanic warrior-hero who had created a great world-movement by preaching a popular anti-Jewish faith fused with intense patriotic idealism. Jesus's crown of thorns was his 'struggle against the Jews', now made to serve as a model for Hitler's own war against the materialistic 'Jewish spirit'. It was 'as a Christian', the Nazi leader insisted, that he had a duty to see that society did not suffer the same collapse as the Greco-Roman civilisation of antiquity which had been driven to its ruin by this same Jewish people.[6] On 12 April 1922 he emphatically declared in Munich: 'I would be no Christian ... if I did not, as did our Lord 2000 years ago, turn against those by whom today this poor people is plundered and exploited.'[7] Draping himself in the colours of a fundamentalist anti-Semitic Christianity, he confessed to his Bavarian audience: 'In boundless love, as a Christian and a human being, I read the passage which tells us how the Lord at last rose in his might and seized the scourge to drive out of the Temple the brood of vipers and adders. How terrific was his fight against the Jewish poison. I realise more profoundly than ever before the fact that it was for this that He had to shed His blood upon the cross.'[8]

In another fiery speech in Munich, in December 1926, Hitler even claimed Jesus as a model and 'pioneer' for the National Socialist cause.

> The birth of The Man, which is celebrated at Christmas, has the greatest significance for National Socialists. Christ has been the greatest pioneer in the struggle against the Jewish world enemy. Christ was the greatest fighting nature which ever lived on the Earth ... The struggle against the power of capital was his life's work and his teaching, for which he was nailed to the Cross by his arch-enemy the Jew. The task which Christ began but did not finish I will complete.[9]

When Count Lerchenfeld, a former Prime Minister of Bavaria, stated in a local Landtag session that his feeling 'as a man and a Christian' prevented him from being an anti-Semite, Hitler's reply unequivocally rejected any pacific, humanitarian stand-point. 'I say my feeling as a Christian points me to my Lord and Saviour as a fighter. It points me to the man who once in loneliness, surrounded by only a few followers, recognised those Jews for what they were and summoned men to fight against them and who, God's truth! was greatest not as a sufferer, but as a fighter.'[10]

Hitler's vision of a militantly anti-Jewish Jesus developed in large measure out of the fin de siècle Austrian Catholicism that he had imbibed in his childhood and adolescent years. As a young man in Vienna he had admired the political virtuosity of Karl Lueger's Christian-Social movement, in which an anti-Jewish and anti-capitalist populism, fostered by the clergy, had played a central role. The devotion of the lower clergy to the poor and their sense of mission had made them – in Hitler's words – 'stand out of the general morass like little islands'.[11] Indeed, the Catholic Church in his native Austria had, as he liked to recall, served as an important vehicle for the social mobility of many able individuals from the ranks of the people.[12] There were also other features of his boyhood religion, like the 'mysterious artificial dimness of the Catholic churches', the burning candles and the incense, that made a strong impression upon the young Hitler.

Learning from the experiences of his pre-war apprentice years in Vienna, he concluded that any open confrontation with the Catholic Church must be avoided. The earlier failure of Bismarck's *Kulturkampf* against German Catholics in the 1870s and of Schoenerer's crusade against Rome in 1900 were object lessons. Hence, from the early days of the Nazi *Kampfzeit* he had avoided any involvement in the religious disputes that could adversely affect his own image or the unity within his movement. Those who attempted to introduce a Protestant religious sectarianism into the NSDAP, such as the Thuringian Nazi leader Arthur Dinter, were either expelled or accused of national betrayal and of 'consciously or unconsciously fighting for Jewish interests'.[13] This ultimate disqualifying charge was even levelled at Hitler's former comrade-in-arms General Erich von Ludendorff, the vehemently anti-Catholic hero of the German *völkisch* Right. Both Ludendorff and his second wife, Mathilde von Kemnitz, who had founded the *Tannenbergbund* in 1926, became obsessed with Jesuitism and the Roman Church as implacable enemies of Germandom, no less deadly than 'Judah' or Freemasonry. Hitler denounced this fanatical anti-

Romanism and the internecine war between the Christian denominations in Germany as a disastrous diversion away from the 'Jewish peril'.[14]

Hitler's concern not to alienate traditionalist opinion was eminently *political* and made sense in a rural Catholic region like Bavaria, which had been the cradle of the Nazi movement between 1919 and 1925.[15] Moreover, Hitler recognised the affinity between local anti-Jewish religious traditions typified by such popular festivals as the Oberammergau Passion Play (which highlighted the Jews' primary role in Christ's crucifixion) and his own violent anti-Semitism. The potency of this inflammatory strand of folk prejudice accentuated by the linkage in the popular mind between Jews and Communism in post-1919 Munich, explains why Hitler sought to appropriate the Christian anti-Jewish tradition for his own demagogic ends. It is succinctly summed up in that notorious passage in *Mein Kampf* where he rails: 'in defending myself against the Jews I am acting for the Lord' (*vollziehe ich das Werk des Herrn*).[16] The continuity is equally evident whenever Hitler's speeches passionately evoked Jesus as 'the scourge of the Jews' or praised the 'utterance(s) of the great Nazarene', who had always despised the golden mean, whether in politics or in life.[17] Small wonder then that the Nazis were eager in the early years to tap into the centuries-old tradition of Christian anti-Semitism for electoral purposes and present their doctrines as being compatible with 'positive' Christianity. To understand what Hitler meant by this propagandist phrase it is important to remember that his ideas in the 1920s were strongly influenced by the 'spiritual' godfather of Nazism, the Bavarian Catholic journalist Dietrich Eckart, whom he admired as 'an outstanding writer and thinker', and to whom *Mein Kampf* was dedicated.[18] Twenty years older than Hitler, Eckart had introduced his raw if energetic new protégé to Munich society, improved his social graces and his German, reshaping his racist anti-Semitism and grooming him for the role of messianic saviour of Germany. Eckart had invented the Nazi battle-cry 'Deutschland Erwache!' (Germany Awake!), the title of one of his poems. In 1919 he began publication of the ultra-nationalist weekly Auf Gut Deutsch, which attacked the Versailles Treaty, Jewish war profiteers, Bolshevism and social democracy.

Eckart's eclectic combination of völkisch racism with Catholic mysticism and his Manichean view of the world as a battle between the forces of light and darkness (embodied by Aryan and Jew) strongly appealed to the early Hitler. He looked up to Eckart as a prophet, teacher and father figure whose services to National Socialism were 'inestimable' and identified with his view that 'the Jewish Question is the chief problem of humanity, in which, indeed, every one of its other problems is contained ...'[19] Equally, he shared Eckart's conviction that Christ's revelation had been radically distorted by St Paul and overlaid with a cold 'Jewish' materialism, from which all social evils subsequently proceeded.

In post-1918 Germany, whose decadent condition Eckart compared to the late Roman Empire (where 'Judaism' under the 'cover' of Christianity had first engineered a moral collapse), the situation was perilous in the extreme. The prime causes of 'decomposition' were capitalism, Bolshevism and Freemasonry – three deadly modern agents of Verjudung.[20] The only salvation for the German Volk from the threat of extinction lay in a fusion of nationalism, socialism and 'positive Christianity'. This new trinity would have to be stripped of any Jewish component and reinterpreted in a fundamentally 'anti-materialist' spirit. After Eckart died in 1924, Adolf Hitler would implement his millenarian programme of redemptive anti-Semitism to devastating effect.[21]

By brandishing the slogan of 'positive Christianity' and projecting their leader as a deeply religious figure (Hitler's frequent references to 'Divine Providence' made this easier) Nazi party

image-makers could suggest that their movement defended traditionalist values, especially against 'godless Marxism'. The
fervent nationalism that had seized hold of so many German
Christians in 1914, and was especially common in Protestant
circles, further played into Nazi hands.[22] Among the evangelical
Protestants, who under the Weimar Republic remained vulnerable to nationalist appeals, there was a significantly large
minority who became enthusiastic supporters of Nazism. They
established their own 'Reich Church' under Ludwig Müller, a
militarist pastor already known for his hard-line nationalistic
sermons and *völkisch* anti-Semitism in the 1920s. His Association of *Deutsche Christen* (German Christians) professed
'heroic piety' and a virile racism that sought to harmonise belief
in Christ with the 'blood and soil' doctrines of Nazi ideology.[23]
The 'German Christians' were especially intent on banning
mixed marriages between Jews and Germans. But despite Müller's dogged loyalty to the regime, Hitler remained unimpressed
by his efforts.

Among Protestants, only the breakaway *Bekenntnis-Kirche*
(Confessional Church) – whose strongholds were in northern
and central Germany – considered Christianity to be manifestly
incompatible with the Nazi world-view. They were especially
exercised by the introduction of an 'Aryan' paragraph into
church life (which removed converts of Jewish origins) and by
the demand of German Christians to eradicate the Old Testament.[24] Nevertheless, even in the Protestant opposition, political anti-Semitism was common enough. The guiding spirit of
the anti-Nazi Confessional Church, Pastor Martin Niemöller,
had like many German Protestants originally welcomed Hitler's
rise to power as the beginning of a national revival. He fully
shared the anti-communism of the Nazis and their detestation
of the Weimar Republic, which he himself had once branded as
'fourteen years of darkness'. Nor was he immune from the
German Protestant tradition of hostility to Jews and Judaism,

with its impressive continuity from Luther through the court preacher Adolf Stoecker during the Second Reich to the theologians of Nazi Germany.[25] The Confessional Church only once raised its voice (in a secret memorandum of 1936 to Hitler) to protest against the campaign of hatred against the Jews, as well as the concentration camps and the pervasiveness of the Gestapo.

The Roman Catholic Church in Germany was to prove more resistant to the incursions and blandishments of Nazi ideology.[26] In contrast to the Protestants they did not have a Trojan horse in their ranks comparable to the Nazified German Christians. Moreover, they could look to the Vatican in Rome for institutional support and powerful moral encouragement. True, in the 1930s the Vatican under Pius XI did feel some affinity (like many Catholics in Europe and beyond) for anti-communist authoritarian regimes that espoused some local version of corporatist, military or clerico-fascist dictatorship. Moreover, in July 1933 in response to Hitler's own urgent requests, the Holy See took a more fateful step, signing a Concordat with the Third Reich, thereby giving a degree of much desired international legitimacy to the Nazi regime. From the Nazi point of view the Concordat, by neutralising the Catholic Centre Party (which consented to its own self-dissolution after agreeing to give Hitler special 'emergency powers' in 1933), had removed a potential source of troublesome opposition. The Concordat henceforth restricted the Church to its purely religious, educative and charitable roles. The Vatican, for its part, believed that a Concordat could help secure the religious freedoms and legal status of the large Catholic minority in the Third Reich.[27]

In his first policy statement in the Reichstag, Hitler had set out to be as reassuring as possible, proclaiming that the new Reich government saw 'in both Christian denominations the most important factor for the maintenance of our society'.[28] In April 1933, in his first conversation as Reich Chancellor with the Catholic Bishop Berning from Osnabrück, Hitler reaffirmed this intention and insisted that his anti-Jewish policy was based on principles that had been pursued for fifteen hundred years by the Catholic Church. However, he deplored the fact that in the modern liberal era the Catholic Church no longer appeared to grasp the reality of the Jewish danger as clearly as it had in the past.[29] Hitler still seemed hopeful that he could win over the Catholic Church to join him in a common anti-Jewish struggle in support of his racial legislation. The fact that Berning breathed not a single word of criticism in response to Hitler's claims that Nazi anti-Semitism was based on Catholic principle and practice could only have encouraged him.

Not only had the Concordat inhibited Church opposition to the regime but numerous Catholics now began to flock to the Nazi Party, attracted like their Protestant counterparts to the call for a national renaissance. Nevertheless there were limits to this *Gleichschaltung* and some unease in the German Catholic hierarchy. Shortly before Christmas 1933, Cardinal Michael von Faulhaber, Archbishop of Munich and a central figure in the German Catholic establishment, preached a series of bold sermons to overflowing crowds at the St Michael's Church in Munich, in which he defended the Hebrew Bible and the Jewish origins of Christianity against vilification by *völkisch* racists. The sermons, published shortly afterwards, under the title *Judentum, Christentum, Germanentum* (1934) eloquently condemned unbridled nationalism and racial intolerance in theological terms.[30] At the same time, Faulhaber insisted that the indispensability of the Old Testament to Christianity had no bearing on 'antagonism to the Jews of today', which he did not s⟍ ⟋to oppose. Indeed, he denied suggestions made abroad ⟍ ⟋blic addresses had constituted a defence of German ⟍ ⟋lied any criticism of Nazi policy.[31] Cardinal Faul- ⟍ ⟋alence continued to surface in the coming years, ⟍ ⟋f the German Catholic hierarchy as a whole and of the Vatican itself. On 4 November 1936 he visited Hitler at Berchtesgaden for a three-hour discussion. The Reich Chancellor demanded, among other things, that the Catholic Church openly support the Nuremberg racial laws against the Jews (officially there had been no clear Catholic response). Against the background of the Spanish Civil War, Hitler warned Faulhaber that if National Socialism did not triumph over Bolshevism, then there would be no future for Christianity and the Roman Church in Europe.[32]

Faulhaber evidently came away impressed by Hitler's diplomatic finesse, believing that he would continue to respect the rights of the Catholic Church in Germany. This proved to be a fatal illusion, one that the Vatican itself corrected in the 1937 papal encyclical *Mit Brennende Sorge* (With Deep Anxiety) issued in German by Pope Pius XI.[33] This was the only serious and unequivocal public criticism of National Socialism that the Vatican would allow itself to venture. The encyclical was to a large extent authored by Archbishop Von Faulhaber himself (helped by his German Catholic colleagues) with the active assistance of Eugenio Pacelli, Cardinal Secretary of State in Rome (and the future Pope Pius XII). The encyclical did contain a sharp condemnation of Nazi racism as a form of atheistic 'neo-paganism' and also a denunciation of totalitarian state doctrines, but no mention was made either of anti-Semitism or the persecution of German Jews. Despite the devastating *Kristallnacht* pogrom that followed a year later, neither the German Catholic hierarchy nor the Vatican officially protested, though it seems that Cardinal Faulhaber did privately aid the Chief Rabbi of Munich to try to salvage some religious articles from his burning synagogue.

But the ambivalence towards National Socialism did not end there. Like the Protestant churches, the leading German Catholic bishops appeared to be generally supportive of German foreign policy at the time of the *Anschluss* with Austria and the

Czech crisis of 1938. Furthermore, both Cardinal Faulhaber and Cardinal Bertram found it appropriate to congratulate Hitler on 'miraculously' surviving Johann Georg Elser's assassination attempt on 8 November 1939 with a 'Te Deum' being sung in Munich's cathedral to give thanks to Divine Providence at the Führer's escape. Cardinal Adolf Bertram of Breslau had already distinguished himself, earlier in 1939, with a congratulatory telegram on the occasion of Hitler's fiftieth birthday, a gesture that he repeated in the following years.[34]

The German Catholic hierarchy fell silent during the war in face of the horrifying atrocities against Poles and Jews, with only a few honourable exceptions. This lack of response was not due to ignorance of what was happening in their midst or in the German occupied territories. The Bishop of Osnabrück, Monsignor Berning, in notes written down on 5 February 1942, remarked that 'the plan for a total elimination of the Jews clearly exists' ('Es besteht wohl der Plan, die Juden ganz auszurotten.').[35] He plainly wondered whether or not he and his fellow bishops should launch a public protest from their pulpits. Monsignor Conrad Gröber, Archbishop of Fribourg, informing the Pope on 14 June 1942 about the massacres of Jews being perpetrated by the Einsatzgruppen in Russia, ominously concluded: 'The Nazi conception of the world is characterised by the most radical anti-Semitism, going as far as the annihilation [Vernichtung] of Jewry, not only in its spirit but also in its members.'[36] But despite the efforts of a small minority like the valiant Margarete Sommer (head of a Catholic relief organisation attached to the Berlin Curia) who urged a public denunciation of the Nazi murders, silence was maintained. At the conference of Bavarian bishops of 30–31 March 1943 Cardinal Von Faulhaber reminded his audience that 'nothing could render a better service to the greatest adversaries of the Church than to have recourse now to heavy artillery. At a moment when we are in difficulty that would allow once again the stab in the back to be revived. My impression is that this is precisely what they are waiting for.'[37]

Faulhaber believed that the German bishops would be accused of treason, of breaking national solidarity and serving enemy propaganda with irreparable consequences for German Catholicism. When the mass deportations of German Jews began in October 1941, the episcopate limited its intervention with the government to Catholic 'non-Aryans'. It was significant that in late 1941, when the German bishops did bring themselves to protest against proposed legislation that would force partners in mixed marriages to divorce, Cardinal Bertram immediately felt obliged to emphasise his unstained patriotism. He pointed out that he was by no means deficient in love for the German *Volk* and for its dignity, 'or [guilty] of underestimation of the harmful Jewish influence upon German culture and national interests'.[38]

Even the most outspoken of all the high-ranking German prelates, the aristocratic Clemens August Graf von Galen (Cardinal Archbishop of Münster) was very careful to emphasise his patriotism. Von Galen consistently exhorted the faithful to defend the Fatherland and 'to fight against the external enemy', though he did preach against vindictiveness, the killing of hostages and the murder of unarmed prisoners of war.[39] In the summer of 1941 Von Galen began his series of blistering sermons against the government's euthanasia programme or so-called 'mercy killings', which he bluntly called 'plain murder' – probably the most effective, single *episcopal* protest against the Nazi regime in the twelve years of its rule.[40] The strong public echo his words aroused sufficiently rattled the Nazi leadership (which to that point had put to death over 70,000 predominantly ethnic Germans suffering from a variety of congenital mental or physical defects) that it was felt obliged to officially suspend the programme of mass gassing. Henceforth, however, euthanasia would be redirected rather than abandoned, in such a way that the killings would be easier to conceal. Hitler, who still wanted to avoid a public confrontation with the Catholic Church, swore to exact retribution from Von Galen, but only after the end of the war – a vain threat as it turned out.

Neither Von Galen nor the ecclesiastical establishments in Germany (Catholic or Protestant) made any comparable pronouncements or interventions in favour of unconverted Jews or gypsies.[41] Nor, when they eventually received reports about the mass murder of Jews in the death camps (from officers serving in the east, from civil servants or from other sources) did the vague pronouncements of the German bishops specifically mention the Jews. The harsh truth is that few Protestants or Catholics in Germany and Austria were ready to expose bloodthirsty Nazi anti-Semitism, not least because the boundaries had long been blurred by the Churches' 'teaching of contempt' towards Judaism. When the genocide began, they appeared to be paralysed. Even more striking was their failure to grasp how dangerous racist anti-Semitism was to the future of Christianity.

For at the heart of Nazism, despite its cunning pretence of standing for 'positive Christianity', there was a deep-seated revolt against the entire civilisation that had been built on Judaeo-Christian ethics. Indeed, the leading Nazis – Hitler, Himmler, Rosenberg, Goebbels and Bormann – were all fanatically anti-Christian, though this was partly hidden from the German public. Had ordinary Germans been privy to Hitler's *Table Talk*, some of them might have been deeply shocked. On 17 February 1942, for example, in the presence of Himmler, and shortly after the first gassings of Jews, the Führer of the Nazi Reich proclaimed in one of his rambling wartime monologues: 'The notions represented by Jewish Christianity were strictly unthinkable to Roman brains ... The Jew who fraudulently introduced Christianity into the ancient world – in order to ruin it – reopened the same breach in modern times, this time taking as his pretext the social question. It's the same sleight of hand as before. Just as Saul has changed into St Paul, Mordechai became Karl Marx.'[42]

The conviction that Judaism, Christianity and Bolshevism represented the same pathological phenomenon of decadence seemed to have become a veritable leitmotif for Hitler once he embarked upon the 'Final Solution' as an operational plan. On the night of 11–12 July 1941, shortly after the invasion of Soviet Russia, Hitler asserted that the coming of Christianity had been 'the heaviest blow that ever struck humanity.[43] It had been responsible for the extinction of the Roman Empire and the destruction of fifteen hundred years of civilisation at a single stroke. In comparison with the tolerance of the Greco-Roman world, Christianity sought 'to exterminate its adversaries in the name of love'.[44] Worse still, Bolshevism was 'Christianity's illegitimate child' and both were 'inventions of the Jew'.[45] Christianity had first introduced the deliberate lie of religion into the world, but Bolshevism was based on a similar kind of lying 'when it claims to bring liberty to men, whereas in reality it seeks only to enslave them'.[46]

It is a striking fact that as he launched the Holocaust, Hitler increasingly sought to emphasise the parallels between Christianity and Bolshevism as doctrines destructive of human culture. In both cases, he insisted that they derived their 'levelling' inspiration from the same tainted Jewish 'ferment of decomposition'. On 21 October 1941 we can find another variant on this theme: 'Whilst Roman society proved hostile to the new doctrine, Christianity in its pure state stirred the population to revolt. Rome was Bolshevised, and Bolshevism produced exactly the same results in Rome as later in Russia.'[47] With the collapse of culture in the twentieth century, 'the Jew restores to pride of place Christianity in its Bolshevistic form'.[48] Under Jewish-Marxist rule in Russia, for example, hundreds of thousands of men had been deported and their women delivered 'to males imported from other regions'. Deliberate race-mixing had become in Hitler's fevered imagination a primary feature of the Judaeo-Christian-Bolshevik *Unkultur* which National Socialism was committed to destroy.

Nor did Hitler forget to repeat again his obsession with the 'crypto-Marxist' instigator of revolt, St Paul. ('Saul has changed into St Paul, and Mordechai into Karl Marx.') Following Dietrich Eckart, he saw in Paul 'the first man to take account of the possible advantages of using a religion as a means of propaganda'. St Paul had found an ideal terrain in the decadent Roman Empire for his 'egalitarian theories', which contained 'what was needed to win over a mass composed of innumerable uprooted people'.[49] St Paul's proto-Bolshevism had marked the end of the reign of 'the clear Greco-Latin genius'.[50] The Jews, using the disguise of Pauline Christianity, had deliberately invented the fiction of a transcendent 'Beyond', in place of aesthetic harmony in the cosmos and the natural 'hierarchy amongst nations'. Under the mask of monotheistic religion, the Jews 'introduced intolerance in a sphere in which tolerance formerly prevailed'.[51] Above all, Judaeo-Christianity had deliberately subverted the *natural order*.

> It constantly provokes the weak against the strong, bestiality against intelligence, quantity against quality. It took fourteen centuries for Christianity to reach the peak of savagery and stupidity. We would therefore be wrong to sin by excess of confidence and proclaim our definite victory over Bolshevism. The more we render the Jew incapable of harming us, the more we shall protect ourselves from this danger. The Jew plays in nature the role of a catalysing element. A people that is rid of its Jews returns spontaneously to the natural order.[52]

At first sight, these thoughts seem no more than the crude and malevolent rant of an unhinged mind. While the *Einsatzgruppen* were busy massacring countless Jews and 'Bolsheviks' on the Russian steppes, why engage in hysterical diatribes against St

Paul? Why insist that Christianity and its offshoots
Reformation (and more dubiously in modern revolutions)
the death of all empires and of human civilisation itself? And
yet, there was a method in this madness. Indeed, it reveals one
of the deepest reasons why Hitler ordered the Holocaust. For at
the root of Hitler's anti-Semitism was an apocalyptic vision
of the future of civilisation and of the 'Aryan' destiny that
necessitated the complete eradication of a rival Jewish mes-
sianism. It was the Judaeo-Christian ethic (of which St Paul was
for Hitler the ultimate symbol) that had alienated humanity
from the harmony of the natural order in pursuit of the 'lie' of
a transcendent God. Judaeo-Christianity in its secularised form
had, so he believed, given birth to contemporary teachings of
pacifism, equality before God and the law, human brotherhood
and compassion for the weak, which Nazism had to uproot.
There could be no place for Christian ideals of charity, meekness
and humility in the Nazi New Order for Europe.[53]

Since 1937 it had seemed to Hitler that the Churches were
'allies' of Judaism rather than of National Socialism. The mainstream churches still persisted, for example, in treating the Old
Testament as a major source of Christian revelation and they
had rejected the cult of the 'Aryan' Jesus. In Protestant circles
the Confessional Church had openly challenged the Nazi-spon-
sored *Deutsche Christen*. Nor can there be any doubt that
the Nazis were infuriated by Pius XI's 1937 papal encyclical
protesting against the regime's many violations of the Concordat with the Holy See and sharply criticising certain mani-
festations of National Socialist neo-paganism. True, German
Catholic and Protestant leaders did not express any public sympathy for persecuted Jews, confining themselves strictly to a
defence of the Biblical Hebrew heritage of Christianity. But even
church passivity on the 'Jewish Question' was interpreted by
Hitler, Himmler, Goebbels, Ley and others as proof that Christianity was irredeemably tainted by 'Jewish' influences. It was

no accident that in the reports of the SD (Security Services) the churches after 1937 figure prominently, alongside Jews and Communists, as 'ideological enemies' of the regime.[54]

The real chasm between Nazism and Christianity was perhaps best summed up by Hitler's *eminence grise*, the head of the Party Chancellery and private secretary of the Führer, Martin Bormann. On the night of 29 November 1944, he ominously remarked: 'In the same way any doctrine which is anti-Communist, any doctrine which is anti-Christian must *ipso facto* be anti-Jewish as well. The National Socialist doctrine is therefore anti-Jewish *in excelsis*, for it is both anti-Communist and anti-Christian.'[55]

For the National Socialists, with the outbreak of the Second World War, it was already clear that there would eventually have to be a 'final solution' of the 'religious question', though for tactical reasons they preferred to postpone any major confrontation with the churches in wartime. But from an ideological standpoint – especially from the summer of 1941 – Judaeo-Christianity was seen as the embodiment of universalist, rationalist and humanitarian values antithetical to the Nazi creed. Hence the annihilation of the Jews also had a profoundly symbolic as well as ideological and political meaning. It simultaneously brought the Christian anti-Semitic tradition to a twisted and horrific climax while negating every positive value that Christianity had ever contained.

The danger that National Socialism represented to Christianity in general was not unfamiliar to the new pope Pius XII (Eugenio Pacelli) who had been elected to his position on 2 March 1939. Having spent twelve years as papal nuncio in Munich and Berlin before 1929, his personal knowledge of German Catholicism as well as his love of the German language and culture was unrivalled in the Roman hierarchy. Well informed about domestic conditions in the Third Reich, Pacelli had been the architect of the Concordat in 1933 but had also played a role in formulating the 1937 papal encyclical that condemned National Socialism.[56] In 1939, however, once installed as Pius XII, he sought to achieve a détente with Hitler in order to preserve the vital interests of the Roman Catholic Church in Nazi Germany.

At a meeting in the Vatican in early March 1939 with the German cardinals, Von Faulhaber from Munich, Bertram from Breslau, Schulte from Cologne and Innitzer from Vienna, he emphasised that he considered the 'German question' to be *the* most important and that 'he reserved its treatment' to himself alone.[57] He further told the German cardinals (on 9 March 1939) that he had no intention of initiating a break with the Nazi regime, having earlier successfully persuaded Pius XI against precisely such a drastic step. Moreover, he forbade the Vatican newspaper, *L'Osservatore Romano*, from engaging in any further criticism of events in Germany. Such polemics had rarely mentioned the Jews, focusing rather on Nazi harassment of the Church or disapproval of the 'neo-pagan' aberrations of biological racism. Objections to German anti-Semitism before the war generally related solely to its violence and brutality, not to the intrinsic right of the state to discriminate against Jews.[58] The 'Jewish Question' did not have a high priority for Pius XII and his closest collaborators any more than it did for the leading German cardinals. Hence it is no surprise that Pius XII's letters to the German bishops contain so few comments about the outrages committed against Jews in Poland or elsewhere after September 1939. Yet there was no lack of information on the subject nor of appeals to the Pope for his intervention. Konrad von Preysing, the Bishop of Berlin (the most perceptive and anti-Nazi of the front-rank German Catholics) wrote to Pius XII on 17 January 1941, anxiously noting: 'Your Holiness is certainly informed about the situation of the Jews in Germany and the neighbouring countries. I wish to mention that I have been asked both from the Catholic and Protestant side if the Holy

See could not do something on this subject, publish and appeal in favour of these unfortunates.'[59]

As with other appeals of this kind requesting the Pope to make a public declaration about the persecution of Jews, he felt unable or unwilling to respond. But a year later, a great deal more information was becoming available. In the Vatican, as in other European capitals, knowledge was fast growing about the 'horrible deportations' (*orribile deportazione*) of Jews to the east. On 30 January 1942 Cardinal Maglione (Vatican Secretary of State) had commented to the British ambassador at the Vatican, Sir Francis d'Arcy Osborne, about a Hitler speech in which the Nazi leader had promised: 'The Jews will be liquidated for at least a thousand years!'[60] Much more concrete information soon began to pour in to Rome from many sources. In March 1942, the Vatican received news from Guiseppe Burzio, its representative in Bratislava, that the deportation of 80,000 Slovak Jews to Poland meant 'certain death' for a large number of them.[61] On 18 March 1942, Gerhart Riegner of the World Jewish Congress and Richard Lichtheim of the Jewish Agency for Palestine sent a remarkably detailed report on the fate of the Jews in Poland and the rest of Europe, which reached the Vatican through the Swiss nuncio in Berne, Filippo Bernardini. It spoke of more than a million Jews 'exterminated by the Germans', pointing out that the old, the sick, women and children were being systematically deported, a measure that clearly could not have been implemented for the purposes of forced labour.[62] Then, towards the end of June 1942, the London *Daily Telegraph* began to publicise a series of reports on the exterminations in Poland, which were broadcast on the BBC. These reports were specially summarised for the Pope by Osborne, who continued to supply His Holiness with similar material on a regular basis. On 30 June 1942, for example, Osborne noted down and passed on to the Pope, the following item: 'The Germans have killed over a million Jews in all, of whom 700,000 were in Poland.

Several million more have been deported or confined in concentration camps.' On 9 July 1942 he reported to the Pope the condemnation by Cardinal Hinsley, the highest ranking Catholic in Great Britain, of the 'utter bestiality of German methods'.[63]

From the autumn of 1942 not only Osborne but the Vatican ambassadors representing Brazil, Poland, Belgium and the United States began a series of steps to pressure Pius XII to speak out on behalf of the mercilessly oppressed Poles and Jews. The Roman Curia was upset at these moves, claiming that a public protest would only make the victims' suffering even worse and oblige the Vatican to condemn other atrocities besides those of the Germans. Moreover, so Maglione argued, the massacres were still not verifiable as hard fact and the Pope had already deplored such actions in general terms. Furthermore, he made it clear that it was out of the question for the Pope to condemn *by name* either Hitler or Nazi Germany.[64]

These arguments did not overly impress President Roosevelt's personal representative to the Pope, Myron Taylor. On 22 September 1942, in an interview with a top Vatican official, Domenico Tardini, he spoke 'of the opportunity and the necessity, of a word from the Pope against such huge atrocities by the Germans'. Tardini privately agreed, even as he wearily repeated the standard refrain that Pius XII 'has already spoken several times to condemn crimes by whomsoever they are committed.'[65] Such answers did not reassure the American or British representatives. Osborne, writing to British Foreign Secretary Anthony Eden on 3 October 1942, noted with some irony and regret that the 'occasional declarations in general terms do not have the lasting force and validity that, in the timeless atmosphere of the Vatican, they might perhaps be expected to retain ... A policy of silence in regard to such offences against the conscience of the world must necessarily involve a renunciation of moral leadership...'[66]

On 13 December 1942, Osborne angrily confided to his diary: 'The more I think of it, the more I am revolted by Hitler's massacre of the Jewish race on the one hand, and, on the other, the Vatican's apparently exclusive preoccupation with the effects of the war on Italy and the possibilities of the bombardment of Rome. The whole outfit seems to have become Italian.'[67] The next day he urged the Vatican to reconsider its duties 'in respect of the unprecedented crime against humanity of Hitler's campaign of extermination of the Jews, in which I said that Italy was an accomplice as the partner and ally of Germany'.[68] On 18 December he pressed Tardini hard to get the Pope to say something clear in his upcoming Christmas Eve broadcast. The evasive reply suggested to Osborne 'that His Holiness is clinging at all costs to what he considers to be a policy of neutrality, even in the face of the worst outrages against God and man, because he hopes to be able to play a part in restoring peace'.[69]

Finally, on 17 December 1942, the Allies themselves issued a public declaration condemning the German massacres of the Jews, which Osborne promptly brought to the Pope, hoping for an endorsement. The reply from Maglione was again negative, though he deplored the cruelties inflicted on innocent people. The Holy See, he explained, could only condemn atrocities in general, not particular crimes. Moreover, it was not in a position to verify Allied reports on the number of Jews who had been murdered and to know how reliable such estimates really were.[70] This was a remarkably unsatisfactory statement given the volume of increasingly detailed information that had reached Rome from a wide variety of sources during the past six months.

Slovakia was a good example of important knowledge available fairly early to the Vatican from its energetic representative, Giuseppe Burzio, information on which it had indeed acted. Anti-Jewish laws had been introduced almost immediately after Slovak 'independence' was declared on 14 March 1939. The fascist Slovak state was ruled by a cleric, Father Jozef Tiso, leader of the *Hlinková Garda* (Hlinka Guard) but it also included a pro-Nazi group in the cabinet led by the Prime Minister Tuka and Alexander Mach, the Interior Minister. After September 1941, on its own initiative the Slovak government began to proceed with the expropriation of Jewish property and then with deportations in March 1942. Initially at least, the government enjoyed the tacit support of the Catholic bishops in Slovakia, who seemed to be concerned only with making sure that Jewish converts be granted appropriate facilities for observing their new faith.[71]

The Vatican had protested against the planned deportations of Jews on 14 March 1942, expressing some astonishment that a nation supposedly committed to Catholic principles could act in this manner. The papal chargé d'affaires (who had tried unsuccessfully to persuade the Slovak bishops to take a unified position against the earlier codex of September 1941) now warned Tiso of serious consequences if he ignored the Vatican protest. On 23 May 1942, the Slovak government sent a chilling communication to the Vatican proudly defending its anti-Semitic policy. It clearly stated that the mass deportation of Slovak Jews was 'part of a much larger general plan' put into operation in agreement with the German government. 'Half a million Jews would be transported to eastern Europe. Slovakia was to be the first State whose inhabitants of Jewish origin would be accepted by Germany.'[72] The very detailed elaboration of government policy that followed (transmitted by the Slovak representative to the Holy See, Karol Sidor) spoke of the imminent deportations of Jews from France, Holland, Belgium, Bohemia, Moravia and the German Reich. The Slovak report announced that they would be settled in areas near Lublin where they would be 'under the protection of the Reich' (*sotto la protezione del Reich/Schutzbefohlene*). The official Slovak communication observed that Hungary, too, would be requested to deliver up its 800,000 Jews. While washing its hands of its own Jewish citizens, the Slovak government told the Vatican that the Germans had promised 'that the Jews will be treated humanely'.

Vatican Secretary of State Maglione seemed taken aback at the brutality of Slovak government policy and the continuing deportations of Jews to Poland, especially since Slovakia was a self-proclaimed Catholic nation whose leader, Monsignor Tiso, was an ordained priest. His involvement in such massive crimes could after all compromise the honour of the Vatican and the Church. On 13 July 1942 Maglione's top assistant Tardini pointedly noted the fact: 'It is a real misfortune that the President of Slovakia is a priest (*un sacerdote*). That the Holy See cannot bring Hitler to heel, everyone knows. But who will understand that we cannot even control a priest?'[73]

The Vatican record in Croatia was particularly open to condemnation, and much worse than in Slovakia, because of the monstrous crimes committed by a piously Catholic regime headed by Ante Pavelic, the *Poglavnik* (leader) of the Croatian Ustashe movement, which had come to power on 10 April 1941. Ustashe violence directed against the 'schismatics', i.e. the Orthodox Serbs, resembled a 'religious crusade'. The Vatican deplored preaching the gospel out of the barrel of a gun, but it also knew how proud the new regime was of its thirteen-hundred-year-old links with the Holy See. The Croatian state had wasted no time in passing racial laws against the Jews – accomplishing in a matter of weeks what it had taken the Nazi regime years to achieve in Germany.[74] As early as May 1941 Jews were being rounded up and sent to concentration camps. The Croatian archbishop, Cardinal Stepinac of Zagreb, watched these events with anxiety and perhaps with ambivalent feelings. He approved of certain Ustashe actions, for example against abortion and indecent advertisements, and he welcomed the intensely public Catholicism of the new regime. At the same time he felt bound to protest against the forced conversions of Serbs and the 'brutal treatment of non-Aryans during the deportations and at the camps'.[75] Yet, while he appealed to Pavelic for measures against Serbs and Jews to be 'carried out in a more humane and considerate way', he did not challenge the racist policy as such. In this respect Stepinac was acting consistently with the line adopted by Vatican officials during the Holocaust.

By October 1942, the Vatican had received reliable information on the massacres of Jews collected by Father Pirro Scavizzi (an Italian hospital train chaplain), who reported to the Pope that two million deaths had occurred up to that point. From this and many other sources (Allied, Polish, Jewish, etc.) as well as its own nuncios, the Vatican knew by the autumn of 1942 that the systematic killing of Jews was taking place all over Nazi-occupied Europe. Eventually, in his Christmas message of 1942, Pius XII did say something. In one single sentence that lasted for the duration of a breath, he mentioned that 'hundreds of thousands of people, through no fault of their own and solely because of their nation or race (*stirpe*), have been condemned to death or progressive extinction'.[76] As the British historian Owen Chadwick has observed, 'the Pope was very careful to guard against exaggeration'. Rather like the high officials of the British office, 'he thought that the Poles and Jews exaggerated for the sake of helping the war effort'.[77] Hence the numbers mentioned in his broadcast were far lower than the estimates in the reports that the Vatican had earlier received. Nor was there any mention of Nazis, let alone Jews, Poles or other particular victims.

The Pope's general appeal to the world's conscience, while angering some and pleasing others, was well understood by at least one of the German bishops. On 6 March 1943, Konrad von Preysing evoked the message when writing to Pius XII, asking him to try and save the Jews still in the Reich capital, who were facing imminent deportation, which would lead to certain death.

> Even more bitterly, the new wave of deportations of the Jews that just began in the days before 1 March particularly affects us here in Berlin. Several thousands are involved: Your Holiness has alluded to their probable fate in your Christmas Radio Broadcast. Among the deportees are also many Catholics. Is it not possible that Your Holiness tries once again to intervene for the many unfortunate innocents (die vielen unglücklichen Unschuldigen)? It is the last hope for many and the profound wish of all right-thinking people.[78]

Pius XII's lengthy reply (dated 30 April 1943) covered many themes that had preoccupied him all through his wartime correspondence with the German bishops. He expressed his pain at the fierce Allied aerial bombardments of German cities and reported on Vatican efforts to secure information about German soldiers captured or missing in Russia. Pius XII did not directly respond to Von Preysing's appeal to speak out about the Jews. But he did articulate his satisfaction at the fact that it was specifically Berlin Catholics who had shown such fraternal love towards 'the so-called non-Aryans' (Nichtariern) in their distress. He also wrote of the 'charitable action' of the Holy See on behalf of both 'Catholic non-Aryans' and those 'of Jewish confession' (Glaubensjuden), emphasising that the Vatican had spent considerable sums 'for the transportation of emigrants overseas' (much of this money had come from American Jewish sources, which was not mentioned).[79]

The Pope also noted that while the Holy See expected neither heavenly nor earthly rewards for its humanitarian gestures, it had received 'the warmest recognition for its relief work' from Jewish organisations. Pius XII even found a word of 'fatherly recognition' for Father Lichtenberg, a Catholic bishop who had been imprisoned by the Nazis for his courageous sermons (in solidarity with the deported Jews) and who would die on his way to Dachau shortly afterwards. No less significantly, Pius XII told Von Preysing that he gave to his pastors at the local level 'the duty of determining if and to what degree the danger of reprisals and diverse forms of repression ... seem to advise caution, to avoid the greater evil (*ad maiora mala vitanda*) despite alleged reasons to the contrary'.[80] The Pope felt that under wartime conditions he had to exercise great care in order not 'to impose useless sacrifices on German Catholics, who are already so oppressed for the sake of their faith'.[81]

Perhaps in a delayed response to Von Preysing's appeal for a further statement about the fate of the Jews, Pius XII did allusively refer to the subject in an allocution to the cardinals on 2 June 1943. This was the second and last time that he would touch in public on what we now call 'the Holocaust'. 'Do not be astonished,' he said, 'if we lend our ear with particularly profound sympathy to the voices of those who turn to us imploringly, their hearts full of fear. They are those who, because of their nationality or their descent, are pursued by mounting misfortune and increasing suffering. Sometimes, through no fault of theirs, they are subjected to measures that threaten them with extermination.'[82] This short section was suppressed by the Axis powers in their reports on the Pope's speech, but Vatican radio did broadcast it to Germany, adding that those who make 'a distinction between Jews and other men' were unfaithful to God and the divine commands.

Only at the end of the war, on 2 June 1945, before the Sacred College of Cardinals, did Pacelli feel free to fully unburden himself and call things by their proper names. The Pope now claimed to have foreseen the disaster of National Socialism 'when it was still in the distant future, and few, We believe, have followed with greater anxiety the process leading to the inevitable crash'.[83] He pointed out that 'the Church did everything possible to set up a formidable barrier to the spread of

ideas at once subversive and violent'. In no way had the Concordat implied 'any formal approval to the teachings or tendencies of National Socialism'.[84] Pacelli recalled how the 1937
encyclical of his predecessor, Pius XI, had boldly exposed
Nazism as 'an arrogant apostasy from Jesus Christ, the denial
of His Doctrine and of His work of redemption, the cult of
violence, the idolatry of race and blood, the overthrow of human
liberty and dignity'.[85] This sharp drawing of the lines in 1937
had opened the eyes of many, though regrettably not of all
Catholics. There were some, he admitted, who had been 'too
blinded by their prejudices or tempted by political advantage'
to oppose National Socialist ideology with sufficient vigour.

But the Pope's own record after the German military occupation of Rome in September 1943 also left something to be
desired. More than a thousand Roman Jews (out of a population
of 8,000) were deported to Auschwitz from under the windows
of the Vatican, so to speak. True, there were also Roman Jews
who were hidden in monasteries, convents and even in the
Vatican itself. But it is not clear how much Pius XII had to do
with the rescue actions, or whether he directly approved them.[86]

On 16 October 1943, the SS and German military police
surrounded the Roman ghetto, rounding up and transporting
Jews to the Italian Military College – less than half a mile from
the Vatican. The same morning the Pope ordered Maglione to
summon the German ambassador Ernst von Weizsäcker. The
Cardinal told him how 'painful beyond words it is for the Holy
Father that here in Rome itself, under the eyes of the Common
Father (*sotto gli occhi del Padre Commune*), so many people
should be made to suffer uniquely because they belong to a
certain race (*appartengono ad una stirpa determinata*)'. Maglione appealed to the ambassador's 'tender and good heart – to try
to save these many innocent people', invoking his sentiments of
humanity and 'Christian charity'.[87] He also suggested that 'the
Holy See did not want to be put in a position that forced it to

protest (*non deve essere messa nella necessità di protestare*)', if the German deportations continued. In such a case, 'it would have to trust for the consequences in the Divine Providence'. Most remarkable of all was Maglione's admission that 'the Holy See had been prudent enough not to give to the German people any impression of having done or wanting to do anything against Germany during this terrible war (*per non dare al popolo germanico l'impressione di aver fatto o voler fare contro la Germania la minima cosa durante una guerra terribile*)'.[88] Neither Pius XII, Maglione nor any other high Vatican official wanted a rupture with Nazi Germany.

Pius XII's refusal to make a public denunciation of the Roman *razzia* was no different from the position he had adopted when vast numbers of Jews had been deported from across Europe in 1942 (including from Catholic countries such as Slovakia, Croatia, Belgium and France) or murdered in Russia, the Ukraine and Poland. Had such a protest been made it is quite possible that more Catholics might have helped to rescue Jews in occupied countries or that more Jews might have fled in time from their Nazi hunters. Nor did the Vatican oppose discriminatory laws against Jews or the social segregation that resulted, even as the Holocaust was raging in the heart of Europe. In the autumn of 1941, a report by the French ambassador to the Holy See, Leon Bérard, confirmed to Marshal Pétain that the Vatican had no objection to Vichy's draconian anti-Jewish statutes provided that the French government acted with 'justice and charity'.[89] The pattern in Croatia, Slovakia, Hungary, Romania and other countries that passed anti-Semitic legislation was almost always the same. Vatican objections were rarely directed against the principle of discrimination *per se*, though it did object to violence, murder and racist assumptions about baptised Jews that conflicted with Catholic doctrine or church prerogatives. As late as August 1943, the Jesuit father Pietro Tacchi Venturi observed that according to the principles and traditions of the

Catholic Church the Italian anti-Jewish laws had '... dispositions that should be abrogated but contain others worthy of confirmation'.[90]

Such hesitations and ambivalence cannot be divorced from the deep suspicion in which the Church still held the Jews, a distrust that the unfolding Holocaust was unable to significantly dent. They were still identified theologically as a 'deicide' people in most Catholic minds; they were seen as being linked with the forces of liberalism, Freemasonry, rationalism and secularism in the democratic west and with a dictatorial and ruthless Bolshevism in the east. The Jews embodied in Catholic tradition a secular 'modernity' that was considered inimical to the ideals of Christian society and its vision of redemption. The Churches, both Catholic and Protestant, were unable – with a few honourable exceptions – to shake off the age-old 'teaching of contempt' towards the Jews, though they neither conceived, collaborated in nor approved of the Holocaust. To quote Emil Fackenheim, the 'Final Solution' was 'the nemesis of a bi-millennial disease within Christianity *itself*, transmuted when Nazism turned against the Christian substance'.[91]

# VI   *Collaboration across Europe*

> It takes a lot of imagination to find something new. In fact, after the expropriation of real estate, after the deportations and assassinations – all the rest becomes grotesque ... Sometimes there is something diabolic in anti-Semitism, but now, when we don't swim in blood, we are splashing through muddy, petty theft.
>
> **Journal of Mihail Sebastian**, Bucharest, 12 November 1941

> Hitler, keep your dirty hands off our dirty Jews!
>
> Wartime graffiti in Amsterdam

> ... the immediate factors favourable to Jewish rescue during the Holocaust must be placed in the context of the customs and traditions of individual countries. The most pertinent tradition, of course, is the existence or absence of anti-Semitism. For many reasons, modern Italy lacked an anti-Semitic tradition.
>
> **Susan Zuccotti**, *The Italians and the Holocaust* (1987)

The Nazi Holocaust had begun on Soviet soil and was initially directed at the three and a half million Jews living in the USSR, including the recently annexed Baltic states. One of its most striking features was its openly *public* character, so different from the secrecy surrounding the gassings later conducted in the death camps of Poland. As the Wehrmacht struck more deeply into the Soviet Union, the death toll rapidly mounted.[1] According to Raul Hilberg, by the end of 1943 the Germans had succeeded in killing close to two million Jews within the pre-invasion borders of the USSR, mostly by shooting in pits close to their homes. Only in the Soviet Union did the Germans and their helpers repeatedly shoot down hundreds of thousands of unarmed Jewish men, women and children in broad daylight, almost within the sight and hearing of their neighbours. Despite the high visibility of these murders, the Soviet regime was not interested in publicising more than the barest details that directly related to the genocide of the Jews. It was equally determined to cover up the evidence of extensive collaboration with the Nazi invaders by 'peaceful Soviet citizens'.

The example of the Ukrainians is particularly pertinent since their 'collaboration' with the Germans had assumed such a wide-ranging character. In the Ukraine, local police zealously rounded up Jews and herded them into ghettos, isolating them from their neighbours and weakening their physical and psychological resistance. When the mass shootings began in the late summer of 1941, it was they who took the Jews to the killing sites, seeing to it that they would not escape. Although the Germans always directed and co-ordinated the killing of Jews through their regional SS and police leaders, the Security Police and units of the mobile Order Police, recent research has confirmed the vital auxiliary role of the indigenous local police collaborators (*Schutzmannschaft*).[2] Together with the German gendarmerie, Ukrainian police were not only responsible for the round-ups but on occasion participated directly in the pit shootings so characteristic of mass executions in the east.

In the Ukraine and western Belorussia, the *Schutzmannschaft* specialised above all in search-and-kill operations, looking for Jews still hidden in the ghettos or who had fled for refuge to the neighbouring forests.[3] The local police were especially dangerous since they were often the only people able to clearly identify their former Jewish neighbours. In the areas under German civil administration, more than 25,000 men had volunteered in the first few months of the occupation for service in the *Schutzmannschaft*. There never seemed to be any shortage of such volunteers to round up and escort Jews to their deaths or to join in the notorious 'Jew hunts' in the countryside. In the rural districts of Ukraine and Belorussia at the time of the 1942 ghetto 'liquidations', these local policemen often outnumbered the German gendarmes by a ratio of more than five to one. Thus not only the German Order Police were 'willing executioners' in the face-to-face killing process described by Daniel Goldhagen. Indeed, some of the more zealous perpetrators, who sought to win promotion through their prowess as murderers, were later described by eyewitnesses as even more callous towards Jewish women and children than the Germans themselves.

The local perpetrators included a mixture of nationalist activists, brutalised anti-Semites, rank opportunists, former criminals and simple peasants looking for a more secure source of income. Their motives were equally mixed. Some were primarily influenced by sheer personal greed, driven by alcoholism, careerism or peer group pressure, others by a vicious anti-Semitism and a burning hatred of the Soviet regime.[4] Ukrainians had not, for example, forgotten Stalin's deliberately induced 'terror famine' in their homeland, which had led to four million deaths in the early 1930s during the forced collectivisation of agriculture. Although the Stalinists could not – any more than the Nazis – realistically aim at wiping out the entire 36 million strong Ukrainian people, both sought by different totalitarian methods to break the back of a tenacious Ukrainian nationalism.[5] As had happened elsewhere in eastern Europe, Ukrainian nationalists in the 1930s frequently identified Jews with the hegemonic oppressor nationality (in this case, the Russians) and with the hated Soviet yoke. This 'Judaeo-Bolshevik' amalgam fatally intensified the anti-Semitism woven deep into the fabric of Ukrainian popular consciousness since the seventeenth century – an ethnic and socio-economic hatred that periodically erupted into bloody pogroms in 1881, 1905 and again during the Russian Civil Wars.[6]

Collaboration with the Nazi invaders, welcomed by many Ukrainians as a 'liberating' force from Soviet Communism and the Jews, was all too common in the early stages of the German occupation. Such co-operation would have assumed much greater proportions had it not been for the unbounded racial hubris and folly of the German conquerors, who treated millions of their Ukrainian subjects as if they really were Slavic *Untermenschen* – exploiting and killing them in large numbers.[7] Yet, in the initial euphoria of the German invasion, there had been no shortage of Ukrainians who seized Jewish possessions and occupied their homes once Jews were forced to abandon them.

In Lithuania, too, the Germans and their local collaborators had begun to murder Jews systematically, almost immediately after the invasion of the USSR. Heydrich's instructions to the *Einsatzgruppen* had been to encourage the local population 'to act spontaneously' against the Jews. In the event, Lithuanians needed no prompting, such was the zeal and frenzy with which they carried out pogroms. The first killings of 1,500 Jews in Kovno on the night of 25–26 June 1941, was perpetrated by Lithuanians with a bestial savagery that surprised the Germans themselves.[8] It was the ultra-nationalist, anti-Soviet Lithuanian 'partisans' who most eagerly volunteered to kill many thousands of Jews in Kovno, Vilna and the numerous *shtetlach* in the Lithuanian provinces. In these *Aktionen* they outstripped the Germans both in the scale and intensity of their involvement and the number of victims they wiped out. Perhaps as much as two thirds of Lithuanian Jewry were extinguished by local units, who could even give lessons to their 'liberators' in how to murder women and children without mercy.

Altogether, over 90 per cent of Lithuanian Jewry were killed in the Holocaust, the highest single death rate for any major Jewish community in Europe. The great majority were murdered very swiftly indeed, in the five months between the end of June and December 1941. None of these horrors would have been possible without what Dina Porat has described as 'a fatal combination of Lithuanian motivation and German organisation and thoroughness'.[9] She points out that though the Germans provided the framework and 'legitimacy' for the killings, Lithuanian national aspirations and hatred for Communism were the fuel driving the murder machine. Feelings that had been bottled up during the oppressive Soviet rule of Lithuania (1940–1), when its indigenous citizenry saw their independence erased, exploded into a crazed anti-Semitic fury once the Germans arrived. Though there was no pogrom tradition analogous to Poland, the Ukraine, Romania or Russia, Lithuanians proved to be highly proficient in face-to-face killing. Once local police battalions (numbering about 8,500) were close to completing their macabre work, some of them were sent to Belorussia and Poland to continue their murderous activities in small towns, camps and ghettos. Their members could also be found as guards in death camps such as Treblinka or Maidanek and as auxiliaries assisting General Stroop's forces in crushing the Warsaw ghetto uprising. As hangmen and sadists their reputation was second to none.

Croatia stands out as another example of human bestiality closely allied to fanatical nationalism. The ruling clique under Pavelic required no encouragement from the Germans to kill Jews and even less to murder almost half a million Serbs. Here, too, the German army was momentarily taken aback (despite its own appalling record in Serbia) by the bloody fury of the Ustashe fascists who had come to power in April 1941.[10] For the Croats, the prime enemy remained the Orthodox Serbs, who were designated to be exiled, killed or returned to Catholicism – allegedly the 'true faith of their fathers'. The 'new Croatia' did indeed forcibly convert hundreds of thousands of Greek Orthodox Serbs at gunpoint, amply confirming Jonathan Steinberg's description of it as 'the only Axis satellite to have murdered more non-Jewish than Jewish civilians'.[11] Genocide was official, state-directed policy in wartime Croatia and it did not spare the 38,000 Jews and 27,000 gypsies who died during the four years of Ustashe rule.[12] Within three weeks of coming to power, the new regime had passed anti-Jewish race laws (May/June 1941), which prohibited intermarriage, removed Jews from the civil service and professions, forced them to register their property, marked their stores and 'Aryanised' their capital. Following the example of the Nuremberg laws, Jews were forbidden to employ 'Aryan' female servants. Soon the bulk of Croatian Jews would be sent to the notorious Ustashe concentration camps, while an additional seven thousand were deported by the Croats at German request.[13] In the summer of 1943 Archbishop Stepinac deplored the 'inhumane and brutal treatment of non-Aryans during the deportations and at the camps, and even worse, that neither children, old people nor the sick are spared'.[14] Pavelic did not even respect the human rights of Jewish converts to Catholicism, much to the dismay of Stepinac and the accredited Apostolic Visitor, Monsignor Marcone.[15]

Romania was another example of primitive, Balkan-style ferocity where 'even the SS were taken aback, and occasionally frightened, by the horrors of old-fashioned, spontaneous pogroms on a gigantic scale'.[16] In the nineteenth century, Romania had rivalled Tsarist Russia in its persecution of Jews and intransigent insistence on regarding them as aliens. Under enormous pressure from the Western Allies it had grudgingly granted citizenships to its Jewish minority after the First World War, a step that the Romanian government eventually cancelled in December 1937. At that time, Romania had a very large Jewish population of 750,000. Within a short period, several hundred thousand Jews lost their civil rights, possessions and jobs. Neither the Romanian government nor the fanatical ultra-nationalists in the fascist Iron Guard movement needed any prodding from Nazi Germany. Romanian nationalism had become almost synonymous with anti-Semitism and slogans connecting the Jews with Communism, capitalism and plu-

tocracy fell on fertile soil.[17] An extremist anti-Semitic movement like the Iron Guard could win 15.5 per cent of the vote in
the 1937 elections, forcing even the 'moderates' in Romania to
engage in racist and xenophobic rhetoric simply to keep it
in check.[18] In August 1940, the head of the new Iron Guard
dictatorship, Marshal Ion Antonescu, declared almost all Romanian Jews stateless (only about ten thousand Jews placed in a
special privileged category were exempt), initiating some of the
harshest anti-Jewish legislation hitherto seen in Europe. This
step prompted Hitler to remark that 'Antonescu proceeds in
these matters in far more radical fashion than we have done up
to the present'.[19]

In January 1941, the Iron Guard carried out a savage pogrom
in Bucharest in which 170 Jews were murdered. The following
month, Romania entered the war and its legions were soon
involved in horrific massacres of Jews in the east, especially in
the Crimea and southern Ukraine. In Odessa alone, Romanian
troops butchered about 30,000 Jews with unsurpassed cruelty.
Even after the Iron Guard left the government, the slaughter
continued unabated in the summer of 1941. Romanian troops
were further used to send thousands of Jews into designated
killing areas on forced marches, to drown them in the Dniester,
or push them into the German zone of the Ukraine. The deportations of nearly 150,000 Jews to the newly annexed province of
Transnistria were especially horrific. The Jews were herded into
freight cars and often died of suffocation as the trains travelled
through the countryside for days on end. The ghettos and concentration camps in Transnistria were as dreadful as anything
in the German Reich. Not surprisingly, three quarters of the
Jews in Transnistria perished.

Although Antonescu's government acted with complete ruthlessness against the non-assimilated and non-Romanian-speak-
ing Jews of Bessarabia and Bukovina (seized from the Soviet
Union in 1941), it was much less inclined to co-operate with

German demands to deport the acculturated Jews of the Romanian heartland to the East.[20] Antonescu made no secret of his opposition to any encroachment on his national sovereignty. Probably he also felt that Romania had already achieved its territorial ambitions by the autumn of 1942 and was better off disengaging itself from Nazi Germany. His regime had already killed about a quarter of a million of its own Jews, mostly without German assistance. But as the tide of war turned against Germany, Antonescu preferred to hedge his bets, maintaining his channels to the west and gradually distancing himself from Hitler's 'Final Solution'.

From the end of 1942 a flourishing trade in exemption certificates for Jews developed, as Romanian officials discovered that the sale of Jews abroad for hard currency could be a profitable business. Romania now became an enthusiastic convert to the idea of Jewish emigration and an outlet for Jews seeking to reach Palestine. The one country in Europe (outside Germany) that had practised mass extermination of Jews entirely on its own initiative had also proved to be the most mercenary. This corruptibility led to a new 'moderation' on the Jewish question. Antonescu first tried and ultimately failed to persuade the Nazis to permit the departure of Jews to the Middle East. Then, ignoring German pressure, he decisively obstructed the deportation of Jews from the Regat region of old Romania. At the end of the war, despite Antonescu's earlier record of murderous anti-Semitism, about 300,000 Romanian Jews (over half the Jewish population) had survived the Holocaust.

Hungary was an exceptionally tragic case, for had the Germans not invaded the country in March 1944, far more Jews would have been spared than in Romania. Instead, in a dizzying, accelerated process of destruction that took less than four months, over 60 per cent of Hungary's 725,000 Jews were packed off to the gas chambers of Auschwitz. By 8 July 1944, almost 440,000 Jews had been deported and towards the end of the year, except for the Jews of Budapest, the country was virtually *judenrein*. The speed of dispatch seemed all the more shocking given the late stage of the war, the certainty that Nazi Germany would be defeated, the widespread knowledge of the Holocaust and repeated Allied warnings to the Hungarian government. The two hundred Germans in Adolf Eichmann's *Sondereinsatzkommando* (Special Operations Unit) aided by another six hundred Gestapo men sent to Budapest to supervise the deportations could hardly have deported Hungarian Jewry to the death chambers on their own. The collaboration of the Hungarian army, the gendarmerie (who played the key role), politicians, civil servants, fascist Arrow Cross militia and transport workers was essential. It was made much easier by the spinelessness of the Hungarian Regent, Admiral Horthy, and the hostility of ordinary Hungarians, who seemed to sympathise more with the persecutors of the Jews than with the victims.[21] There were no less than 35,000 Hungarian denunciations of Jews in the first weeks of the German invasion. Moreover, the Christian churches and the Primate of Hungary, Cardinal Justinian Seredi, displayed remarkably little resistance (except on the issue of converts) to the anti-Jewish measures that ultimately led to the deportations.[22]

Jewish resistance, while difficult in Hungary's flat, open terrain, was also minimal. One of the reasons why so few Hungarian Jews resorted to arms lay in the depth of their integration in Hungarian society, ever since their emancipation in 1867. Before 1914 they had been important allies for the Magyars in the framework of a multi-ethnic Hungarian state that was still part of the Habsburg Empire but faced with constant demographic and political challenges from Romanians, Germans, Slovaks, Serbs and Croats.[23] During the First World War, however, the short-lived Soviet Republic established by Béla Kun and his associates (two thirds of whom were Communists of Jewish origin) changed perceptions decisively for the worse, even though the revolutionaries were no less hostile to Judaism than to the Christian Churches. This was especially true for the conservative, landowning elites who had traditionally looked to Jews as their natural business partners.

In 1920, Hungary had been the first modern state in post-war Europe to institute a *numerus clausus* in order to reduce Jewish admission in the universities to 6 per cent. In 1938, the first anti-Jewish law limited Jewish representation to 20 per cent in commercial, financial and industrial concerns as well as in journalism and the professions. A second anti-Jewish law of wider scope followed in May 1939, restricting Jewish participation in professional and economic life to 6 and 12 per cent respectively. The third anti-Jewish law of July 1941 was much more openly racist, forbidding mixed marriages between Christians and Jews, and narrowing exemptions.[24] This barrage of legislation reflected in its own way the exceptional importance of the role that Jews had played in Hungary's economic and cultural life for many decades.

As in Romania during the 1930s, successive Hungarian governments tried to outflank the far Right by adopting more moderate anti-Semitic legal measures. But this tactic did not stop the Nazi-style Arrow Cross from winning forty-five out of 260 parliamentary seats in the May 1939 elections. The Arrow Cross immediately demanded far sterner measures against the Jews, which were partly satisfied by the new legislation of July 1941. Then, in June 1942, Prime Minister Kállay, a cosmopolitan Catholic aristocrat, introduced a bill to expropriate Jewish-controlled estates. A few weeks later, the Jewish religion was deprived of equal treatment with other denominations, which it had enjoyed ever since 1895. But Kállay firmly rejected German demands to expropriate all Jewish wealth, to impose the yellow star or deport the Jews to the east.[25] When Hitler summoned Admiral Horthy to Klessheim Castle on 17–18 April 1943, it was evident that both he and Ribbentrop were profoundly irked by the fact that Jews (whether baptised or not) still held positions of economic and political influence in Hungary. This was almost certainly a factor in the German invasion of Hungary nearly one year later.

After the March 1944 invasion the new Hungarian Prime Minister, Döme Szótay, was ready to give the Germans what they wanted. Adolf Eichmann soon found three Hungarians on whom he could completely rely for the concentration of Jews in the provinces with 'lightning speed' and then for the transportation to Auschwitz of nearly half a million Jews. His Hungarian collaborators-in-chief were Lieutenant Colonel Ferenczy, who had direct charge of the deportations; László Baky, in the Interior Ministry, who controlled the *gendarmerie*; and László Endre, State Secretary in Charge of Political Jewish Affairs, a particularly rabid anti-Semite.[26] Collaboration now proceeded on a very broad scale. Deportations in every locality required the intervention of the mayor, the police chief and gendarmes as well as civil servants, who, along with other Hungarians, often enriched themselves by plundering the belongings and property of the departing Jews. The lack of resistance by most Hungarian Gentiles to this forcible uprooting within a matter of days of so many Jews (some of whom had lived continuously in certain communities for centuries) was all the more stunning, given the extent of assimilation on which Hungarian Jewry had long prided itself. Eventually Admiral Horthy did buckle to outside pressure and stop the deportations on 7 July 1944. He bowed to vigorous representations from the Western Allies, Pope Pius XII, the King of Sweden and other dignitaries; undoubtedly, he also feared retribution after the American bombing raids on Budapest (2 July 1944), the approach of the Red army from the east and the Allied advances in Normandy. He could not but take note of President Roosevelt's ultimatum that 'Hungary's fate will not be like any other civilised nation ... unless the deportations are stopped.'[27]

But in mid-October 1944, the Germans overthrew the Horthy government, appointing the violently anti-Semitic Arrow Cross leader, Ferenc Szálasi as head of state. Now began the gruesome last phase of the Hungarian Holocaust – a reign of terror in which the Danube turned red with the blood of more than 20,000 Jews, tormented and butchered by Arrow Cross fanatics.[28] It was a period of feverish appeals by World Jewry to Allied governments, to the International Red Cross, the Vatican and neutral countries, imploring them to save Jewish lives. Protective passes, an idea inspired by Raoul Wallenberg – the heroic Swedish diplomat – saved at least 15,000 Jews in Budapest. Jewish lives were also saved by the energetic Papal nuncio Angelo Rotta and through Swiss diplomatic protection in buildings specially acquired as safe houses.[29] Interestingly enough, it was a sustained Swiss press campaign that did much to ignite the indignation of Western leaders at the fate of Hungarian Jews in the summer of 1944.[30]

The position of Jews in the 'independent' Slovak state established with German help in 1939 was even shakier than in Hungary. The fascist militia (the Hlinka Guard) in this small, weak, backward puppet state was Catholic in outlook but also ultra-nationalist, pro-German and very anti-Semitic. Most of the Catholics in the Slovak government did not fully share the 'modern' racism of the Nazis. They still favoured the traditional Catholic distinction between baptised and unconverted Jews.[31] They were certainly interested in deporting the Jews and taking over their property but as yet unaware of the 'Final Solution'. However, there were powerful figures such as Alexander Mach (the Interior Minister) and the German-oriented Prime Minister, Vojtech Tuka, who wished to imitate the Nazi handling of the 'Jewish Question'. These men were the driving force behind the deportation of nearly 90,000 Slovak Jews that began in early 1942. The evidence suggests, as Yehuda Bauer has argued, that it was the Slovaks, rather than the Germans, who initiated the deportations.[32] The Slovak leaders did not definitively know until May 1942 of the mass murders in Poland, though they had probably received some indications before then. By the end of July 1942, however, 52,000 Jews had been transported to Poland, including women, children, the very young and the infirm. Nazi Germany demanded five hundred Reichsmarks for every Jew received but did not make any claim on their property. The Slovak government, eager to co-operate in the Nazi new order, expected to benefit handsomely from the massive expropriation of Jewish possessions.

It was in Slovakia that a Jewish Centre (*Ustredna Zidov*) first emerged that tried to prevent the deportations by bribing Slovak officials and by conducting negotiations with Eichmann's representative in Bratislava, Dieter Wisliceny. Though nominally part of the Tiso regime's apparatus (and including at least one collaborator with the Germans), the Jewish Centre's members tried to subvert the machinery of destruction as best they could. They established intelligence networks, smuggled and assisted some 8,000 Jews to the comparative safety of Hungary, passed information about deportations on to the West and engaged in other underground activities. There was also a working group that emerged apart from the Centre, led by a courageous woman Zionist, Gizi Fleischmann, and the ultra-orthodox Rabbi Michael Dov Ber Weissmandel, who conceived the plan of trying to stop the deportations by offering a major bribe to Wisliceny.[33] Towards the end of 1942, the working group suggested a much more sweeping idea to Wisliceny, called the Europa Plan, which was intended to halt all the deportations to Poland (and perhaps even the killings) in return for an initial down-payment of $200,000 with more cash to follow. Rabbi Weissmandel (who wrongly assumed that the first payment to Wisliceny had succeeded in halting the deportations from Slovakia in the summer of 1942) would later denounce the outside Jewish world for having failed to save European Jewry, by not sending the money

in time. But his accusations were based on ignorance of what
had really happened in Slovakia, of the financial constraints
operating on the Jewish side as well as a misreading of Nazi
intentions.[34]

There were, as we have seen, countries like Slovakia, Croatia,
Lithuania and Romania that had at different times preceded or
even rivalled the Germans in their brutal treatment of Jews. But
there were also opposite cases where the 'Final Solution' was
partially or wholly sabotaged. A dramatic example was Bulgaria,
whose 50,000 indigenous Jews survived the war, despite considerable German pressure on its wartime ally to deliver them
up for deportation.[35] The Bulgarian monarchy had enjoyed
extensive territorial aggrandisement (at the expense of Greece,
Yugoslavia and Romania) thanks to its alliance with Nazi
Germany. Unlike Hungary and Romania, however, it did not
send even a token force to fight against the Soviet Union. Also,
in contrast to Slovakia, Croatia, Romania and Hungary, its
native fascist movement was small and without political influence. Moreover, the country had a highly respected parliament
which worked harmoniously in tandem with the monarchy.
Above all, Bulgarians were strikingly free from the anti-Semitism that was so pervasive in most of eastern Europe – a critical
factor in their opposition to surrendering native Jews to the
Nazis. The predominantly Sephardic community, which was
well integrated into national life, was simply not regarded by
most Bulgarians as a threat to their society.[36]

It is true that, in January 1941, the Bulgarian government did
pass some anti-Jewish laws. But they were far milder than in
most European countries and mitigated by many exemptions.
For example, *all* baptised Jews (irrespective of their conversion
date) were automatically exempted. Five thousand Jews – a tenth
of the entire Jewish population – were given special privileges. A
*numerus clausus* was imposed, but it was based on the percentage of Jews in the cities, which made it rather high. The

most severe measure, to mobilise six thousand able-bodied men for work, was hardly guaranteed to enthuse the German Nazis, who bemoaned Bulgaria's failure to understand the 'Jewish problem'. Even when a yellow badge was briefly introduced (and then removed) it was extremely small and most Jews did not even bother to wear it. An SD report to the Foreign Office in November 1942 noted that those who did wear it received much sympathy from 'the misled population'.

When Hitler asked King Boris III of Bulgaria to transfer the Bulgarian Jews for work in Germany's eastern territories, the monarch resisted, claiming that the Jewish workforce was required in the country to build roads and railway trucks. Not even the arrival of the zealous SS Jewish expert Theodore Dannecker in Sofia, early in 1943, succeeded in changing the situation, largely because the parliament and a wide section of the Bulgarian population was opposed to deportation. Nonetheless Dannecker did negotiate an agreement with Aleksandur Belev, Commissar for Jewish Affairs, to deport 20,000 Jews. None, however, would leave the country. Politicians, clerics, intellectuals and civil servants were on the side of the Jews.[37] As soon as the news reached the King, he instructed the Prime Minister to cancel the deportations. The Jews were resettled from the capital to rural areas which, much to German displeasure, dispersed rather than concentrated them. The Greek Orthodox metropolitan Stephan of Sofia declared publicly that 'God had determined the Jewish fate, and men had no right to torture Jews, and to persecute them'. This was considerably more explicit than anything Pope Pius XII could bring himself to say in public.

In his study of the subject, Michael Bar-Zohar gives special credit to the efforts of Dimitâr Peshev, vice-president of the Bulgarian parliament, who with forty-two MPs pressured the Prime Minister to save the Jews. He also reveals the intense lobbying by the Bulgarian Jews themselves and the secret action of Belev's Bulgarian Secretary, who warned a leading member of the Jewish community when the first deportations were imminent. As a result of the rescue action, local German officials became unsure of themselves. The German ambassador in Sofia wrote in June 1943 to his Foreign Minister that the situation was hopeless: 'There is no point in pressing Bulgaria any further to hand over their Jews for deportation because the Bulgarians do not have the same concept and ideas about the Jews as prevail in Germany. The Bulgarians have been accustomed to living for centuries in harmony with their minorities of Turks, Jews, gypsies, Armenians, etc., simply because no distinct differences in characteristics separate them, as in other countries.'[38]

The Germans soon abandoned their efforts and not a single native Bulgarian Jew was deported during the war. But the 11,363 Jews living in the newly occupied territories of Macedonia and Thrace were deported by the Germans with the help of Bulgarian police units under their command. The sovereignty of the occupied territories had not yet been determined and possibly there was not much that King Boris or the Bulgarian state could have done. But unlike the case of Denmark (of which Bulgaria is reminiscent in other respects) there is no evidence of any action planned or undertaken to rescue the Jews of these territories.

Denmark was the one country in Nazi-occupied Europe where the *entire* Jewish community was saved as a result of massive *popular* opposition to Nazi policy.[39] Although it had been conquered in April 1940, the country was treated by the Nazis as if it were a neutral state, retaining an independent government with which the Germans did not interfere until the autumn of 1943. Unlike neighbouring Norway, there were no enthusiastic collaborators organised into a serious fascist or Nazi movement. In contrast to Germany itself, the Lutheran tradition had spawned no significant religious anti-Semitism and Protestant pastors were in the forefront of protests on behalf of the Jews. Like Bulgaria and Italy, Denmark was relatively immune to Judaeophobia, but it did not feel the need to go through any complex contortions and double-dealing to rescue its Jews. In Denmark, the Germans did not even introduce their favoured ploy of softening resistance by distinguishing between the 6,400 native Jews and the 1,400 'stateless' refugees from Germany who had been given asylum before the war.

The Jewish community in Denmark was not only small, relatively homogeneous and highly assimilated – it had the good fortune of living in a country where a democratic civic consciousness extended through the whole society.[40] This seemed to influence some of the German occupiers themselves, including the military commander, General Von Hannecken. The German plenipotentiary Dr Werner Best also played a some-what ambiguous role in Denmark after November 1942. Despite his fearsome record as a 'desk murderer' and close collaborator of Heydrich, there is evidence that he helped to sabotage Himmler's orders to deport the Danish Jews. No more than 477 out of more than 7,000 Jews were finally rounded up by German troops, who were forbidden by Dr Best to break into Jewish departments. Jewish leaders, who had been tipped off by Danish government officials about the deportation plan, which had been set for 1 October 1943, had the news communicated in the synagogues during the New Year services, which allowed just enough time for Jews to go into hiding. Here, too, they were fortunate that their Danish neighbours stood ready to receive them.

Through October, the Jews were ferried across the narrow strip of water to neutral Sweden, where even the non-Danish Jews were given permission to work. The Danish fishing fleet helped with the transportation and the costs were largely paid for by wealthy Danish citizens. This generosity stood in stark contrast to many other countries, where Jews had to pay extortionately large sums simply to obtain an exit permit. The open resistance demonstrated by Denmark to Nazi Jewish policy during the Holocaust was in fact unique, though it was much helped by having an understanding neighbour in Sweden, one which by 1943 (despite its 'collaboration' with Germany) was willing to take in Jews without conditions.[41] Finland, too, which categorically refused to even discuss with Nazi officials the deportation of its 2,000 Jews, proved that resistance to German demands was feasible. Ironically enough, the Nazis experienced their biggest failure on the 'Jewish Question' among their Scandinavian 'blood brothers'. With rare exceptions, their fellow Nordics proved most unhelpful whereas all too many of the so-called *Untermenschen* of the east, reviled by the Nazis, collaborated with alacrity in the despoliation and murder of their Jewish neighbours.

Holland also shared with the Scandinavian countries a fairly modest level of anti-Semitism (though German Jewish refugees before 1939 had not received a specially warm welcome), and there was widespread hostility to the anti-Jewish measures imposed under the German occupation. Support and assistance for Jews was especially prevalent among Dutch Calvinists. Equally, the Catholic Archbishop De Jonge of Utrecht forbade his constituents to assist Germans in rounding up Jews.[42] In February 1941, after widespread arrests of Jews and outbursts against them by the local Nazis, the workers had called for a general strike in Amsterdam, which lasted for two days. This was the first public demonstration against Nazi Jewish policies anywhere in wartime Europe. But the Nazis were able to crush most of the local Dutch resistance with comparative ease, not least because of the flat, open terrain that made methods of guerrilla warfare unfeasible. The Germans also learned a lesson from the public protests by halting police raids in the streets and subsequently carrying out their persecution of Jews through decrees published in official newspapers. They had Dutch helpers, too. They could, for instance, rely on Anton Mussert's National Socialist Movement, which was relatively strong in the Netherlands. Though it was not notably anti-Semitic before 1939, it later proved more than willing to help ferret Jews out of their hiding places. Still more important was the assistance given by the Dutch bureaucracy, with its meticulously precise information about the Jews' addresses, jobs and personal backgrounds. Not only that but respected Dutch stock exchange, insurance, and bank officials readily participated in the pillage of Jewish properties on their own initiative.

The Dutch police, too, played a vital and *deliberate* part in collaborating with the SS in the removal of the Jews. They were responsible for the cruel round-ups at Jewish homes which preceded the deportations, though it is unlikely that they knew the final destination of the victims. Much of the blame for the zeal of the police can be attributed to the charismatic wartime superintendent of the Amsterdam police force, Sybren Tulp, a fervent admirer of Hitler. Because Amsterdam contained the majority of Holland's 140,000 Jews (especially after other Dutch Jews were forced to move there in 1942) his influence was especially disastrous.[43] Only 25,000 Dutch Jews were able to successfully hide from the police, though this might be regarded as a relatively high figure for a small country without the cover of mountains or big forests. Nevertheless, 107,000 Dutch Jews were deported from Westerbork and less than 5,000 returned alive, after the war.[44] The deportations in Holland turned out to be a catastrophe unparalleled in any other western European country, with over 80 per cent of the Dutch Jews ending up in the death camps of Poland. The gullibility of the Dutch Jewish leadership was, unfortunately, also a factor in this disaster.

The Dutch Jews had been organised by the Germans into a *Joodsche Raad* (Jewish Council), which published the Nazi anti-Jewish ordinances in its newspaper, distributed yellow badges and generally enjoyed a 'privileged' status. It assisted in deportations, avoided any resistance and even handed over the names of seven thousand council members to the Germans. The leaders of the *Raad* persisted for a long time in believing that only German Jewish refugees or other 'foreigners' would actually be deported. Their policy of collaboration was bitterly opposed by a rival Jewish group that objected strongly to working with the Nazis in any way. The Jewish Council and its leaders may simply have refused to believe the worst, naïvely trusting in universal respect for the law and something they called 'civilisation'. Perhaps there was little that they could objectively do to avert the 'evil decrees'. But a less benign interpretation would have to say that, as happened elsewhere, they allowed themselves to become part of the machinery of destruction, with particularly disastrous results.

In neighbouring Belgium, the situation of the Jews was different in virtually every respect. Before the war, there had been about 90,000 Jews, of whom one third were German Jewish refugees, while an even higher number came from other European countries such as Poland and Czechoslovakia. By the end of 1942, nearly 40,000 Jews had fled (including the most prominent leaders) and there were barely five thousand native-born Belgian Jews out of the 50,000 still remaining in the country.[46] The majority of stateless or recently naturalised Jews were easily identifiable and it was difficult to hide in such a small, highly urbanised and industrialised country. By the end of 1942, about 15,000 of these mainly foreign Jews (30 per cent of Belgian Jewry) had been deported to Auschwitz. But when the Germans began to round up native Belgian Jews in 1943, there were public protests, which led to the release of some of the internees. What helped in this and other cases was the attitude of the top German military authorities – the Governor, General Alexander von Falkenhausen (later involved in the 1944 conspiracy against Hitler) and Brigadier General Eggert Reeder. Both had opposed the imposition of the yellow star in Belgium, and successfully restricted the authority of the SS and Gestapo. It was also significant that (unlike in Holland) the Belgian police chose not to co-operate with the Nazis, and railway workers were at times deliberately lax with the deportation trains, permitting some Jews to escape. In Belgium there were relatively few collaborators with the Germans, except among the Flemish-speaking population. Even the fascist Rexist party headed by Léon Degrelle (which lost influence after 1939 among the French-speaking Walloons) was much less collaborationist than Mussert's National Socialist movement in Holland. As a result of these factors, the death count of about 25,000 Jews in Belgium (44 per cent) was considerably lower than in Holland.[47]

France, on the other hand, had both the largest Jewish community in western Europe and an indigenous tradition of anti-Semitism, unrivalled in its literary brilliance by any other nation in Europe.[48] At the same time it had been the cradle of European Jewish emancipation – an achievement that remained intact for 150 years until the fall of France in 1940. The Jews of France were already well integrated into French society, culture and politics under the Third Republic. In the 1930s, however, the earlier climate of tolerance had become frayed, as thousands of refugees (many of them Jewish) entered the country. In 1940 it was estimated that of the 330,000 Jews in France, about 195,000 were native French and the other 135,000 were foreign Jews. It is undoubtedly significant that about 50 per cent of the *foreign* Jews would be deported to their deaths as opposed to roughly 10 per cent of the *israélites français*. Altogether about 80,000 persons (one-quarter of all French Jews) would die in the Holocaust, which was a terrible stain on modern French history but a relatively low body-count in the larger European chamber of horrors.

The military debacle of June 1940 and subsequent German occupation was the prerequisite for the institution of Marshal Pétain's 'national Revolution' and the Vichy regime in the southern half of the country. The French government, as a result of the armistice, retained some attributes of sovereignty and could therefore limit the German power of intervention on the 'Jewish Question' in their own zone. Thus, for example, the yellow star, which had been decreed in the German-occupied zone after 7 June 1942, was *not* introduced by Marshal Pétain at Vichy.[49] On the other hand, the French government did energetically persecute the Jews during the war years; indeed, it passed anti-Semitic laws on its own initiative after October 1940, which were as severe as anything the Germans had yet invented. This legislation was an autonomous act based on a home-grown French tradition combining traditionalist Catholicism, xenophobia, integral nationalism and racist assumptions about the inferior character of Jewry.[50] The law of 4 October 1940 authorised prefects (as agents of the French state) to intern foreign Jews in 'special camps' or to place them under police surveillance in remote villages. On 7 October 1940, the French state summarily deprived the Jews of Algeria by decree of the French citizenship that they had possessed for seventy years.

The Vichy *Statut des Juifs* spoke explicitly about race. It classified persons with only two grandparents 'of the Jewish race' as being Jews if they had a Jewish spouse – a definition that was harsher than the existing German legislation. The Vichy government was especially concerned to prevent further immigration of Jewish refugees and to promote the re-emigration of those already in France. It was determined that everything foreign, 'non-French' and 'unassimilable' had to be driven out of French culture. Already, in October 1940, Vichy laws had sealed off public service and certain professions from those not born of a French father. A quota on Jews in the professions would soon follow. There can be no doubt that the Vichy regime was thoroughly permeated by anti-Semitism. It even established a special department for Jewish Affairs, headed first by the more traditional conservative-Catholic nationalist Xavier Vallat and then by the fanatically racist and anti-Semitic Darquier de Pellepoix.[51] It was self-evident for Vallat that Jews were dangerous, unassimilable foreigners 'whose implantation tends to form a state within a state'. At the same time, he favoured a more moderate 'state anti-Semitism' in the tradition of the right-wing *Action Française*, which would drastically reduce Jewish numbers and influence while avoiding the more extreme positions of the Nazis and pro-German French collaborationists.

Between June and December 1941, a string of Vichy decrees limited Jews to 2 per cent of the professions (medicine, law, etc.) and 3 per cent of the students in higher education. Vallat also introduced a detailed census of all Jews in the unoccupied zone as well as proposals (that became law on 22 July 1941) to 'organise' Jewish property and enterprises. The object was 'to eliminate all Jewish influence from the national economy'. In November 1941 Jews were removed from a whole range of commercial and financial activities, including banking, merchant shipping, real estate and wholesale trading as well as publicity, news services, publishing, film, theatre and radio. They were forbidden to buy land unless they cultivated it themselves. Vichy France, by this draconian legislation, hoped to assert its own sovereignty in Jewish affairs while fulfilling the anti-Semitic programme that was an integral part of its ideology.[52]

But by the spring of 1942 the Germans had developed more far-reaching anti-Jewish projects for France, starting with the mass deportations that would begin a few months later. In May 1942 Vallat was replaced by the more radical De Pellepoix – a move that followed Pierre Laval's return to power and the intensification of German police operations in France. Already on 27 March 1942, the first trainloads of Jews had left the Drancy concentration camp for Auschwitz, ostensibly in reprisal for attacks on German servicemen in France. When railway cars were made available in June 1942, more Jews were dispatched. But the Reich Security main office could not pursue its anti-Jewish actions in France unless it had the active help of the French administration, public services and police force, not to mention railroad officials. The Germans did not, however, have to bargain too hard to persuade Laval to agree to the deportation of its foreign and stateless Jews. But there is no evidence that mass extermination was any part of French government plans. The Vichy regime was none the less eager to get rid of the foreign Jews in its own zone (pressing the Germans to include them in transports) even as it opposed touching the French Jews. On 4 July 1942 René Bousquet, head of the French police, relayed to the Gestapo the agreement of Pétain and Laval to the deportations as 'a beginning' for removing 'all stateless Jews from the Occupied and Unoccupied zones'. For the Germans, this was merely a temporary limitation. On the other hand Laval was aware of the negative reactions in French public opinion to the radicalised German policy during the summer of 1942. The introduction by the Germans of the yellow star in the occupied zone had provoked the first open resistance to anti-Jewish persecution in wartime France. It exposed the full gravity of anti-Semitism in a much more concrete way to many French people who had previously gone along with racist laws against the Jews.[53]

The Germans in mid-1942 did not have enough men (no more than three battalions of police numbering just under 3,000) to carry out their policy of round-ups, internment and deportation. Hence, the far more numerous French police force with its efficient card-file system, listing almost 150,000 Jews in the department of the Seine alone, was indispensable to their aims. The vast collaborative effort in which the French police engaged with the Germans proved to be the critical factor in the deportations. Perhaps the most notorious example of such collaboration was the Vel d'Hiv round-up of 16 July 1942 by the

Paris police, which packed 7,000 Jews (including over 4,000 children) like sardines in the Parisian indoor sports arena, so that there was barely space to lie down. Altogether 12,884 Jews were netted in the two-day *Aktion*, but this was less than half the number that the Germans had hoped to seize.[54]

By September 1942, more than 27,000 Jews had been deported from both zones of France. A month earlier, Laval told an American Quaker group that 'foreign Jews had always been a problem in France and that the French government was glad that a change in the German attitude towards them gave France an opportunity to get rid of them'.[55] It was evident to the American chargé d'affaires in Vichy, who also spoke with Laval about the deportations at this time, 'that he had neither interest nor sympathy in the fate of any Jews, who, he callously remarked were already too numerous in France'.[56] Pétain's response seemed equally detached. He gave petitioners the impression that he only vaguely understood the full seriousness of the round-ups and the deportations. Indeed, one of the blackest stains on Vichy's record was that it offered to deliver the children of foreign Jews to the Germans for deportation even before the Nazis asked for or were ready to accept them. Over 1,000 children under six years old as well as a further 2,557 under twelve years and almost 2,500 Jewish adolescents between thirteen and seventeen were packed off at French initiative to Auschwitz during 1942 alone. For the Vichy administration there was never any question of taking them in hand through public charity or rescuing them. In mid-September 1942, Laval made crystal clear that nothing would deter him 'from carrying out the policy of purging France of undesirable elements, without nationality'.[57]

After women and children were put into the cattle cars by French police along with the men (some of whom were French citizens) and they were never heard from again, public opinion began to turn. Voices of protest were raised in the Catholic Church (previously very supportive of Pétain and Vichy) and among the Protestants, led by Pastor Boegner. Archbishop Saliège of Toulouse on 23 August 1942 drafted his famous pastoral letter which attained a wide distribution: 'That children, that women, fathers and mothers be treated like cattle, that members of a family be separated from one another and dispatched to an unknown destination, it has been reserved to our own time to see such a sad spectacle.'[58] Saliège reminded the French public that Jews and foreigners 'are real men and women', 'part of the human species', who could not be abused without limit. Others like the bishops of Montauban and Marseille followed suit, though the protesters actually represented fewer than half of the prelates of the unoccupied zone. Laval tried, at first, with only partial success, to warn Church officials against mixing in politics. But the initial crisis between the regime and the Church had faded by the end of October 1942 and the furore in public opinion about the deportation of the Jew died down. Nevertheless, the legitimacy of the Vichy regime had suffered a blow.

On 11 November 1942, the period of full German occupation began as Hitler's armies swept down to the Mediterranean coast of France, to counter the American landings in North Africa. With regard to the Jews, the powers of the German police were now extended across France, though their manpower was severely overstretched in the southern zone. But the French police continued and even increased their repressive actions, with mass arrests of foreign Jews in February 1943. In the northern zone, too, deportations from Drancy to Auschwitz resumed in January/February 1943. By 6 March 1943, according to German calculations approximately 49,000 Jews from France had already been sent to the east. As the pressure intensified through 1943, some of the hunted Jews fled to Spain and to Switzerland or more often found refuge in French homes and religious institutions, especially in the countryside.

Through 1943 the French police continued to accompany

convoys and escort trains carrying Jews for deportation, as well as hunting down escapees. But they were noticeably less enthused about deporting French Jews and the Germans now felt that they lacked the requisite initiative in the 'struggle against Judaism'. German pressure on Vichy to strip French Jews of their citizenship (*dénaturalisation*) grew in the summer of 1943. Darquier de Pellepoix ardently supported this idea (especially for Jews naturalised after 10 August 1927) but Laval prevaricated and then retreated from this step on 7 August 1943. Pétain, too, resisted the idea of indiscriminate deportation of French Jews based on denaturalisation. He had to maintain order in France and for the sake of his own conscience he also wanted to examine each case individually. Vichy's new-found obstructionism on the Jews was probably connected with shifting military fortunes and the increasing likelihood that Germany would lose the war. There was the growing anti-German mood in France to reckon with and the displeasure of the Vatican to consider. Foreign opinion, especially in the United States, also entered into the calculations at Vichy.

Moreover, French public opinion was itself becoming more restive and disenchanted with the Vichy regime. German arrests of French Jews were regarded by growing numbers of French people as a national humiliation – a perception that sapped the legitimacy of Vichy. Thus, while Laval scarcely sought a confrontation with the Germans over (what was to him) the relatively minor Jewish issue, he did reject the denaturalisation programme as too extreme. The Nazis therefore turned to direct action, dispatching one of the most ruthless SS Jewish experts, the Austrian-born Alois Brunner, from Salonika (where he had helped to speedily deport over 50,000 Greek Jews to Auschwitz) to take over the deportations from France. Brunner and his SS team descended on the south of France in the fall of 1943, continuing their sweeps until the spring of 1944, this time without much support from the French police. They were, however, assisted by the Milice, a French paramilitary force that relentlessly pursued Jews and acted out of a certain level of ideological conviction.

Although they no longer had the full resourses of the French police to help them, the Germans still managed to send 33,500 Jews to the East in 1943–44. Most of them were gassed immediately – mainly in Auschwitz – and a mere 2,500 out of the deported 80,000 survived.[59] Nevertheless, from the Nazi standpoint, the overall results in France were disappointing. Only one in four Jews had been trapped in the web of the 'Final Solution'. From August 1943, some Gestapo officials were convinced that Vichy was no longer co-operative and even sabotaged their work. This seems like an overstatement. There is little evidence that Pétain and Laval *consciously* sought to protect native French Jews by willingly accepting the deportation of foreign Jews. But it seems clear that they did become obstructive once a German victory appeared in doubt and they were certainly concerned at their loss of face in French public opinion.

What is less obvious is when Vichy officials realised the true meaning of the 'Final Solution'. The official French (and German) line about the deportations was that Jews were being transferred to work colonies in Poland. But after the end of June 1942, the inclusion of women and young children on the transports, as well as the sick and the aged, made this fiction seem scarcely credible. By the end of August 1942 Jewish organisations in France (like the Consistoire Central des Israélites de France) were telling Laval that Jews were being exterminated 'pitilessly and methodically', though they could not as yet verify the existence of a total plan.[60] Pastor Boegner also talked with Laval in September 1942 about the mass murder but was fobbed off with stories about Jews building an agricultural colony in the east. Vichy officials nonetheless knew that many Jews would die, simply from looking at the atrocious conditions of departure from France. After 1943 French officials said as little as possible about the Jews, which in the circumstances can only be regarded as a guilty silence.

French complicity in the 'Final Solution' cannot be separated from the deeply entrenched anti-Semitic tradition that had been sharpened by the trauma of defeat in 1940. Vichy's racist measures against the Jews were inhuman, its despoliation of Jewish property rapacious and its anti-Semitic propaganda repulsive, though it never sank to the truly venomous abyss of the pro-Nazi French collaborationist press based in Paris.[61] Vichy did partially protect native Jews (as did Romania and Hungary before the German invasion) but its efforts in this direction were hardly vigorous or robust. It zealously volunteered to hand over foreign Jews from the unoccupied zone of France and to add Jewish children to the transports well before the German asked for them. These were actions of a particularly vile character. On the other hand, the Vichy leaders never deliberately planned to murder Jews en masse or encourage executions comparable to those in Germany, Austria, Croatia, Romania, the Ukraine or Lithuania. Through its perfidious policy, Vichy sought to reduce the number of Jews in France by every possible means, but its role in the 'Final Solution' remained ambivalent.

While three quarters of French Jewry survived under Vichy, it must also be said that the French government proved much more severe towards the Jews than the Italians. Laval was infuriated by Italian actions to help Jews in the eight departments of southern France that they occupied after November 1942 and even requested German intervention, though this failed to change the situation. In February 1943 the Italians not only blocked the attempts of French police and prefects to round up and transfer Jews (French or foreign) from their zone, but formally brought them all under Italian protection. As a result, thousands of Jews made their way to the Italian zone of France on the Côte d'Azur. Nice even became a Jewish cultural and political centre under Italian military rule, much to the disgust of Berlin and Paris. Only with the Italian evacuation in September 1943 and the entry of the German forces could the anti-Jewish terror in the south of France finally begin.

The Italian sabotage of the Holocaust was at first sight all the more astonishing given that Italy was the leading ally of Nazi Germany in Europe. Until the *coup d'état* by Marshal Pietro Badoglio on 8 September 1943, it had been treated by the Germans as a sovereign, independent State. Already in *Mein Kampf* Hitler had pointed to Fascist Italy (along with Great Britain) as a natural ally for Germany against French hegemonic ambitions.[62] He greatly admired Mussolini as the founder of Fascism, from whom he had learned much about techniques of mass mobilisation. It was from Mussolini that he adopted in the early 1920s the use of uniforms, coloured shirts and the arm-extended salute. Paramilitary methods, shock troops (*fascio di combattimento*), the *Führerprinzip*, militarism, extreme nationalism and militant anti-Bolshevism were innovations of the Italian Fascist programme, adapted by the Nazis for their own needs.[63] Both fascist and Nazi ideologies exalted youth, activism and movement for its own sake. They thundered against the decadence of a moribund bourgeois era while declaring a war to the death against Marxism. Both looked back to myths of power and imperial greatness rooted in the past – Hitler to the German Reich and Mussolini to ancient Rome. But it was Mussolini who was the first to pioneer a new-style Caesarism based on mass politics and spectacular ritualised displays of power.

For no other living statesman did Hitler feel a comparable sense of loyalty or reverence. During the Duce's visit to Berlin at the end of September 1937 he had acclaimed his Italian visitor as one of those 'lonely men of the ages on whom history is not tested, but who themselves are the makers of history'. Unlike other leading Nazis, Hitler never seemed to fully grasp the ideological gulf separating his own movement and outlook from

Mussolini's Fascism, despite many outward similarities. For example, 'race' for most Italian Fascists was not a biological concept but tended to be synonymous with the nation. Until the mid-1930s, Mussolini treated the Germanic version of 'Nordic' racism as pretentious, pseudo-scientific nonsense offensive to a sophisticated Mediterranean Latin people. Similarly, he regarded the persecution of the Jews as an embarrassing mark of Nazi 'immaturity', although he still tolerated fanatic Jew-baiters in his own party, such as Giovanni Preziosis and Roberto Farinacci. In periodic outbursts of anti-German resentment, he could be particularly scathing about Hitler and his quirks. In November 1934 he told the Zionist leader, Nahum Goldmann: 'I know Herr Hitler. He is an idiot, a rascal, a fanatical rascal, an insufferable talker. It is a torture to listen to him. You are much stronger than Herr Hitler. When there is no trace left of Hitler, the Jews will still be a great people.'[64]

The Duce knew perfectly well that the 45,000 Jews in Italy were model patriots, thoroughly integrated into Italian society. They had blended easily enough into the Italian population and apart from their religion they were physically, linguistically, and culturally little different from their neighbours. Since the *Risorgimento* in the mid-nineteenth century, Italian Jewry had played a prominent part in economic life (especially banking, business and insurance), in journalism, education, the sciences, arts and literature. They had produced (despite the small size of the community) two prime ministers, a defence minister and fifty Jewish generals – a record unmatched in Europe. Assimilation was a reality in Italy, not a mere ideology, myth or self-deception as it often proved to be elsewhere. There was no genuine 'Jewish Question' in Italy and no political anti-Semitism comparable in its severity to those of France, Germany, Austria or eastern Europe.

The Italian Jewish community did not suffer any serious harassment or persecution for sixteen years after the Fascist seizure of power in 1922. Jews, like other Italians, flocked into the Fascist movement without encountering any popular opposition. Mussolini himself acknowledged their patriotism and his official stance was to encourage intermarriage and full integration of the Jews into the Italian nation. This was the exact opposite of Nazi German policy. Hence the new Race Laws of 1938 stunned public opinion and were immediately unpopular, both with the established elites, ordinary Italians and the Catholic Church. The legislation was widely seen by many Italians as a somewhat ridiculous kowtowing to Nazi Germany, a pathetic attempt by Mussolini to ideologically and politically align himself with Hitler, though this lack of popular enthusiasm was small consolation for Italian Jewry. Nevertheless, Italian policy continued to deviate considerably from the German pattern. There were numerous exemptions – for example war veterans, Jews with high decorations and former members of the Fascist Party, including their parents, grandparents, wives, children and grandchildren. The 'Aryanisation' policies in Italy were also far more liberal than in Germany or Austria. Even more importantly, the Italians after 1939 defended foreign Jews as well as their own nationals, not only in Italy but also in southern France, Tunisia, Greece, Albania, Montenegro and Croatia.[65]

It is a striking fact that wherever the Italian army was in occupation during the war years, the Jews did not come to any serious harm.[66] For example, when they left France in 1943, the Italian military helped to transport Jewish refugees across the mountains; while in those parts of Yugoslavia occupied by Italy, Jews fleeing from the Croatian Ustashe and the Nazis were helped by Italian soldiers, appalled by the atrocities inflicted upon them. Many were taken on to Italian army trains, dressed in military uniforms, and brought to Italy, where they were concealed. One can hardly fail to notice the chasm separating the ruthlessness of the German military, with its rigid discipline, obedience and clockwork efficiency, from the Italian army, which though stunningly ineffective as a fighting force, showed mercy and compassion in many instances. The Wehrmacht and the German air force were responsible for the massive destruction of whole cities, small towns and villages, the uprooting of populations and repeated cold-blooded murders of Jewish civilians in Russia, the Ukraine, Serbia and other areas in the east. The Italian military, while its record towards colonial populations was far from exemplary, often behaved with impeccable humanitarian sensitivity towards Jewish refugees who were complete strangers. As Jonathan Steinberg has pointed out, even classic Italian vices of laziness, corruption, inefficiency and chaotic indiscipline became virtues in the context of the Holocaust, allowing rules to be constantly bent in the name of common humanity. On the other hand, Prussian military virtues of punctilious order, the sense of duty, blind obedience and rigid perfectionism, turned into a fearsome machine of destruction when hooked up to the dictates of Hitler's racial war.[67]

After 1940 Mussolini was certainly guilty of co-operating fully with Hitler in the prosecution of war. Even before then, he had implemented his own Fascist version of anti-Semitism through the Italian educational system, in the press, radio, and throughout cultural life. Most Italian Jews were shattered by the shock of their sudden social exclusion, having been robbed of their citizenship and deprived of their livelihoods in a nation that they had served loyally and well. But inexcusable though these actions were, their impact was partially mitigated by the scale of the exemptions, the resourcefulness of the Italian Jews themselves and the help they received from their neighbours.[68] Even Italian government officials and some veteran Fascists seemed to be infected by this popular mood and a general unwillingness to toe the Nazi line. The Germans were well aware of the 'lack of zeal' shown by Italian officials in the implementation of anti-Jewish measures. On 13 December 1942, Goebbels noted in his diary: 'The Italians are extremely lax in the treatment of Jews. They protect the Italian Jews both in Tunis and in occupied France and will not permit their being drafted for work or compelled to wear the Star of David. This shows once again that Fascism does not really dare to get down to fundamentals but is very superficial regarding problems of vital importance.'[69] On 23 June 1943, after a conversation with Hitler, Goebbels recorded that the Führer apparently expressed dissatisfaction with the Italians for failing to deal radically with the Jewish question. Mussolini, he reportedly said, was no revolutionary like himself or Stalin. Despite these private criticisms, Hitler's loyalty to his ally still remained intact.

On 25 July 1943, the Duce was summoned by King Victor Emmanuel III to his villa and arrested. Not long afterwards, the Italian army surrendered to the Allies. Mussolini was nonetheless rescued by the Nazis and set up the Italian Social Republic of Salò in northern Italy, which lasted from September 1943 until his execution by Italian partisans on 28 April 1945. The Duce quickly issued a manifesto declaring Jews to be 'enemy aliens' and had an anti-Jewish law passed that dissolved the Jewish communities and charitable institutions, as well as confiscating their property. German troops invaded Italy and the SS began to subject Italian Jews to deportation, including the seizure of over 1,000 Jews from Rome in mid-October 1943. This was to be the blackest period in the history of Italian Jewry, when the most fanatical elements in Italian society surfaced to terrorise the Jews, kill partisans and execute German orders. Some had their hiding places betrayed by Italian citizens, usually motivated by greed. Thousands of Jews were arrested and interned by the Fascist police – many ending up in concentration camps near the Austrian border. The most notorious of these camps was the one established in October 1943 at La Risiera di San Sabba, near Trieste, which had a gas chamber and crematoria.[70] About 5,000 Jews, as well as Italian anti-Fascists and Slovenian partisans were killed there. Several thousand foreign Jews (and some native Italian Jews as well) who were interned at the Ferramonti-Tarsia concentration camp in southern Italy, occupied by the Allies in 1943, were, however, able to survive the war.

In the spring of 1944 the Germans broke an earlier promise and began transporting Jews from Italy to Auschwitz. Altogether some 8,000 Jews would die as the Holocaust descended upon northern Italy with unexpected force, bringing death and destruction to about 15 per cent of Italian Jewry. The casualties would certainly have been far higher without the humanity shown by many ordinary Italians, whether clerics or lay persons, resisters or non-resisters, soldiers or civilians, nominal fascists, liberals or communists. Jews found hiding places in the cities and the countryside, in the hills and farms, in convents, monasteries – and a few were even concealed in the Vatican. They were received and spontaneously assisted, despite the risks involved, because they were seen as human beings with an equal right to live. The history of collaboration in the Holocaust was all too often a story of indescribable cruelty, callousness, indifference and insensitivity. But there were also islands of charity and simple human decency that stand out all the more sharply as a testament of hope in the prevailing darkness.

# VII Britain, America and the Holocaust

> ... Let my death be an energetic cry of protest against the indifference of the world which witnesses the extermination of the Jewish people without taking any steps to prevent it.
>
> **Shmuel Zygelboym**, (Bundist deputy to the exiled Polish National Council in London) shortly before his suicide on 12 May 1943

> [The guilt] lies with the Nazis ... But can we escape blame if, having it in our power to do something to save the victims, we fail to take the necessary action, and take it swiftly? ... if the British and American Governments were determined to achieve a programme of rescue in some way commensurate with the vastness of the need, they could do it.
>
> **George Bell**, Bishop of Chichester (England), 18 May 1943

> ... What have you done to us, you freedom-loving peoples, guardians of justice, defenders of the high principles of democracy and the brotherhood of man? What have you allowed to be perpetrated against a defenceless people while you stood aside and let them bleed to death ...? If instead of Jews, thousands of English, American, or Russian women, children, and the aged had been tortured every day, burnt to death, asphyxiated in gas chambers – would you have acted in the same way?
>
> **David Ben-Gurion**, Speech on Mount Scopus, Jerusalem, 10 July 1944

The Allied response to the Holocaust has been overladen with charges of 'complicity', 'abandonment' and culpable indifference to the unfolding Jewish tragedy. Some historians have implied that the American and British governments could have saved hundreds of thousands of Jews by a more energetic rescue policy. David Wyman, for example, believes that President Roosevelt, though well informed about the murder of the Jews, was not prepared to take any risks for them and that this indifference was 'the worst failure of his presidency'.[1] Political expediency largely determined his policy, but like most other Allied decision-makers he had only the most superficial understanding of Jewish issues. Roosevelt most probably did not think much about what was happening to the Jews in the midst of the gigantic global confrontation in which the United States was engaged, except when specific Jewish requests were made. Then, the standard answer that the Americans (like the British) always gave to such pleas would be forthcoming: the only way to help the Jews is to win the war as swiftly as possible. But while no serious historian would deny that there were strategic realities that limited the chances of rescue, reluctance to help Jews or open doors to them sent a negative message to perpetrators, bystanders and victims alike. This message, though rarely spelt out, suggested that Jews were expendable, an idea that encouraged Hitler in his belief that the outside world would not seriously obstruct his desire to destroy them.

The criticism directed at the United States (and to a large extent Great Britain) usually contains a triple indictment. First, the American government adopted a highly restrictive immigration policy (which was never modified between 1933 and 1945) and did so in response to racist and xenophobic pressures in American society, which it was unwilling to seriously confront.[2] Second, it refused or obstructed (knowingly in the case of the State Department) German offers of negotiation or other possibilities to remove Jews from Hitler's clutches; and finally (again like the British) the US Air Force was itself unwilling and was not instructed by the American government to bomb the railway lines leading to Auschwitz or to destroy the extermination facilities within the camp itself.[3]

Of these indictments, the best documented is the general hostility in the inter-war period to an 'alien' influx into American society.[4] There is no doubt that the US Immigration Act of

1924, which set tight quotas by country of origin with a particular bias against eastern and southern Europe, was driven by a desire to exclude as many Jewish, Slavic and Italian immigrants as possible. Its underlying assumptions of 'Nordic supremacy', while not driven exclusively by anti-Semitism, were in their own way analogous to Hitler's notions of racial purity. A xenophobic climate of opinion in the aftermath of the First World War had favoured racist and anti-Semitic organisations such as the Ku Klux Klan, which reached the peak of its influence in the 1920s. It was also a decade that witnessed the efforts of automobile millionaire Henry Ford (much admired by the Nazis) to spread his fantastic anti-Semitic theories about the world Jewish conspiracy in the *Dearborn Independent*.[5] There were evangelical fundamentalist preachers like Gerald L. K. Smith and Gerald Winrod who peddled anti-Semitism, as did William Dudley Pelley's Silver Shirts and Fritz Kuhn's German-American Bund in the 1930s.[6] As the Great Depression deepened, the receptivity towards such bigotry broadened considerably in America. A good example was the impact of the Catholic radio priest, Father Charles Coughlin, who reached an audience of millions with his ranting against the New Deal and the Jews in 1938–39.[7] Particularly worrying for American Jews was the developing link between powerful isolationist currents in the United States and anti-Jewish sentiments as the European war approached. In September 1941 (three months before America's entry into the Second World War) the aviator folk hero Charles Lindbergh – himself a long-standing admirer of Hitler – made the connection fully explicit. In a notorious speech on behalf of the America First Committee, he warned that Jews should not push the United States into war (they were indeed strong supporters of Roosevelt's interventionism) because they would be the first victims.

Although anti-Semitism in America never crystallised into a coherent, organised political movement or seriously infiltrated into the mainstream political parties, it was nonetheless pervasive enough in the 1930s and 1940s to affect American responses to the Holocaust. Opinion polls (while always subject to numerous qualifications) showed that on the eve of the war 75 to 85 per cent of Americans opposed relaxing the drastically prohibitive immigration quotas to help Jewish refugees. At the end of the 1930s, anti-immigration sentiment was so strong in the Congress that proposed legislation to open America's doors to refugees had to be withdrawn.[8] The same fate awaited Senator Robert Wagner's bill in 1938 to admit twenty thousand Jewish children over the existing narrow quota.

America's entry into the war, ostensibly to make the world safe for democracy against Nazism and fascism weakened the potential impact of anti-Jewish sentiments. Yet opinion surveys indicate that after the Japanese and the Germans, Jews were considered the greatest menace to American society during the war years. In 1944, no less than 65 per cent of Americans declared that Jews had too much power (a figure about three times higher than estimates for Great Britain) and stereotypes of Jews as dishonest, greedy, materialistic, aggressive and subversive were rather widespread.[9] Such prejudices played a role in negatively shaping or encouraging the behaviour of top State Department officials like Assistant Secretary of State, Breckinridge Long, Jr, responsible for refugees in the Roosevelt administration. Long was himself a paranoid anti-Semite who thought Hitler's *Mein Kampf* 'eloquent in opposition to Jewry and to Jews as exponents of Communism and Chaos'.[10] Not surprisingly, in the light of such attitudes, when Henry Morgenthau's Treasury Department attempted to license the transfer of money from Jewish charities to fund a programme for the relief and rescue of Jews, the State Department delayed it for months. They were encouraged in this prevarication by the British government, which in December 1943 cabled Washington that they were opposed to such relief programmes because 'of the difficulties of disposing of any considerable number of Jews should they be rescued'.[11] This callous response stung Morgenthau and Secretary of State Cordell Hull into action. An internal investigation of the State Department's handling of the question of rescue produced a document dated 13 January 1944 and starkly entitled 'Report to the Secretary on the Acquiescence of this Government in the murder of the Jews'.[12]

This unrelenting indictment, which was submitted to Morgenthau, demonstrated that not only did certain State Department officials fail to use the American governmental machinery at their disposal to rescue Jews from Hitler, they sought to prevent it. Not only did they fail to co-operate with private organisations seeking to develop their own relief programmes, but they obstructed them. Further, they had surreptitiously tried to stop the obtaining of information concerning the murder of European Jews and then issued false and misleading statements to cover up their guilt. Roosevelt was shocked by the report and realised that if the facts became known, it would be political dynamite. The result was the creation in January 1944 of the War Refugee Board to assist in rescuing the Jews in Europe.[13] It was the only such Allied government agency created during the war, but it was too little and too late. No military resources whatever were diverted to it and it succeeded in obtaining the admission of a mere thousand refugees.

The prevailing anti-Jewish climate inhibited the willingness of most American Jews to intervene forcefully with the Roosevelt administration in order to change the policy of the United States in the face of the Holocaust. American Jewry was profoundly shaken by what it took to be a steep rise in anti-Semitism in America. Many Jews still felt insecure as recent immigrants, about their own position and their rights in American society. Hence, they were reluctant to do anything to 'make *rishis*' – to create a fuss – for fear that their own loyalties would be questioned and the wrath of the Christian world might be stirred up.

The American Jewish community, which numbered close to 5 million during the war years, was far from being monolithic. Indeed, never had its internal ideological and political divisions seemed greater than in the 1930s. There were Orthodox and Reform, uptown and downtown Jews, 'Germans' and 'Russians', not to mention the *Galitzianers* and secularists of all shades – socialist, communist, labour and 'revisionist' Zionists. The bonds of religious and ethnic solidarity had been considerably eroded by secularisation and acculturation to American life, weakening the cultural ties with the Jews of Russia, Poland, Germany or Palestine.[14] What united most American Jews much more than links across the ocean was the desire to prove their new-found American patriotism. This imperative was spectacularly demonstrated by the fact that more than half a million young Jews served in the armed forces of the United States. Responses of American Jews to the Holocaust were very much shaped by such acculturating trends. For example, the more Americanised Jews tended as a rule to marginalise or underestimate the scale of the disaster, much like Gentile Americans. This was less true of Jews in the immigrant centres such as the Lower East Side of Manhattan or Williamsburg in Brooklyn, for whom the European Jewry that was being destroyed was far from being an abstraction. Not surprisingly, the Yiddish-language press covered the events of the Holocaust more closely and intensely than its counterparts in the English language news media.[15]

But the harsh truth is that rescue was not a particularly high priority for the major American Jewish organisations and barely featured on their wartime agendas. There were a few private approaches by representatives of the individual Jewish organisations to the President and high government officials, but even these feelers were not intensively followed up. Such apathy notwithstanding, the leaders of American Jewry did find a common voice in condemning the activities of the Emergency Committee to Save the Jewish People of Europe, founded by a complete outsider, the militant Peter Bergson, a representative of the Palestinian Jewish Irgun in the United States.[16] They objected to the Committee's loud, provocative style of advertisement in reminding the American public and Congress of what was actually happening in Europe; they disliked the violence of its anti-British tone, its insistent emphasis on the need for a Jewish army and its emotionally raw, immoderate language.[17] Above all, the Jewish establishment was displeased at this unexpected invasion of their organisational territory and at being upstaged by a tiny group, linked from 1944 onwards with the terrorist activity of the Irgun against British colonial rule in Palestine.

Mainstream American Zionists also disapproved of the extremism of the Bergsonites, despite their own opposition to British policy. Having observed the American government's unwillingness to open the door to Jewish refugees in the 1930s, they concentrated their energies on helping to build up the Jewish National Home in Palestine. They co-operated with David Ben-Gurion and the rest of the Palestinian *Yishuv* leadership in protesting against the British White Paper of 1939 and were sufficiently convinced to rally around Ben Gurion's arguments in favour of Jewish statehood as an immediate postwar goal. This aim was formally endorsed on 6 May 1942 at the Biltmore Hotel in New York.[18] At the Conference, Chaim Weizmann (at that time still the leader of world Zionism) grimly predicted that a quarter of east European Jewry would probably perish as a result of Nazi atrocities, while some four million homeless post-war Jewish survivors would remain suspended somewhere between heaven and hell.[19] The Gentile world would, however, be persuaded by Zionism because Palestine offered the only practical solution to the Jewish tragedy of homelessness. At long last, Weizmann suggested, Jews would relieve non-Jews 'of the trouble of settling our problems'.[20]

In August 1942, three months after Biltmore, the best-known American Zionist (and leader of the World Jewish Congress) Stephen Wise was finally given the telegram from Dr Gerhart Riegner (representing the WJC in Geneva) outlining the existence of a German plan to systematically destroy all the Jews of Europe at one blow.[21] The State Department had initially withheld this information from him but he was finally authorised by Secretary of State Welles to release it on 24 November 1942. The devastating news had a brief galvanising effect on Jews in the United States, with American Zionists in the forefront of efforts to lobby the Roosevelt administration to undertake a more serious rescue programme. On 1 March 1943, over 20,000 people (mobilised primarily by the WJC), jammed into Madison Square Garden in New York to express support for the millions of European Jews threatened with extinction.[22] A week later, a similar number attended the spectacular ninety-minute pageant *We Will Never Die*, which included a searing recitation of some of the atrocities that the Nazis had perpetrated against Jewry. Its initiator, the popular author and dramatist Ben Hecht, hoped to pierce the veil of silence around the tragedy of the Jewish people with flaming rhetoric: 'The corpse of a people lies on the steps of civilisation. Behold it. Here it is! And no voice is heard to cry halt to the slaughter, no government speaks to bid the murder of human millions end.'[23] The *New York Times* and some of the regular daily press were sympathetic to the pageant, helping to reopen the public debate about whether nothing could be done to help the Jews. One indirect result was the Bermuda conference of April 1943, in which British and American officials (belatedly aware of the political risk of doing nothing) announced that they would try to develop plans to aid European Jewry, a vain promise as it soon turned out.

The Anglo-American conference began on the first day (19

April 1943) of the doomed Warsaw ghetto uprising, which also happened to coincide with the first night of the Jewish Passover. The coincidence of dates was a particularly cruel irony since the outcome of the Bermuda conference would reveal that the Allies had abandoned European Jews to their fate, despite the optimistic pronouncements to the contrary. The two delegations categorically ruled out any approach to Hitler to release Jews in Nazi-occupied countries, any exchange of Nazi prisoners of war and internees for Jewish people, or the sending of food (through the Allied blockade) to help feed the Jews of Europe.[24] After quickly and smoothly settling the problem of dealing with non-Jewish Polish and Greek refugees, the delegates had much more difficulty in agreeing about even a relatively small item such as the temporary settlement of Jewish refugees in North Africa. Eventually an Anglo-American compromise was struck, based on one fundamental and tacit assumption: that the Americans would not press the British over Palestine, while the latter would act with similar discretion about Jewish immigration to the United States.[25]

After the conference, Richard Law, Minister of State at the British Foreign Office, wrote to Foreign Secretary Anthony Eden commenting on the different internal pressures concerning refugees that faced both the American and British governments. In Britain, he alleged that public officials felt considerable pressure from an alliance of Jewish organisations and archbishops 'but as yet no counter-pressure from the many people who feared and opposed alien immigration'.[26] In America, in addition to Jewish pressure, Law observed that there was a body of opinion 'which, without being purely anti-Semitic, is jealous and fearful of an alien immigration *per se*. And in contradistinction to the position at home, that body of opinion is very highly organised indeed. The Americans, therefore, while they must do their utmost to placate Jewish opinion, dare not offend "American opinion".'[27] Law was partly correct in his assessment, which would explain why the American government, early in 1939, had callously turned back German Jewish refugees on the ocean liner *St Louis*, who had been refused Cuban entry visas. President Roosevelt may also have been eager not to give any credibility to anti-Semitic claims that he was an 'instrument of the Jews', especially in the years between 1939 and 1941. He was, after all, strenuously seeking to involve America more closely in the war, against the powerful weight of isolationist and nativist opinion.[28] He also knew, as a practical political matter, that reversing Congressional or popular sentiment on the immigration laws, was not a feasible proposition.

What of later possibilities of rescue or slowing down the German genocidal machine by the bombing of Auschwitz? After September 1943, American and British bombers were able to reach targets all over the Nazi Reich, especially from airfields in southern Italy. On 4 April 1944 an Allied reconnaissance plane had taken off from an Italian base and managed to photograph the new industrial installations at Auschwitz after a flight that took two and a half hours. The photographs showing the synthetic oil refinery were minutely examined but no attention was paid to the gas chambers and crematoria.[29] On 20 August 1944, 127 Flying Fortresses escorted by a hundred Mustang fighters successfully dropped their bombs on a factory less than five miles from Auschwitz. On other occasions, too, the Allies targeted Auschwitz III (Buna-Monowitz), passing over the death camp and railway lines leading to it, which were not viewed as military targets.[30]

Already in the summer of 1944, as hundreds of thousands of Hungarian Jews were being deported to their deaths in Auschwitz, Jewish leaders in Slovakia, especially Rabbi Weissmandel, pleaded that Auschwitz be bombed.[31] Some Jewish organisations and the War Refugee Board (created by the Roosevelt administration specifically for rescue purposes) also called, though more circumspectly, for action.[32] But by no means all Jewish leaders were agreed. Some of them, including the Jewish Agency for Palestine Executive, feared the resulting casualties among the inmates of the camps.[33] American Jewish leaders seemed far from enthusiastic. The proposal was initially opposed even by Leon Kubowitzki (head of the World Jewish Congress Rescue Department) who had forwarded the formal request to John J. McCloy, American Assistant Secretary of War. The reply from McCloy misleadingly claimed that a feasibility study had been made and that experts concluded that 'the diversion of considerable air forces now engaged in decisive operations elsewhere ... would be of such doubtful efficacy that it would not warrant the use of our resources'.[34] McCloy added that such rescue action might provoke even more vindictive action by the Germans. These were not trivial arguments as is sometimes claimed. But it would have made more sense for McCloy to say that the Germans could always revert to mass shooting if the gas chambers were rendered inoperable. One should not automatically deduce from this negative response (or the similar British refusal) that there was a deliberate cover-up or sheer malevolence at play. However, a disinclination to act upon Jewish requests, along with bureaucratic routinism, indifference and more than a tinge of anti-Semitism did indeed exist among high-ranking American and British officials as well as among Allied military leaders.[35]

Above all, one must not forget that the 'Jewish Question' was ultimately marginal to Roosevelt, who certainly had little understanding of its centrality to the Nazis. Once America became involved in the war, it became even less important compared to the supreme goal of an Allied victory. Like Churchill, Roosevelt was far too involved in the larger details of global military and diplomatic strategy to devote much time after December 1941 to specific issues of Jewish rescue. Nevertheless, he did periodically make himself available to Jewish organisations. When Stephen Wise finally asked him in December 1942 to draw world attention to the Nazi 'Final Solution', he did not refuse. Nor did he try to discourage Wise from pursuing a plan for the evacuation of Jewish refugees from Romania (which unfortunately led nowhere). More importantly, from the end of 1943 Roosevelt supported the Treasury and its high officials in taking the initiative on rescue actions.[36]

The creation of the War Refugee Board, in early 1944, however belated an act, was an important and positive step. For the first time during the war years, the issue of relief for Jews was partially freed on the Allied side from the obstruction of the American State Department and the British Foreign Office. After the German invasion of Hungary, Roosevelt (once again over some internal opposition) warned in a statement of 24 March 1944 that those who took part in deporting the Jews would be punished. The fourth paragraph of his statement referred to the 'wholesale systematic murder of the Jews of Europe', describing it as 'one of the blackest crimes of all history'.[37] Again, on 26 June 1944 (the day after a rare public plea by Pope Pius XII), President Roosevelt demanded that Horthy halt all deportations from Hungary.

Having said that, it must be acknowledged that Roosevelt was not immune to a 'liberal' version of anti-Semitism. At Casablanca in January 1943, he had proposed to the French Governor-General of Morocco that 'the number of Jews engaged in the practice of the professions (law, medicine, etc.) should be definitely limited to the percentage that the Jewish population in North Africa bears to the whole of the North African population'.[38] To justify such discrimination Roosevelt recalled 'the specific and understandable complaints which the Germans bore towards the Jews in Germany, namely, that while they represented a small part of the population, over fifty per cent of the lawyers, doctors, school teachers, college professors, etc., in Germany were Jews'.[39] Equally simplistic and prejudiced notions surfaced in Roosevelt's meeting with King Saud in February 1945. No doubt influenced by American oil interests, he declared himself very impressed by the Saudi monarch's (highly partisan) view of the Middle East conflict, which mixed open anti-Semitism with total negation of a Jewish state. Roosevelt added that 'the Germans appear to have killed three million Polish Jews, by which count there should be space in Poland for the resettlement of many homeless Jews'. This assumption, shared by British officials, was a truly stunning misconception of the Jewish condition and mindset in the aftermath of the Holocaust.[40]

For the Zionist movement, Roosevelt's sudden death in April 1945 was a stroke of luck since his successor, Harry S. Truman would prove considerably more sympathetic to its aspirations. American Zionists had already drawn their own conclusions from the miserable failure of the Bermuda conference two years earlier.[41] The unseemly farce in the Caribbean seemed like another glaring illustration of the general indifference of the Christian world (including supposedly 'friendly' governments like those of Roosevelt and Churchill) to Jewish suffering and demonstrated the futility of relying on humanitarian appeals. Abba Hillel Silver, the firebrand of American Zionism, angrily summed up this sentiment on 2 May 1943, not long after Bermuda: 'The enemies of Israel seek us out and single us out but our friends would like to forget our existence as a people.'[42] Silver believed that if only the Jews had possessed their own Palestinian state in 1933, then German, Austrian and east European Jewry would have found a refuge in large numbers. This was also the argument made by another leading American Zionist, Emmanuel Neumann, who added that if American Jews in 1943 did not put an end to the long history of their people's persecution by supporting a post-war Jewish commonwealth in Palestine, 'we shall be contemptible in our own eyes'.[43]

The Zionist leadership of the *Yishuv* (Palestine Jewish community) was fully committed to fighting for the realisation of a Jewish National Home and had for the past twenty years urged that everything be subordinated to this priority. The 1933 *Ha'avarah* agreement to facilitate the transfer of German Jews and part of their property to Palestine offered the Zionists an unexpected opportunity to strengthen their demographic position, even if it meant undercutting the world-wide Jewish anti-Nazi boycott.[44] The *Yishuv* was still rather small (278,000 Jews) and substantially outnumbered by the Palestinian Arabs. Never the less in 1937, the British appeared ready to offer to the Jews a mini-state in a partitioned Palestine. But this proposal rapidly vanished from the table as the international situation deteriorated. By May 1939 it was clear that the Balfour Declaration was dead and the Zionist enterprise in serious danger of being derailed by the British Mandatory Power at the very moment when a deadly trap was closing in on the Jews of Europe. The foremost leader of Palestinian Jewry, David Ben-Gurion, was fully aware of the weak position of the *Yishuv*, dependent as it was on the doubtful goodwill of Great Britain. However, Zionism and world Jewry had little choice after September 1939 but to support the Allied war effort despite increased British hostility to their national aspirations. At the same time, Ben-Gurion was determined to arouse world public opinion against the White Paper policy and to endorse illegal immigration, without renouncing the *de facto* pact with Great Britain.[45] Despite widespread anger at the Mandatory Power's restrictions on *aliyah* and on any military organisation by the *Yishuv*, young Palestinian Jews were encouraged to enlist in the British army.

The *Yishuv* and its leadership were nonetheless beset by deep-seated anxieties of impotence, aware of the disparity between the virile self-image of Zionism and its limited capacity to rescue the Jews of Europe. Moreover, by 13 November 1942, the earlier reports of the massacres of European Jewry had been reliably confirmed by the arrival of some seventy Palestinian Jews held in Europe since the outbreak of the war.[46] They were part of a civilian exchange agreement with Germans resident in Palestine. The new arrivals came from different parts of Nazi-occupied Europe (including Poland) and their vivid, first-hand accounts provided a shocking glimpse into the scale of the genocide. Zionist leaders began to wonder if the complete extermination of European Jewry would not mean the end of the movement, as Chaim Weizmann had already hinted in June 1942. This 'terrifying vision' also haunted Ben-Gurion at nights, though he kept it to himself and tried to play down the magnitude of the tragedy in public.[47]

Ben-Gurion none the less became increasingly active after November 1942 in pressing the Allies to intervene on behalf of European Jews. He proposed that they offer the Nazis an exchange for Germans held in the western hemisphere in return for their agreement to let the Jews leave Europe; that neutral countries be encouraged to accept Jews against the promise that the West would provide food supplies to keep them alive and guarantee their removal after the war. He wanted bombings of German cities carried out openly as reprisals for the massacre of Jews, together with a propaganda campaign using leaflets over German cities to explain the policy. He thought that Allied warnings to Hitler's allies not to deport or harm their Jews could also be an important deterrent to their further collaboration.[48] Above all, he and other Zionist leaders wished for an easing of the British White Paper restrictions, so that Palestine could absorb more of the survivors. Nor were the death camps ignored. Chaim Weizmann and Moshe Shertok (a future Prime Minister of Israel) pressed the British Foreign Secretary for Allied bombing of the death camp at Auschwitz–Birkenau. Shertok conceded that this might not save too many Jewish lives but there were still compelling reasons to undertake such an action.

Shertok composed a memorandum of 11 July 1944, which seems to have impressed Eden and Churchill with its cogency. He pointed out that bombing Auschwitz would show 'that the

Allies waged direct war' on the perpetrators of genocide. It would undermine repeated German assertions 'that the Allies are not really so displeased with the work of the Nazis in ridding Europe of the Jews'; it would help dissipate scepticism 'in Allied quarters with regard to the report of mass extermination perpetrated by the Nazis'. Furthermore, it would lend weight to the threat of reprisals against the murders 'by showing that the Allies are taking the extermination of the Jews so seriously as to warrant the allocation of aircraft resources for this particular goal, and thus have a deterrent effect'. Finally, it might create some internal German pressure against continuing the massacres.[49]

Despite Churchill's enthusiasm, the British Air Ministry (like their American counterparts) rejected the proposal on technical grounds.[50] The fact that these requests for bombing were turned down demonstrated how difficult it was to change fixed Allied positions whether for political, strategic or bureaucratic reasons. The same was true of the 'trucks for blood' deal that became known as the Joel Brand Affair in 1944 – something to which Ben-Gurion devoted a great deal of time but which was quickly squashed by the Allies as a Gestapo plot.[51] Brand, a Hungarian Zionist who had met Eichmann in Budapest, travelled to Turkey on orders to present the Jewish Agency with a German proposition: namely, to halt the extermination of Hungarian Jewry in exchange for trucks and other equipment. He was arrested by the British on suspicion of being a Nazi agent. No attempt was made to explore the offer, if only to play for time. These and other examples underlined the fact that every rescue and aid proposal emanating from the *Yishuv* was dependent on Allied approval – a major restriction on the ability of Zionists to do anything substantial for the Jewish victims of the Holocaust. For example, the transfer of Transnistrian Jews out of Romania in late 1942 depended on British agreement, which was not forthcoming. The plan to evacuate Jews from Bulgaria came closer to success but ultimately failed because of opposition from the British ambassador in Ankara. Where British immigration permits were granted, as in the case of Romanian Jews arriving in Istanbul in 1944, it was due to the co-operation of the local British consulate and of the American War Refugee Board representative, Ira Hirschman. But such assistance was only given grudgingly to the *Yishuv*, usually where it suited British military and intelligence operations.

Thus the relatively powerless *Yishuv* found itself trapped between a ruthless German annihilation policy and relative Allied indifference during the Holocaust. The Zionist movement lacked extensive funds or any influential allies. It did not control admission to Palestine or to any other country. The Zionists did not have the ability to declare war on Germany, nor indeed did they possess any independent means of action, except in the most limited sense. An effective response to the Holocaust was therefore almost wholly dependent on the ability of the *Yishuv* to persuade the British and the Americans to try to stop the slaughter or provide a refuge for fleeing Jews. Ben-Gurion and his colleagues had to constantly take into account these very severe constraints. With one eye on the coming confrontation with the Arabs (which they judged to be inevitable) they sought to strengthen the *Yishuv* and prepare for the future. As a result, rescue was subordinated to long-range political priorities and to a degree of instrumental thinking that in retrospect sometimes seems chilling.[52] At a Jewish Agency Executive meeting on 6 December 1942, Ben-Gurion evoked, for example, the Jews of Poland as 'the sacrifices of a nation without a homeland'. The only proper response to the Holocaust was 'redoubled pressure for Jewish independence'.

British responses to the Holocaust were also very much influenced by the Arab–Jewish struggle in Palestine. After 1938, imperial decision-makers became increasingly concerned with their strategic and political position in the Middle East as the danger of a new world war drew near. Although the British had crushed the Palestinian Arab rebellion by 1939, they now resolved to appease Arab aspirations at the expense of the Zionists. Thus, any further Jewish immigration to Palestine would be made dependent on Arab acquiescence. To this end, after 1939 a supposedly sympathetic Britain was busy sealing off the escape routes for Jewish refugees, especially those bound for the Jewish National Home in Palestine. An intense British diplomatic effort was undertaken to pressure European governments during the war to *actively prevent* 'illegal' Jewish immigration.[53] British naval forces were diverted to the eastern Mediterranean for the express purpose of intercepting ships carrying such immigrants, who, if caught, usually faced deportation and exile. This grimly inhumane policy, backed to the hilt by the army, the Colonial Office and the Foreign Office, continued (undisturbed by knowledge of the Holocaust) until British withdrawal from Palestine in 1948. Naturally, if Palestine, which had been expressly given to Britain to help build a Jewish National Home was *a priori* excluded, then possibilities for rescue were greatly reduced. So draconian was Britain's policy that by 1945 even the miserly permitted quota of 75,000 Jewish immigrants to Palestine throughout the war years had not yet been achieved.

This obstinacy led to such tragedies as the sinking of the *Struma* refugee ship in February 1942, a disaster that was in large measure the result of British government pressure on Turkey to send this rickety vessel back into the Black Sea, despite all the known risks.[54] It produced responses like the British High Commissioner cabling the Colonial Office in July 1940 about Polish soldiers to be evacuated from south-east Europe to Palestine, and adding that 'only non-Jews be regarded as acceptable'.[55] The plain truth was that all branches of the British government, from the cabinet, the Foreign and Colonial Offices in London to the army command in the Middle East and the colonial administration in Palestine itself were determined to keep the Jews out of their homeland at the very moment at which they faced their greatest danger. Almost any argument could be used in this perverse endeavour, including the grossly exaggerated fear that some Jewish immigrants might be Nazi agents. Nor did Jewish and Zionist demonstrations of loyalty to Britain's war against the Nazis cut much ice, especially since government officials felt that they could take such support for granted. As one Foreign Office minute in 1941 concluded: 'When it comes to the point, the Jews will never hamper us to put the Germans on the throne.'[56] The contrast with the days of the Balfour Declaration and the First World War, when Great Britain had actively wooed 'world Jewry' (convinced that its friendship was of vital importance to the Allied war effort) could not have been greater.

The scale of the repudiation is the more remarkable since Great Britain was governed in the Second World War by the most powerful prime minister in living memory, Winston Churchill, an ardent pro-Zionist. When in opposition, Churchill had been a fierce critic of the British retreat from its 'solemn engagements' given in the Balfour Declaration. What then was Churchill's attitude to the Jews, Zionism and the Holocaust as it unfolded during the Second World War? Certainly, he had from the beginning of the war been supportive towards Zionist aspirations for 'a strong Jewish armed force in Palestine', to provide for their own defence. But his unequivocally expressed views (before he was Prime Minister) had no support from his cabinet colleagues in February 1940. A year later he dismissed General Wavell's objections to the idea of arming Palestinian Jews as typical of the strong pro-Arab sentiments of most British army officers who had deliberately exaggerated fears of negative repercussions in the Arab world. Churchill felt that 'the Arabs, under the impression of recent [British] victories, would not make any trouble now'.[57] But in order to avoid an unnecessary confrontation on what to him was a secondary matter, he delayed the Jewish army project for six months. On 5 July 1942, he intervened in support of Weizmann's request to renew it, writing to the Colonial Secretary that to indulge the 'bias in favour of the Arabs against the Jews' that was still rampant in the Colonial Office and among British military authorities was wrong; indeed he was in favour of making 'an example of some of these anti-Semite officers and others in high places' by recall or dismissal.[58]

There were other factors, too, that influenced Churchill. He was convinced that, given the growing strength of feeling in the United States in favour of a Jewish army, delay in this matter could damage the British image in America. Moreover, in 1942, when the *Yishuv* was in direct danger from a German invasion of Palestine by Rommel's Afrika Korps, Churchill thought that 'we should certainly give them a chance to defend themselves'.[59] But the opposition to the idea of a Jewish army in Whitehall remained determined and insistent, while the War Office continued to be obstructive. Only Churchill's energetic intervention finally overcame these objections. On 26 July 1944, he wrote to Secretary of War Grigg (who had been firmly opposed): 'I like the idea of the Jews trying to get at the murderers of their fellow-countrymen in Central Europe, and I think it would give a great deal of satisfaction in the United States ...'[60] In a message to Roosevelt on 23 August 1944, to bring him on board, he added that 'surely they of all other races have the right to strike at the Germans as a recognisable body'.[61] Churchill told the American President (who was himself basically favourable to the idea) that he had no objection at all to the Jewish Brigade flying their own flag, the Star of David, whatever 'the usual silly objections' that would be raised. 'I cannot see why this should not be done. Indeed I think that the flying of this flag at the head of a combat unit would be a message to go all over the world.'[62] Such sentiments were consistent with Churchill's long-standing personal support for the creation of a Jewish state (including the

Negev Desert), which he repeated to Chaim Weizmann in November 1944. But the Jewish army was the only clear instance of Churchill doing anything specific to help the Jews during the Holocaust. This is a sobering fact in the light of his enormous contribution to saving Western civilisation from Nazi barbarism and it demonstrates how low the fate of the Jews was on his list of priorities.

Churchill, however, did respond positively to Weizmann's appeal to bomb Auschwitz after Eden had informed him of the matter, replying on 7 July 1944: 'Get anything out of the Air Force you can and invoke me if necessary.'[63] Unfortunately, the Air Ministry rejected the plan as impractical and some officials evidently felt 'that this idea would cost British lives and aircraft to no purpose'.[64] As Bernard Wasserstein notes: 'this was a striking testimony to the ability of the British civil service to overcome ministerial decisions'.[65] All too often ministerial officials in Whitehall had their way in decisions affecting the Jews, when intervention on a higher level might have made a difference. Churchill, at least, did have the historical imagination to comprehend the magnitude of the tragedy: on 11 July 1944 he wrote to Eden in the following terms about the Nazi Holocaust: 'There is no doubt that this is probably the greatest and most horrible crime ever committed in the whole history of the world, and it has been done by scientific machinery by nominally civilised men in the name of a great State and one of the leading races of Europe.'[66]

Yet Churchill's statements on the subject remain meagre considering that he had access to earlier and better information on the massacres of Jews than any other major Allied leader. The crucial British success in breaking German codes meant that he received regular decrypts of German radio messages, along with intelligence interpretations, soon after becoming Prime Minister in May 1940. By the summer of 1941, the British knew through their own cryptanalysts of massacres carried out against Jews in Russia by the German Order Police and Waffen-SS. In a speech of 24 August 1941 Churchill actually made an intensely emotional allusion to the 'mass murder' and 'frightful cruelties' of the Germans, which reflected the information in the reports he had received.[67] However, his emphasis was on the strength of Russian patriotic resistance to the German invaders, not the Jews, whom he never mentioned at all. This pattern continued, despite his access to police decodes. As Richard Breitman has noted, Churchill very seldom went much beyond the limits of the British government consensus about the fate of the Jews in public broadcasts or speeches.

An exceptional case was the sympathetic message to the *Jewish Chronicle* that he sent in November 1941, remarking that the Jews had borne 'the brunt of the Nazis' first onslaught upon the citadels of freedom and human dignity'.[68] They were now suffering beyond endurance, Churchill acknowledged, but their spirit was not broken nor their will to resist. Unfortunately, this statement had a rather limited audience and was only a pale echo of what Churchill already knew about the Nazi killings. Moreover, it was a rare instance of his addressing Jews at all. Churchill was not, for example, interested in meeting with Anglo–Jewish deputations. In this respect, he was even less accessible than Roosevelt.

A good example of this detachment was his lack of any personal response to the desperate appeal written on 16 January 1943 by Lady Reading about 'the horrible plight of the Jews'. She had implored Churchill to help break asunder 'the iron fetters of red tape'.[69] How, she asked, could British members of Parliament 'stand to show sympathy to the Jewish dead' in the House of Commons while 'her officials are condemning these same Jews to die?' 'You cannot know of such things. I do not believe you would tolerate them. There are still some 40,000 certificates for Palestine even under the White Paper regulations. Mr Churchill, will you not say they are to be used now, for any who will escape, man, woman or child? Is it possible, is it really possible, to refuse sanctuary in the Holy Land?'[70] The cruel answer is that it was all too possible. Mr Churchill knew and did little about it, leaving the Foreign Office to send a characteristically non-committal reply, invoking the usual transport difficulties and the military complications involved in any rescue effort. The consensus in both London and Washington was adamant that any attempted rescue of Jews could only complicate or obstruct the war effort. There is no evidence that Churchill thought otherwise. His Foreign Secretary, Anthony Eden, who 'preferred Arabs to Jews' and was an unshakeable anti-Zionist, remained decidedly unsympathetic to rescue. His position (shared by the Foreign Office) was best summed up in his icy reply to American pressure in March 1943 to help those Jews who were 'threatened with extermination' out of south-east Europe. 'If we do that, then the Jews of the world will be wanting us to make similar offers in Poland and Germany. Hitler might well take us up on any such offer, and there simply are not enough ships and means of transportation in the world to handle them.'[71]

Eden's bland response to the Holocaust in 1943 was not the result of ignorance concerning what it might mean for the victims. But as facts accumulated about what was happening to the Jews, there was also widespread disbelief and a tendency on the part of British officials (like many of their counterparts elsewhere) to treat the news of mass murder as the unreliable product of overactive imaginations. A characteristic exemplar of this proclivity was the Chairman of the Joint Intelligence Committee, Victor Cavendish-Bentinck, who agreed with other officials that the evidence about gas chambers was not to be trusted, adding in a minute of July 1943: 'The Poles, and to a far greater extent the Jews, tend to exaggerate German atrocities in order to stoke us up.'[72] This contemptuous dismissal is the more remarkable since a reasonably detailed picture of the death camps, including Auschwitz with its gassing installations, was available to the British government by December 1942 at the latest, if not well before then.

Particularly revealing was the suspicious reception accorded to the eyewitness account of an intrepid Polish underground courier Jan Karski, who arrived in London in November 1942. Karski, a promising young career diplomat, had soon after the outbreak of war become the means of liaison between the Polish government-in-exile, based in London, and the resistance organisations in his conquered homeland. In the summer of 1942, this practising Catholic and ardent Polish patriot had embarked on a highly dangerous mission. He had toured with Jewish guides in the Warsaw ghetto and seen the results of the deportations at first hand. He had visited Izbica Lubelska in eastern Poland and circulated in the vicinity of the Belzec death camp. Karski also accurately identified Treblinka and Sobibor as places of mass execution for Jews. He reported to the British and Americans that out of the pre-war Polish Jewry numbering nearly $3\frac{1}{2}$ million people 'only a small number remain'. It was not a question of oppression, Karski emphasised, but 'of their complete extermination by all kinds of especially devised and perfected methods of pain and torture'.[73]

In describing what went on in Belzec, he specifically mentioned murder by poison gas. Karski repeated word for word for his listeners the message given to him in Warsaw by a spokesman for the Jewish socialist Bund. 'They [in the West] don't believe what they hear. Tell them that *we are all dying*. Let them rescue all those who will still be alive when the Report reaches them. We shall never forgive them for not having supplied us with arms so that we may have died like men, with guns in our hands.'[74] Both the anguished Bundist and the Zionist leader who took him around the Warsaw ghetto had told him that the Jews in Poland were helpless. They could not rely on the Polish underground or the population-at-large for any help against the Germans. Only the powerful Allied governments could effectively assist but they must take a series of *unprecedented* steps: these included bombing German cities and making it clear that this was in retaliation for the extermination of Jews; using German prisoners of war and German nationals resident in Allied countries as hostages; appealing to the German people through broadcasts and leaflets dropped from the air, to pressure their own government; and spelling out all available data in their possession about Nazi crimes against the Jews.[75]

Karski's mission had an immediate impact on the London-based Polish government in exile (PGE), which on 10 December 1942 formally appealed to the Allied governments to speak out against the extermination of the Jews in Poland. Indeed, it was the prime mover in the Allied declaration a week later that publicly condemned Nazi crimes against the Jews for the first time. But proclamations were one thing and actions another. On 18 January 1943 Count Raczynski, in the name of the PGE and also on behalf of Polish Jews, demanded that the Allies bomb Germany in reprisal for the exterminations. The British Foreign Secretary curtly rejected all demands, offering, as Karski would put it, 'vague promises to intervene in some neutral countries'. In Washington the Polish courier was received rather more warmly by Roosevelt but without much comprehension of his message, and the practical results were meagre. Karski's record of these and other encounters with British and American statesmen, government officials and high-ranking military personnel are essential reading. He felt with good reason that the testimony in his report of November 1942 should have provided them with incontrovertible proof of the genocide and led the Allies *immediately* to undertake special measures to save the European Jews. This did not happen. Instead, what he encountered was a mixture of political hypocrisy and soulless bureaucracy, narrow national self-interest and sheer indifference in those Western political and military leaders who had the possibility of ameliorating the Jewish tragedy in a larger or smaller way.[76] Either they did not care, or they cast doubt on the extent of the annihilation, or else they saw the Jewish tragedy as being essentially a 'Jewish problem', rather than one directly related to the meaning of Western civilisation and to mankind as a whole.

# VIII  *Modernity and the Nazi Genocide*

Der Tod ist ein Meister aus Deutschland.

**Paul Celan,** 'Death Fugue'

Here in this carload
I am Eve
With my son Abel
If you see my older boy
Cain son of Adam
Tell him that I...

**Dan Pagis** (written in pencil
in the sealed freight car)

In no other place and time has one seen a phenomenon so
unexpected and so complex: never were so many human lives
extinguished in so short a time, and with so lucid a combination
of technological ingenuity, fanaticism and cruelty.

**Primo Levi,** *The Drowned and The Saved*

It was a Denial of God. It was a Denial of Man. It was the
Destruction of the World in Miniature Form.

**Rabbi Hugo Gryn** (Auschwitz survivor)

The Nazi genocide has been called 'the most spectacular and
terrifying instance of industrial killing in this century'.[1] It has
been seen in recent years by a growing number of scholars less
as a regression to barbarism or as a uniquely horrible event in
universal history and more as a characteristic expression of
modernity itself: in other words, the Holocaust has been inter- ·

preted as a product of the destructive bureaucratic and technical capacities of modern Western civilisation.[2] This sociological approach, exemplified for instance in the work of Zygmunt Bauman, tries to go beyond the pioneering investigations of Raul Hilberg forty years ago, which first detailed the ice-cold, bureaucratic and industrial efficiency with which the German genocidal programme was carried out; or the more controversial theses of Hannah Arendt concerning the conditioned readiness of masses of human beings to abdicate any sense of collective or individual moral responsibility under the pressure of modern totalitarian regimes.[3] For Bauman, the Holocaust is not so much a totalitarian phenomenon as the consequence of an inherent potential of modern life and its organisational culture, dominated by 'rational' bureaucracies, 'scientistic' ideologies, depersonalisation and the extreme functional specialisation of industrial society.[4] Not surprisingly, perhaps, this has led him to downplay the influence of historical and ideological factors such as the long anti-Jewish tradition that existed in Christian Europe over many centuries.

Even 'scientific' anti-Semitism, while not ignored, is granted only a qualified, purely functional and limited causative role in the Nazi genocide.[5] Bauman regards modern racism as a desperate attempt to redraw boundaries that have been crossed as a result of the ceaseless flux and dizzying changes of industrial society. It was an equally vain effort to check and reverse the social mobility produced by Jewish emancipation and place the Jews once more beyond the pale. There is certainly some truth in this model, but it also ignores the persistence of a host of premodern prejudices, emotions and hatreds for which the Nazi world-view merely provided an updated pseudo-scientific window dressing. Moreover, the Holocaust, while certainly 'modern' in some of its organisational and technical features, had equally as many 'archaic' attributes down to and including its primitive methods of killing. Indeed, as many Jews were eliminated by shooting in the horrific pit exterminations of the Eastern Front as died in the factory-style extermination of Auschwitz.

The German historians, Götz Aly and Susanne Heim, like Bauman, also regard the Holocaust as having been triggered by modern processes of technical rationalisation. However, they claim that the mass murder was primarily designed by technocrats within the German intelligentsia, involved in planning the Third Reich's population policy.[6] The demographic experts were neither fanatical Nazis nor even anti-Semites but essentially opportunist academics and efficient bureaucrats who believed in 'modernisation' and at the same time wished to advance their personal careers by helping to map out the Nazi 'New Order' in Europe. They argued that the deportation or murder of the impoverished Jewish masses in overpopulated agrarian Poland would open the door to greater social mobility and future industrial development. The murder of Jews would get rid of unnecessary consumers and be the first step in a broader plan of genocide against other ethnic groups (gypsies, Russians, Poles, etc.), clearing the way for socio-economic modernisation in eastern Europe. Thus, the Jews were not killed because they were Jews or as the result of an 'irrational' racist ideology: rather, they were eliminated on utilitarian grounds as *Luftmenschen* who stood in the way of modern, rational, 'Western' technocratic civilisation. The young planners of the Third Reich set the agenda in preparing 'the decisions of their superiors, who for their part, attached great significance to the advice of their experts and expressly urged them to research in freedom'.[7]

There are serious problems with such an approach, though few would quarrel with the assumption of complicity by German academic experts, 'strategists' and planners in Nazi crimes. But there are too many facts that simply do not square with this theory. There was, for example, little unanimity among the

'Jewish' experts in the Reich when proposing solutions for the starving Jews in the Lodz and Warsaw ghettos.[8] Furthermore, there is no indication that Hitler, whose contempt for 'experts' of all kinds (even in military matters) was well known, ever paid the slightest attention to the proposals of low-level planners.[9] Moreover, one needs to distinguish between a modernisation strategy and plain straightforward greed for plunder and the stripping of Jewish assets, which was indeed an integral part of Nazi anti-Semitic policy during the *Anschluss*, the pogroms of 1938, the 'Aryanisation' measures and the subsequent deportations. The massive expropriation of Jewish wealth and property undoubtedly made Nazism more attractive to millions of non-Jews.

But what 'modernising' logic underlay the transport in wartime of 2,200 Jews from the Greek island of Rhodes, two thousand miles away from Auschwitz, despite urgent military transport priorities?[10] What economic or political sense did it make to deport half a million Hungarian Jews to Auschwitz in 1944 after the Normandy landings of the Allies and the advances of the Red army from the east had made Germany's defeat inevitable? If social 'modernisation' was the Nazi objective, why deport and murder the highly integrated, economically productive Jews of Germany, Austria, Italy, Holland or France, who were certainly no *Luftmenschen*? The fact that Nazi economists and planners often employed a 'utilitarian' language to mask their prejudices against Jews and Poles by framing their policy proposals in terms of productivity, food supply, public health or 'security threats' should not deceive one as to their underlying racist content. Rationalisations are not the same as causes. Using the label of 'modernisation' to categorise the Nazi policy of genocidal annihilation in effect flattens out and 'normalises' mass murder as if it were a slightly deviant version of normal capitalist development.[11]

Genocidal impulses, as we have shown throughout this book,

were inherent in the Nazi movement, ideology and collective mindset. In peacetime, it is true that the official goals of the regime were still confined to 'racial separation' followed by expulsions. But by 1939 it was already apparent that if a general war broke out, then conditions would exist for the Nazis to 'ethnically cleanse' the physically and mentally handicapped, the gypsies and above all, the Jews.[22] The Nazi leadership did not require planning experts to tell them that in a global war, 'the destruction of the Jews will go hand in hand with the destruction of our enemies ...'[13] Goebbels, commenting on a Hitler speech in February 1942, added: 'The Führer realises the full implications of the great opportunities offered by this war.'[14]

The war against the partisans was a case in point. The SS leader in charge of this warfare, Erich von dem Bach-Zelewski, observed: 'The fight against partisans was gradually used as an excuse to carry out other measures, such as the extermination of Jews and gypsies, the systematic reduction of the Slavic peoples ... and the terrorisation of civilians by shooting and looting.'[15] The 'anti-partisan' struggle and 'security' considerations were typical Nazi methods of camouflage and pseudo-legitimisation for their policy of physical extermination. So, too, social engineering models could be and were used by planners to give an aura of scientific rationality to the genocide. But such concerns never interfered with the primacy of politics in the Third Reich.[16] Nor did they prevent Hitler from cursorily dismissing pressures from the army or industrialists to delay the deportation of much-needed Jewish precision workers.[17] Ghettos, too, were created in Poland on ideological and political grounds even though they disrupted the economy.

When Himmler instructed Rudolf Höss to establish the Auschwitz concentration camp, the reason given was expressly ideological – the need to extirpate the biological roots of Jewry.[18] Invariably, Himmler's orders and those of his speeches that related to the 'Final Solution', spoke of the primordial 'racial struggle against Jewry', not of economic benefits.[19] Moreover, whenever Jews were used for slave labour, Himmler demanded that they should be worked to death or quickly replaced by Poles so that, as he put it on 2 October 1942, 'all the Jews would disappear in accordance with the Führer's wish' (dem Wunsche des Führers entsprechend).[20]

Nor is there any convincing evidence for the claim of Aly and Heim that the Nazis ultimately planned the *extermination* of the Slavs (or even of all Slavic elites) as part of their demographic and 'modernisation' programme. Slav nations such as Croatia and Slovakia, for example, were allies of Nazi Germany (as was Bulgaria) and the Germans envisaged that Croats and Slovaks would dominate and help destroy the Serb and Czech elites. Although the Ukrainians and Belorussians (along with the Balts) were not granted the semblance of independence, they did enjoy a limited, subordinate status as 'helpers' of the Germans, especially in killing Jews. Poles, Serbs and Great Russians, on the other hand, had no rights at all and were subjected to massacres and horrendous injustices but *not* to systematic genocide. As Himmler expressed it in Poznan in 1943: 'Whether the other peoples live in comfort or perish of hunger interests me only insofar as we need them as slaves for our culture. Whether or not ten thousand Russian women collapse from exhaustion while digging a tank ditch interests me only insofar as the tank ditch is completed for Germany.'[21]

In the logic of Nazi racial imperialism, Russians and Poles would be reduced to the position of helots of the Reich. But they did not have to be exterminated in the name of an apocalyptic, millenarist ideology. Even Nazi officials and certainly soldiers of the Wehrmacht saw something contrary to their self image as a *Kulturnation* in trying to wipe out the entire Polish nation. Significantly, Himmler himself did not exclude 'Germanising' those Poles who were considered as being 'racially valuable' elements. The rest of the Polish people would be enslaved and economically exploited, with the exception of the elites (clergy, intellectuals, army officers), who were ruthlessly eliminated. Similarly, with the Russians and Ukrainians, utilitarian criteria and expediency did play some role in Nazi plans. There was to be a controlled form of 'ethnic cleansing' and it was indeed anticipated in 1941 that millions of Slavs would perish in Russia as a result of German conquest, colonisation and a deliberate policy of starvation. But the total extermination of entire Slavic populations was neither practicable for the Nazis nor did it serve any major ideological agenda.

The Slav peoples of Russia were depicted in wartime as racially inferior and sometimes as Asiatic 'subhumans', but not as 'lice', 'vermin' or 'bugs' to be collectively disposed of by industrialised mass murder. Nor was there any Slavic counterpart to the pit killings of the *Einsatzgruppen*. Neither Poles, Serbs, nor Russians (though they were close to the bottom of the racial–biological hierarchy) were considered as a 'world enemy' or reviled as an anti-race that threatened the foundations of 'Aryan' civilisation itself. The struggle against the eastern Slavs was in Nazi terms essentially a war of *Lebensraum* and land colonisation. Had it been successful it might have led to the uprooting of as many as 30 million Slavs (deported to Siberia) and their replacement by German settlers in western Russia, the Ukraine and the Caucasus.

However, this racist vision of a great Germanic Empire to the east gradually crumbled as the Nazi state became embroiled in a desperate life-and-death struggle from late 1941 onwards against a reinvigorated Soviet Russia and the British Empire, newly reinforced by the United States. The military stalemate and the resulting demographic and logistical bottlenecks in early 1942 led to a shift in German policy. In order to make good her manpower losses and preserve her military-industrial complex, Nazi Germany decided to maximise the labour potential of her subject populations. As a result, millions of Soviet prisoners of war (most of whom would later be starved to death), Poles, Czechs and other Europeans, would be brought into the Reich to serve as an essential labour force, even though this clearly undermined the Nazi vision of a racially pure *Volksgemeinschaft*.[22] At the very time that this was happening, the Jews were being deported *out* of the central Reich territories to the east, where they would be subjected to conveyor-belt extermination. The point is that the 'rational' alternative of economic hyper-exploitation was explicitly *rejected* for the Jews.[23]

The significant element of 'modernity' in the Nazi genocidal project did not therefore lie in its mythical 'economic rationality' or in any linkage to a breakneck developmental programme of social transformation (as occurred in Stalinist Russia) but rather in the new methods that it pioneered in organising the killing of 'superfluous' people. At places like Auschwitz-Birkenau, Majdanek, Sobibor, Treblinka and other death camps, the entire apparatus of the modern German State – the resources of its bureaucracy and military-industrial complex – were put at the disposal of the SS in order to carry out a streamlined extermination. All the skills and techniques of modern technology, scientific and medical expertise as well as precise railway timetabling were enlisted in the service of racial murder. Raul Hilberg, who initiated the study of this administrative process, long ago observed: 'The machinery of destruction, then, was structurally no different from organised German society as a whole. The machinery of destruction was the organised community in one of its special roles.'[24]

The organisation of mass murder involved not only the immediate perpetrators but tens of thousands of Germans not physically involved in killing anyone; diplomats, lawyers, doctors, accountants, bankers, clerks and railway workers without whom the trains to the death camps would never have run on time. This monstrous machinery of death could not have been unleashed except in a highly organised and bureaucratised society – methodical, perfectionist and thoroughly 'modern' in its deliberate fragmenting of responsibilities and routinising of killing operations. Furthermore, it happened in a state that was able to efficiently co-ordinate into a single functioning murder machine countless bureaucrats in the relevant Reich ministries, the army, judiciary and medical establishments – as well as Nazi officialdom in the occupied eastern territories, the SS and Order Police. Such relentless systematisation and its end-product – the gas chambers – is what gave the Holocaust its sinister 'modern' aura of depersonalised violence.[25] The gas chambers and crematoria were an *industrial* method for liquidating human beings on the basis of a daily quota: they demonstrated 'the modern world's capability to organise mass death on a new, more advanced and scientifically planned basis'.[26]

This streamlined administrative killing process was also distinctively modern in its ability to draw on state-of-the-art punch-card technology, which enabled the Third Reich to perfect the rounding up of Jews throughout Europe, their deportation to the camps, and the statistics that measured their agonies during the 'Final Solution'. Only after the Jews were successfully *identified* could they be targeted for asset confiscation, deportation, ghettoisation, slave labour and finally extermination. It was American IBM custom-designed technology, as Edwin Black has recently shown, that gave an unprecedented speed and accuracy to the German capacity for identifying Jews in everything from censuses, registrations and racial ancestry programmes to organising railway transportation and concentration camp registrations.[27]

Similarly, mass murder on this scale could not have happened without the trial-run, beginning in 1939, of the Nazi 'euthanasia' programme. The physicians of the Reich massively collaborated in using poison gas and lethal injections in the murder of 80,000 mentally and physically handicapped Germans. This so-called 'T4' programme (named for the central office in Tiergarten Strasse, 4, in Berlin) had been personally ordered by Hitler. As Henry Friedlander has pointed out: 'The success of the euthanasia policy convinced the Nazi leadership that mass murder was technically feasible, that ordinary men and women were willing to kill large numbers of innocent human beings, and that the bureaucracy would co-operate in such an unprecedented enterprise.'[28] The same sinister methods that were used in operation T4 to mask the killing of the handicapped would be applied in the Nazi death camps. SS guards would be dressed in the white uniforms of medical technicians and the victims were always led to believe that they were being taken to a shower house rather than to a gas chamber.

The German perpetrators who staffed the machinery of destruction, whether in the network of offices spanning a whole continent or in the camps, were 'not a special kind of German' but rather 'a remarkable cross section of the German population'.[29] Engaged in a vast murder operation, which was officially shrouded in secrecy, they appeared to be immune from any pangs of conscience. A camouflaged vocabulary of euphemism shielded them from any guilt feelings or doubts about the justice of their enterprise.[30]

Hans Mommsen has argued that using bureaucratic and technocratic methods successfully repressed any moral inhibitions among the perpetrators, turning the death of Jews into a technical problem of killing-capacity. His vision of the Holocaust is that of a rationalised, quasi-automatic process in which the extermination of those 'unfit for work' developed a dynamic its own: 'The bureaucratic machinery created by Eichmann Heydrich functioned more or less automatically; it was symptomatic that Eichmann consciously circumvented Himmler's order, at the end of 1944, to stop the Final Solution. There was no need for external ideological impulses to keep the process of extermination going.'[31]

But the machinery of death did not exist in an ideological void and even a model bureaucrat like Eichmann – though no fanatical anti-Semite – displayed extraordinary zeal in hunting down Jews. His constant complaints about obstacles in the fulfilment of death camp quotas, his impatience with the existence of loopholes such as the free zone in Vichy France or the uncooperativeness of the Italians and other German allies in expediting the Jews were not simply a petty bureaucrat's desire to prove his efficiency. Eichmann rejoiced in the slaughter of the Jews. It made him feel an important part of a gigantic project. Perpetrators like Eichmann fitted themselves effortlessly into the prevailing genocidal ethos because they believed in what they were doing.[32] Their motives were not always identical to those of the top Nazi decision-makers, but that does not mean that they would have implemented mass murder against any arbitrarily designated enemy group.

The so-called 'functionalist' school of historians has long argued that the 'Final Solution' was not the product of any grand design; that the Nazi regime was administered by 'a maze of competing power groups and rival bureaucracies' seeking the favour of a distant Führer.[33] In their view, such lack of co-ordination and fragmentation of decision-making led to a 'cumulative radicalisation' of policies, each more arbitrary, violent and radical in its implementation than its predecessors.[34] The Nazis, it has been said, had no specific plan to 'solve the Jewish question' in 1933 and simply drifted step by step down the twisted road to Auschwitz.[35] Even the annihilations, according to Martin Broszat, had a largely improvisatory character and did not derive from a specific Hitler order or from a clear 'will to exterminate', but rather from a series of local Nazi initiatives aimed at solving local problems (food supply, logistical difficulties, etc.) on the eastern front. For Broszat, the Nazis had to find 'a way out of a blind alley' into which they had manoeuvred themselves. Once the practice of liquidation was established, it gained predominance and eventually evolved in an *ad hoc* manner into a comprehensive 'programme' that was subsequently approved and sanctioned by Hitler.[36] However, Broszat and others who followed him underestimate the favoured *modus operandi* of Hitler which was to deliberately incite against the Jews while covering his tracks and leaving subordinates to deal with the gory details.

Functionalist theories (perhaps unintentionally) tend to normalise Nazism by suggesting that its leaders stumbled haphazardly into the most extreme criminal behaviour. They unconvincingly turn Hitler himself into a weak, indecisive, procrastinating leader whose visionary political perspectives on the 'Jewish Question' had only a minor impact on the practical policy of genocide.[37] The 'functionalists' also downplay the longevity of anti-Semitism, its transformation into 'scientific' racism, the status, testimony and suffering of the Jews themselves as a social and national group, the role of the bystanders (individuals as well as states), not to mention the ideological motivations and mentality of the Nazi perpetrators.

More recent German scholarship has sought to go beyond the earlier abstract debates on 'modernity' and the clash between the 'intentionalists' (who believe in the centrality of Hitler and a co-ordinated decision to murder the Jews of Europe) and the sceptical 'functionalists'. Ulrich Herbert, for example, while adopting the theory of 'cumulative radicalisation' and though stressing the role of bureaucracy, does not assume that local decisions – whether in Serbia, Lithuania or Belorussia – were made outside a context of deeply ingrained anti-Semitism. He believes that the Holocaust was not simply the result of directives from Berlin but of an interaction between the centre and an increasingly radicalised periphery.[38] The empirical studies of Dieter Pohl and Thomas Sandkühler, discussing the General Government and Galicia, highlight the importance of the periphery and the pivotal role of the civil administration in pushing vigorously for a radical anti-Jewish policy.[39] This kind of research into the complex political process at a local level in the German-occupied territories is to be welcomed; unfortunately, it sometimes blurs the decisive role of Hitler, Himmler and others in Berlin in initiating, centralising and unifying the multitude of regional actions that eventually coalesced into the 'Final Solution'. There are also other weaknesses in this new trend in scholarship. The voice of the Jewish victims is rarely heard and there is a tendency to overstate the symmetry between the Holocaust and the 'ethnic cleansing' of other national groups in eastern Europe.

Herbert, like Goldhagen before him, does emphasise both the numbers of the perpetrators involved (more than was previously assumed) and the fact that the murders were frequently carried out in a traditional, even 'archaic' way.[40] Much of the Nazi genocide, he reminds us, is not adequately described by the notion of 'factory-like killing' or a so-called 'clean' death by gassing. I would certainly reinforce this point by reference to the massacres of Jews in Lithuania, Eastern Europe and the Balkans or to the killings by Wehrmacht soldiers and the *Einsatzgruppen* on the eastern front.[41]

Equally, the 'hot-blooded' slaughters and 'Jew-hunts' carried out by Order Police battalions in occupied Poland (described by Browning and Goldhagen) present us with a distinctly unmodern side of the Holocaust – one that aligns it more closely with other twentieth-century genocides. No high technology was required for the 40 per cent of Holocaust victims who died through malnutrition, famine and disease in the ghettos, through being worked to death in labour camps, through deportations late in the war that turned into horrific death marches; or through the gruesome executions in pits, trenches and ravines, using machine guns, rifles and revolvers. There was nothing particularly 'modern' or 'civilised' about such genocidal acts, any more than there is about those we have witnessed since

1945 in Cambodia, Rwanda, Bosnia and other relatively backward parts of the world. No spectacular industrial measures were needed for this purpose. Yet, the moral lesson of the camps, in particular, suggests that what Europe witnessed in the middle of the twentieth century was nonetheless something unprecedented: not so much in the statistics of the dead but in the sufferings inflicted on the victims and the depravity of their tormentors.[42]

In each of the death camps there were between twenty and thirty-five SS men in charge (a high percentage were German Austrians) assisted by a number of Ukrainian auxiliaries. At Treblinka the Germans succeeded in their ruse of presenting it as a transit camp (*Durchgangslager*) where Jews were supposedly to be 'disinfected' before proceeding on to a labour camp (*Arbeitslager*). Abraham Goldfarb arrived at the camp on 25 August 1942. He relates: 'When we reached Treblinka and the Germans opened the freight-car doors, the scene was ghastly. The cars were full of corpses. The bodies had been partially consumed by chlorine. The stench from the cars caused those still alive to choke.'[43] The death and destruction had already begun when the Jews were still in the freight cars deprived of air, water and sanitary facilities, as they rolled towards the extermination camps; purposely overcrowded by the SS personnel, these transports were in fact a death-trap. Oskar Berger, who arrived three days earlier, witnessed 'hundreds of bodies lying all around' as he disembarked from the train. 'Piles of bundles, clothes, valises, everything mixed together. SS soldiers, Germans, and Ukrainians were standing on the roofs of barracks and firing indiscriminately into the crowd. Men, women, and children fell bleeding. The air was filled with screaming and weeping.'[44]

From eyewitness testimonies it is evident that sadism and torture knew no bounds at Treblinka, Sobibor or Belzec, where the cruelty of security guards – Germans, Latvians, Lithuanians, and Ukrainians – was notorious.[45] As in other camps, they carried out their duties without question but showed considerable initiative when it came to torturing their victims beyond endurance. A good example was the deputy commandant of Sobibor (where 250,000 Jews died), the Viennese-born Gustav Wagner. Like many of the SS personnel in the camps, he was a graduate of Schloss Hartheim near Linz, a centre for killing off the mentally sick and handicapped. Master-Sergeant Wagner was in charge of 'selections' and better known to his victims as the 'Human Beast'. One survivor recalled: 'Wagner didn't eat his lunch if he didn't kill daily. With an axe, shovel or even his hands. He had to have blood.'[46] Another victim remembered him as an Angel of Death, for whom 'torturing and killing was a pleasure' – he would snatch babies from their mothers' arms and tear them to pieces in his hands.

Another prize torturer and sadist was Christian Wirth, Inspector of the Operation Reinhard death camps, who had also previously worked in euthanasia institutions and in 1939 had carried out the first known gassing experiments on German 'incurables'. At the end of 1941 he had been assigned to begin the extermination of Jews in Chelmno, the first of the Nazi death camps to become operational. During the next eighteen months, he oversaw, together with Odilo Globocnik (former *Gauleiter* of Vienna), the murder of nearly two million Jews in the death camps of Belzec, Sobibor and Treblinka. In Belzec (where at least 600,000 Jews were murdered) a survivor recalled Wirth as 'a tall broad-shouldered man in his middle fifties, with a vulgar face – he was a born criminal. The extreme beast ... Although he seldom appeared, the SS men were terrified of him.'[47] SS Scharführer Franz Suchamel, who served under him, testified that he could not be surpassed in brutality, meanness and ruthlessness. 'We therefore called him "Christian the Terrible" or "The Wild Christian". The Ukrainian guardsmen called him "Stuka" (a kind of dive-bomber).'[48] At Belzec, in August 1942, Kurt Gerstein personally witnessed how Wirth and his assistants supervised the last journey of the Jews to their destruction:

> They drew nearer to where Wirth and I were standing in front of the death chambers. Men, women, young girls, children, babies, cripples, all stark naked, filed by. At the corner stood a burly SS man, with a loud, priestlike voice. 'Nothing terrible is going to happen to you!' he told the poor wretches. 'All you have to do is to breathe in deeply. That strengthens the lungs. Inhaling is a means of preventing infectious diseases. It's a good method of disinfection.' ... One Jewess of about forty, her eyes flaming like torches, cursed her murderers. Urged on by some whiplashes from Captain Wirth in person, she disappeared in the gas chambers. Many were praying, while others asked: 'Who will give us water to wash the dead?'[49]

The Austrian, Franz Stangl, Commandant of Treblinka and Sobibor, was (like Wirth) a former policeman and had been Superintendent at the Schloss Hartheim Euthanasia Institute. He was a highly efficient and dedicated organiser of mass murder, even receiving an official commendation as the 'best camp commander in Poland'. Unlike Wirth, the soft-voiced Stangl was not a sadist but polite and always impeccably dressed (he attended the unloading of transports at Treblinka dressed in white riding clothes); he took pride and pleasure in his 'work', running the camp like clockwork. Stangl never looked at his victims as individuals or even as human beings but rather as 'cargo'. Regarding the Jews, he told the journalist Gitta Sereny: 'They were so weak; they allowed everything to happen, to be done to them. They were people with whom there was no common ground, no possibility of communication – that is how contempt is born. I could never understand how they could just give in as they did.'[50] He further recalled:

I think it started the day I first saw the *Totenlager* (extermination area) in Treblinka. I remember Wirth standing there, next to the pits full of blue-black corpses. It had nothing to do with humanity – it could not have. It was a mass – a mass of rotting flesh. Wirth said, 'What shall we do with this garbage?' I think unconsciously that started me thinking of them as cargo ... It was always a huge mass. I sometimes stood on the wall and saw them in the 'tube' – they were naked, packed together, running, being driven with whips...[51]

Rudolf Höss, the Commandant of Auschwitz from 1 May 1940 until 1 December 1943, appeared outwardly, like Stangl, to be a kindly, unselfish family man who loved his wife. He, too, took a perfectionist pride in his 'work' at the 'greatest human extermination centre of all time'. In 1944 he was also commended by his superiors as a 'true pioneer in this field, thanks to new ideas and new methods of education'.[52] In his autobiography, Höss emphasised the 'strong awareness of duty' that had been inculcated into him by his pious Catholic parents. 'Every task had to be exactly and conscientiously carried out.' He considered his own compulsion to obey orders and to surrender all personal independence as a hallmark of his own morality and *petit bourgeois* decency. 'I am completely normal,' he observed in his book. 'Even while I was carrying out the task of extermination I lived a normal life.'[53]

Höss embodied the ideal type of the passionless, self-disciplined, disinterested mass murderer who never personally attended mass executions or selections for the gas chambers but treated his job as a purely administrative procedure. What concerned Höss was not the inconceivable suffering of his victims but the practical and technical questions involving timetables, the size of transports, the types of oven and methods of gassing. He took pride in being the first to successfully utilise 'Zyklon B' – like Himmler, the squeamish Höss, who could not bear shootings and bloodshed, found poison gas to be more rational, hygienic and 'humane'. Naturally, the totally depersonalised commandant of Auschwitz (for whom obedience and duty were the highest virtues) did not have a moment's hesitation in executing Himmler's orders concerning the 'Final Solution' to the Jewish question.

Like Adolf Eichmann, Höss emphasised in his memoirs that he had no *personal* hatred of Jews, though he evidently never had any doubts about Hitler's objectives either. Having spent three years in the vast laboratory called Auschwitz, gathering 'indelible impressions and ample food for thought', he still could not resolve the thorny question as to why 'members of the Jewish race go to their deaths so easily?'[54] Like Stangl, it never occurred to him that the whole apparatus of torture and death over which he personally presided was carefully designed to achieve precisely that outcome. No wonder that Höss was so delighted by the grotesque Auschwitz motto *Arbeit macht frei* (Work makes you free) and totally uninterested in its macabre meaning for the victims.

At Auschwitz-Birkenau there were other technical perfectionists, like the gifted thirty-two-year-old chief doctor, Josef Mengele, who knew exactly why they were there and how killing Jews could advance their academic careers. Mengele used Auschwitz inmates as guinea pigs for what he believed was pioneering scientific research into presumed racial differences and physical abnormalities. People afflicted with any sort of deformity would be killed for him, on his orders, upon their arrival in the camp, to provide new material for his studies. He also conducted medical experiments on living Jews, especially twins, hoping to find a method of creating a race of blue-eyed Aryans to realise the megalomaniac dreams of Nazi racial science. In a conversation in Auschwitz with an Austrian Christian woman doctor, Dr Ella Lingens, Mengele said that 'there were only two gifted nations in the world – the Germans and the Jews'. The question, he told Frau Lingens, is 'which one will dominate?'[55]

Mengele's contribution to the millennial struggle for 'domination', like that of other SS doctors, was considerable. He personally killed many prisoners by injecting them with phenol, petrol, chloroform or air; he participated in countless 'selections' at the Auschwitz railway junction, sending all those 'unfit for work' to the gas chambers with a flick of the hand or the wave of a stick. Children, old people, sick, crippled or physically weak Jews as well as pregnant women were instantly sentenced to death. Yet even Dr Mengele, a music-lover and a scientific mind, also had his 'compassionate' moments when he could give individual patients the best of care, between 'selections' for the gas chambers.[56]

Such discontinuities and 'schizophrenic' attitudes characterised many levels of Nazi behaviour, testifying to a high degree of personal fragmentation, an extreme compartmentalisation of the private and public spheres and the constant effort to repress awareness of the genocidal reality that they themselves had created. A good example can be found in the diary of Dr Johann Paul Kremer, a member of the Auschwitz medical corps. On 5 September 1942 he witnessed a 'special action' in the women's camp, calling it 'the most horrible of all horrors' and agreeing with a colleague's description of Auschwitz as the *anus mundi* – the arsehole of the world. Yet, the following day, Dr Kremer could follow up his record of a dreadful execution with details of a splendid dinner: 'Today an excellent Sunday dinner: tomato soup, one half of chicken with potatoes and red cabbage (20 grammes of fat), dessert and magnificent vanilla-cream.'[57]

In the inverted logic of the SS world, embodied in the camps, such seeming anomalies became normal. It was a world where to torture and destroy became a certificate of maturity and the total negation of one's fellow man the royal road to absolute sovereignty over life and death. As Jean Améry (himself a survivor) once put it: National Socialism was the only political system of the twentieth century that 'not only practised the rule of the antiman, as had other Red and White terror regimes also, but had established it as a principle'.[58] The camps were the supreme manifestation of this system, reproducing its structures on a miniature scale but in an amplified way. It was a universe in which all freedom, choice and human solidarity had been virtually abolished, to be replaced by a Hobbesian war of all against all, with survival against the odds as the sole object. Through hunger, beatings, slave labour, exposure to cold and endless tortures, the aim was to destroy individual autonomy and reduce human beings to purely animal reactions.[59] Women, who were treated less severely by the guards, usually survived the ordeal better than men, proving to be more practical, psychologically stronger and more willing to help one another.[60]

Although the crimes committed were appallingly inhuman, the criminals themselves were, as Primo Levi has reminded us, human beings like ourselves – ordinary people who committed extraordinary acts: 'They were made of the same cloth as we, they were average human beings, averagely intelligent, averagely wicked: save the exceptions, they were not monsters, they had our faces.'[61] Franz Stangl was by all accounts a very good husband and father just as Rudolf Höss exemplified the German bourgeois virtues of discipline, obedience and work. Their sleep was never disturbed since they rarely saw any suffering faces, concentrating – as they did – solely on the organisational task at hand. No doubt their impeccable private lives and the watertight compartmentalising of their existence blunted any sense of the monstrous evil they were perpetrating.

Adolf Eichmann exemplified to perfection the same bureaucratised mentality that focused on technical matters without any concern for ultimate ends – a sphere that belonged solely to the jurisdiction of the Führer, the Party and the state.

Like other 'desk murderers' Eichmann was congenitally incapable of accepting any personal responsibility. 'I never killed a single one ... I never killed anyone and I never gave the order to kill anyone.'[62] Of course, such disclaimers were self-serving falsehoods that permeated the whole of German society from the Nazi leadership, the bureaucracy, the army and the industrialists down to the smallest cogs in the killing machine. The decision-makers and the lower-level perpetrators were certainly aware of the enormity of their crimes, otherwise they would not have sought to obliterate all trace of the gas chambers, crematoria and mass executions. The SS was determined that no witnesses should survive to tell the terrible secret of what they had done: hence the insane death marches of 1944–45 with which the history of the Nazi camps came to an end.

Primo Levi has emphasised how the infernal camp system of National Socialism sought to maximise the degradation of its victims by making them similar to itself. Some individuals, like the *Kapos* of the labour squads, were indeed seduced by the material advantage or fatally intoxicated by the power given to them by their tormentors.[63] Perhaps the most demonic of all Nazi crimes was, however, the way in which the SS delegated the filthiest part of their work to the victims themselves – the special squads (made up largely of Jews) who were entrusted with running the crematoria, extracting corpses from the gas chambers and pulling gold teeth from the jaws of the victims.[64] By making the Jewish *Sonderkommando* responsible for the ovens, the Nazis could demonstrate in Levi's words that 'the sub-race, the sub-men bow to any and all humiliation, even to destroying themselves'.[65] The insidious message of the SS was that 'if we so wish and we do so much, we can destroy not only your bodies but also your souls, just as we have destroyed ours'.[66]

Twelve 'special squads' succeeded each other in Auschwitz, operating for a few months before they were liquidated. In October 1944 the last squad rebelled against the SS, blew up one of the crematoria and was wiped out in the only revolt that ever occurred in the history of Auschwitz. To ask why they did not rise up sooner would be to grossly underestimate the hellish sequence of segregation, humiliation, forced migration, total physical exhaustion and rupture with any kind of normality that had accompanied their arrival in the camps and continued with even greater ferocity thereafter. Millions of young, robust, well-trained Soviet military prisoners behaved no differently when they fell into German hands and the few non-Jews among the 'special squads' behaved exactly like the Jews. The camps were deliberately designed to create a debilitating sense of impotence in their victims, to literally reduce them to *Untermenschen* and thereby remake them in the image of Nazi propaganda. The enemy must not only die, but he or she must die in torment. This 'useless' cruelty was not of course unique to the Third Reich, but it certainly was a fundamental feature of Hitlerism.

The question frequently arises as to how far the National Socialist system, the death camps and the Holocaust were a uniquely *German* genocide? This itself presupposes that it is reasonable to speak about 'the Germans' (or any other people) as a single undifferentiated entity and to postulate a distinctive 'national character' which decisively shaped German behaviour in perpetrating the Holocaust. Daniel Goldhagen has no doubts that the mass killing of Jews was not only a German enterprise but that it virtually became a *German national project*. The perpetrators, in his view, are not accurately described as 'ordinary men' (the title of Browning's parallel study of the police battalions) or simply as Nazis. They were ordinary *Germans*. Not only that, but all of German society was permeated by the anti-Jewish policy, with extermination at its very centre. Moreover, there were hundreds of thousands of Germans [who] contributed to the genocide and the still larger system of subjugation that was the vast concentration system.'[67] I can broadly agree with Goldhagen's general assertion that German anti-Semitic beliefs about Jews 'were the central causal agent of the Holocaust' but not with his simplistic explanation of how this came about nor with the exclusive importance he attached to this factor. I also partly accept his analysis of the camps but would seriously question whether all of the perpetrator behaviour that Goldhagen brands as distinctively 'German' was in fact so unique.

The same combination of murderous anti-Semitism, extreme anti-Communism, brutality and sadism can be found in the behaviour of the Lithuanian, Latvian, Ukrainian, Romanian and Croat executioners as Goldhagen discovered in the German perpetrators. The anti-Jewish dynamic was equally, if not even more, present in the Austrians who, though 'German' by language and culture, originated from a very different history, society and civilisation. It was not so much 'eliminationist anti-Semitism' that was peculiar to Germany; rather it was the integrative role of anti-Semitism in a totalitarian movement like Nazism that was able to mobilise all the material and propaganda resources of a highly organised state to further its imperialist and genocidal objectives. To suggest that virtually *all* Germans identified with this totalitarian state and its murderous anti-Semitic goals is surely a gross oversimplification.

Moreover, the 'camp world', although the largest and most significant institutional creation in Nazi Germany, did have a parallel in the Soviet Union, which cannot be ignored. True, there was no precise equivalent of Auschwitz and the industrialised killing process in the Soviet *Gulag*. There were proportionately fewer fatalities and medical care was less inadequate than in the Nazi camps. Arguably, too, Soviet guards may have been more compassionate than their German counterparts. But for a survivor such as Margerete Buber-Neumann who experienced both the German and Russian camps, the experience often seemed identical: 'I ask myself deep down, which is really worse, the lice-infested corncob-walled cabins in Birma (in Kazakhstan) or the nightmare-order of Ravensbrück.'[68] At the 1950 trial of David Rousset, she posed a similar awkward question: 'It is hard to decide which is the least humane – to gas people in five minutes or to strangle them slowly, over the course of three months, by hunger.'[69]

The Germans were well aware that the Russians had annihilated millions of people through forced labour before they even embarked on their own programme of concentration camps. The SS certainly studied this model closely. While one should repudiate Ernst Nolte's false notion that the death camps were a Nazi copy of the *Gulag* 'original', it is important to recall that Hitler admired Stalin and that both dictators and their regimes stood in a macabre symbiotic relationship.[70] Nevertheless, one also needs to underline some key differences between the Soviet and Nazi systems. Stalin did not set out to deliberately murder the population of the *Gulag* precisely because he needed a vast slave empire to finance the modernisation of Russia. In other words, unlike the Nazi experiment, there were *real* economic and utilitarian motives behind the Stalinist projects, however costly and utterly inhuman they may have been.[71] The Soviet camps were undoubtedly used to eliminate political enemies (including many Communists) and millions of innocent people died there; but they were none the less oriented to the production of wealth and the industrialisation of a backward country: the mining of gold, the felling of timber for export and the extraction of minerals were indeed an integral part of the *Gulag*.

Prisoners were not sent to the Soviet labour camps to be transformed into *Untermenschen*, and then into corpses, as the SS did with the Jews. Some visits and correspondence with the outside world (while rare) were permitted to inmates, who were not totally cut off from the past, their historic communities and personal identity. Such gestures were expressly denied to Jews in the Nazi camps, who when they prayed, remembered and learned, did so in defiance of their tormentors. Moreover, as Steven Katz has observed, the Nazis did not even engage in the pretence of ideological 're-education' that (however cynically it was conducted) was part of the organisation of the Stalinist *Gulag*.[72] There was simply no point in re-educating those who were *a priori* defined as vermin or 'lice'.

Similarly, sexual perversity, salaciousness and exploitation played very different roles in the Soviet and Nazi camp systems. Women in the *Gulag* could still hope to trade sexual favours for life and survival. Under Nazi rule such a possibility rarely, if ever, existed since sexual exchanges between Germans and Jews (or even Poles) constituted a 'racial crime'. As Katz bluntly puts it: 'The SS would sexually assault Jewish women and then murder them. They were obligated to murder them.'[73]

More revealing still was the attitude to mothers and children, who even under the Soviet slave-labour system still enjoyed some rights. Despite the terrible material conditions, children could come into the world in the *Gulag* and mothers were not obliged to work during the last month of pregnancy or the first month after their birth. In Auschwitz or other camps, no Jewish child was allowed to live. As one survivor, Olga Lengyel recalled: '... the Germans succeeded in making murderers of even us. To this day the picture of those murdered babies haunts me. Our own children had perished in the gas chambers and were cremated in the Birkenau ovens, and we dispatched the lives of others before their first voices had left their tiny lungs.'[74] Katz makes the very important point that in contrast to the Soviet *Gulag* and all known genocides – past and present – only under the Nazi Reich were (Jewish) mothers and children (one million of them) 'intentionally, systematically, unrelentingly, *and without exception* murdered'.[75] This was an absolute *novum* of the Holocaust, which marks it off from other crimes in history and underlines Améry's point that we are dealing here with a

Kingdom of Night in which the 'Anti-Man' reigned supreme. Despite the horrors of the Stalinist *Gulag*, 'class enemies' of the socialist order were rarely degraded into subhuman 'vermin', outside the realm of human and moral obligation.

Perhaps the closest analogy to the Nazi genocide in this century has been the great massacre of the Armenian people by the Turks during the First World War, which destroyed about 40 per cent of this ancient national community. Under the cover of war, able-bodied male Armenians were separated from their families and murdered. The remaining women and children, the old and the feeble, were driven into the Syrian desert in forced marches, deprived of food and water. Many were tortured, raped and killed both by Turks and marauding Kurds on the way. This bestial treatment was referred to by the then American ambassador to Turkey, Henry Morgenthau, as 'the destruction of the Armenian race'.

The actions of the Ottoman Turkish state in 'solving the Armenian question' led to the deaths of at least 500,000 to a million Armenians – the main body of its population in Asia Minor and the fountainhead of its culture.[26] The lack of Zyklon B gas, gas chambers or crematoria did not hinder the Turks from carrying out a mass murder of the oldest Christian people in existence, who since the late nineteenth century had been perceived as 'aliens' and pariahs by the dominant group. The Turks had at their disposal some of the technical means later used by the Nazis, including railways, the telegraph, bureaucratic machinery and modern propaganda techniques, but the killing itself was still carried out by the extraordinarily primitive methods of a backward society.

The Turkish government's objective was to destroy the Christian Armenian population inside Turkey, which was deemed to be actively seeking full independence or autonomy. Previously regarded as a constituent *dhimmi millet* (a non-Muslim religious community in the Ottoman Empire) the Armenians found themselves stereotyped as an 'alien nationality', especially after the modernising rulers of Turkey adopted the new ideology of Pan-Turkism. This was a xenophobic nationalism intended to underpin their dreams of a new empire stretching from Anatolia to western China, based on Islam and Turkish ethnicity. The Armenian nation, with its ancient ethnic culture and Christian religion, stood in the way of the homogenising nationalism embraced by the young Turks. Armenians were particularly vulnerable and exposed because of their territorial concentration in eastern Anatolia on the border with tsarist Russia – the traditional enemy of Turkey, with whom they were accused of being in league. The Armenians regarded Anatolia (seen by Turkey's rulers as the heartland of the future Pan-Turkic state) as their natural homeland.[77]

Once Turkey had aligned itself with Imperial Germany against the tsarist Russian Empire during the First World War, the Armenians were quickly branded as a 'fifth column', as Russian spies and secessionists – an internal enemy to be deported, starved and pitilessly destroyed.[78] There was no ideology of 'anti-Armenianism' as such but this proved unnecessary in order to carry out the massacres. Armenians were annihilated in the name of modern Turkish nationalism both as a minority with an historical claim to eastern Anatolia and as Christian 'infidels'. In 1894–6 and then again in 1909 the Armenians had endured massacres (involving about 200,000 victims), which led them to stockpile weapons in anticipation of a further onslaught. This, in turn, enabled the Turkish state to rationalise its genocide as a preventive strike to quash a rebellion by those accused of 'stabbing Turkey in the back' in wartime. Unlike the Holocaust, however, the killing operations against Armenians were never carried out by specialised perpetrator groups. On the contrary, they involved large segments of the provincial population, who eagerly participated in regional and local massacres in remote valleys, gorges, hills, rivers, lakes as well as drowning operations in the Black Sea littoral.[79]

It is certainly legitimate to see the Armenian genocide as prefiguring the Holocaust, especially since the decision to slaughter the Armenians was deliberate, firm and implacable. But there were also many dissimilarities between the two events. The brutish 'war against the Armenians' was primarily a *geo-political* rather than an ideological crusade, an expression of raw nationalism directed against a minority seen as disloyal in wartime and favourable to the Entente Powers. Furthermore, the Armenians were never designated as a 'racial' enemy and the war against them remained strictly territorial, without any metaphysical or ontological implications. Those Armenians who converted to Islam (to save their lives) were spared; the majority of Armenians in Istanbul (numbering up to 200,000) did survive and there was no international crusade to seek out and annihilate Armenians wherever they could be found beyond the borders of Turkey. The Armenians were never perceived by the Turks or anyone else as a Satanic force that threatened civilisation as a whole, nor was their murder planned as an end in itself. Nothing should minimise the horror or scope of the slaughter, but it resulted from motivations different from those that influenced the German Nazis.[80]

Comparing genocides is always a difficult exercise, not rendered any easier by pretentious or mystical assertions of 'uniqueness' often made for the Holocaust or by the hostile, irrational responses to such claims. In focusing here on the historical specificity and singularity of the Nazi mass murder there is no implication that other massacres or genocides are in any way less interesting, important or deserving of attention. But it is equally clear that no other event of the modern era has so fundamentally challenged the foundations of European civilisation – its religious values, legal structures, political ideals, trust in science and commitment to humanity. The question might therefore be asked: why has the Holocaust more than any other genocide so deeply affected modern consciousness? Why has precisely this tragedy become *the* axial event sparking a huge and ever-expanding diet of feature films, plays, memoirs, oral histories, television documentaries, scholarly research and fiction? I believe that the answer to this question does not primarily lie in any political agendas, in the sensationalist appetite of the media and the public for horror stories or in the rapacity of the so-called 'Holocaust industry'. Nor can it be adequately explained by the fact that we do regrettably live in a popular culture where victimhood is a source of empowerment. The avalanche of unadulterated kitsch that swamps us is a fact of life that will doubtless continue along with the plague of commercial exploitation and political correctness. But ultimately these are side issues. The reason for the continuing power of the Holocaust to haunt us lies in the 'big question' – why did it happen? Without an answer we may indeed be condemned to repeat this catastrophic past.

In this book I have argued that the Holocaust was driven by a millenarian, apocalyptic ideology of annihilation that overthrew all the enlightened and pragmatic assumptions of liberal modernity. This does not in itself make it different from all other genocides but it does highlight the Holocaust as an extreme case. The centrality of anti-Semitism and of the Jews to this cataclysmic event was no accident, and this essential fact helps to explain why it resonates so strongly. For the Holocaust cannot be divorced from the dominant religious tradition of Western civilisation. In the Christian imagination of the West the Jews are both the 'chosen people' and a (reprobate) 'witness' to the Christian truth. Their fate therefore has a special *religious* significance as an expression of God's role in the drama of history and as an emblematic part of the eternal struggle between salvation and damnation. Richard Rubinstein has aptly characterised the Holocaust as a 'modern version of a Christian holy war carried out by a neopagan National Socialist state hostile to Christianity.'[81] Hyam Maccoby also put it well (though with a different emphasis) when he suggested that the Nazis 'expressed in racialist terms the concept of the final overcoming of evil that formed the essence of Christian millenarianism. The choice of the Jews as a target arose directly out of centuries of Christian teaching which had singled out the Jews as a demonic people dedicated to evil.'[82]

Hitler, masquerading as a Germanic warrior 'Christ', brought this older millenarian tradition to a gruesome end in the death camps – the 'sacred altars' of the new political religion called National Socialism. In the camps, the images and chronicles of Hell to be found in European art and thought were realised in the most macabre fashion. The cataclysmic black passion of the Death's-Head SS units announced the extinction of a God of Love, compassion and mercy. The mass murder of the Jews was in that respect a totalitarian–nihilist assault on the ethics of Christianity as well as the negation of the stern monotheism that Judaism had bequeathed to the West. In this pseudo-Nietzschean transvaluation of values, 'the negation of Judaism had to be transformed into the annihilation of the Jews, this time not spiritually but rather physically, not symbolically but in substance ...'[83] Hitler consistently regarded the *ethics* of Biblical monotheism as the curse of mankind, especially the fifth commandment – 'Thou shalt not kill'. The ideology of National Socialism that climaxed in Auschwitz-Birkenau had to target the Jews as its primary victim precisely because it had chosen Death over Life and perpetual human sacrifice as the road to redemption.

# Notes

## I  Anti-Semitism and the Jews

[1] On the Armenian genocide, Vahakn N. Dadrian, 'The Convergent Aspects of the Armenian and Jewish Cases of Genocide', *Holocaust and Genocide Studies*, (1996), vol. 3, no. 2, pp. 151–69 and Robert F. Melson, *Revolution and Genocide: On the Origins of the Armenian Genocide and the Holocaust* (Chicago, 1992) pp. 145–7 for estimated casualties and pp. 247–57 on similarities and differences. For the wider issues and problems of methodology and comparison, see Leo Kuper, *Genocide: Its Political Use in the Twentieth Century* (New Haven, 1981); R. J. Rummel, *Death by Government, Genocide and Mass Murder* (New Brunswick, 1994); Yehuda Bauer, 'Holocaust and genocide: some comparisons', in Peter Hayes, ed., *Lessons and Legacies: The Meaning of the Holocaust in a Changing World* (Evanston, 1991) pp. 34–46; Alan S. Rosenbaum, ed., *Is the Holocaust Unique?* (Boulder, Colorado, 1996) pp. 101–99.

[2] Robert Conquest, *The Great Terror. A Reassessment* (New York, 1990); idem, *The Harvest of Sorrow. Soviet Collectivization and the Terror-Famine* (New York, 1986) pp. 217–330. For the differences, see Steven T. Katz, 'Auschwitz and the Gulag: A Study in "Dissimilarity" ', in Alan Berger, ed., *Proceedings of the Holocaust Scholars Conference* (Lewiston, ME, 1992) pp. 71–89 and his essay 'Mass Death under Communist Rule and the Limits of "Otherness" ', in Robert S. Wistrich, ed., *Demonizing the Other. Antisemitism, Racism, and Xenophobia* (Amsterdam, 1999) pp. 267–93. Stephane Courtois et al., eds., *The Black Book of Communism* (New York, 1997) highlights the scale of mass killing under Communist regimes in the twentieth century.

[3] Götz Aly, *Final Solution. Nazi Population Policy and the Murder of the European Jews* (London, 1999). Michael Burleigh, *The Third Reich.*

*A New History* (London, 2000) pp. 486–573. See also Richard C. Lukas, *The Forgotten Holocaust. The Poles under German Occupation 1939–1944* (Univ. Press of Kentucky, 1986) pp. 1–39.

[4] Angus Fraser, *The Gypsies* (Cambridge, 1996); Donald Kenrick and Gratton Puxon, *The Destiny of Europe's Gypsies* (New York, 1972) pp. 76–186. Ian Hancock, *The Pariah Syndrome: An Account of Gypsy Slavery and Persecution* (Ann Arbor, 1988). A comprehensive comparative perspective can be found in Wolfgang Wippermann, *'Wie die Zigeuner.' Antisemitismus and Antiziganismus in Vergleich* (Berlin, 1997).

[5] Ian Hancock, 'Gypsy History in Germany and the Neighbouring Lands: A chronology to the Holocaust and Beyond', in *Nationalities Papers* (New York), Winter 1991, XIX, no. 3, pp. 395–412; Henry R. Huttenbach, 'The Romani Porajmos: The Nazi Genocide of Europe's Gypsies', ibid., pp. 373ff.; Sybil Milton, 'Gypsies and the Holocaust', *The History Teacher* 24, 4 (August 1991) pp. 1–13.

[6] Ibid. Also Y. Bauer, 'Gypsies', *Encyclopaedia of the Holocaust*, 4 vols., (New York/London, 1990) 2, pp. 634–8; Fraser, op. cit., p. 260; Kenrick and Puxon, op. cit., pp. 140ff.

[7] Michael Zimmermann, *Rassenutopie und Genozid. Die nationalsozialistische 'Lösung der Zigeunerfrage'* (Hamburg, 1996) pp. 297ff. and idem, *Verfolgt, vertrieben, vernichetet. Die nationalsozialistische Vernichtungspolitik gegen Sinti und Roma* (Rulda, 1989) pp. 61–83.

[8] Klaus Fischer, *The History of An Obsession. German Judeophobia and the Holocaust* (London, 1998) pp. 81–153.

[9] Jakob Wassermann, *Mein Weg als Deutscher und Jude* (Berlin, 1921); Fischer, ibid., pp. 174–5.

[10] Yirmiyahu Yovel, *Dark Riddle. Hegel, Nietzsche and the Jews* (Cambridge, 1998) pp. 127–9.

[11] See Jacob Golomb and Robert S. Wistrich, eds., *Nietzsche: Godfather of Fascism?* (Princeton, 2001) introduction.

[12] Good examples of this annexation are Alfred Bäumler, *Nietzsche als*

*Philosoph und Politiker* (Leipzig, 1931) and Alfred Rosenberg, *Friedrich Nietzsche* (Munich, 1944).

[13] For an imaginative and controversial elaboration, see George Steiner's novel, *The Portage to San Cristobal of A.H.* (London, 1981) p. 120 and his essay, 'The Long Life of Metaphor. An Approach to "the Shoah"', *Encounter* (February 1987) pp. 55–61, as well as Ron Rosenbaum, *Explaining Hitler. The Search for the Origins of Evil* (London, 1998) pp. 304–14.

[14] Ernst Piper, 'Alfred Rosenberg – der Prophet des Seelenkrieges', in Michael Ley and Julius H. Schoeps, eds., *Der Nationalsozialismus als politische Religion* (Frankfurt a.M., 1997) pp. 107–25.

[15] Hermann Rauschning, *The Voice of Destruction* (New York, 1940) pp. 235–42.

[16] Jacob Katz, *Out of the Ghetto: The Social Background of the Emancipation of the Jews* (New York, 1978) pp. 191–219.

[17] James Parkes, *The Conflict of the Church and Synagogue* (Cleveland, 1961) pp. 151–270; Rosemary Ruether, *Faith and Fratricide: The Theological Roots of Anti-Semitism* (New York, 1971); Alan Davies, ed., *Antisemitism and the Foundations of Christianity* (New York, 1979); Edward H. Flannery, *The Anguish of the Jews* (New York, 1985) pp. 47–144; and most recently James Carroll, *Constantine's Sword. The Church and the Jews* (Boston/New York, 2001) pp. 67–342. All of the above are Christian scholars.

[18] Ruether, ibid., p. 113; Carroll, ibid., pp. 92–3. Also Hyam Maccoby, *The Sacred Executioner: Human Sacrifice and the Legacy of Guilt* (London, 1982) p. 146.

[19] Maccoby, ibid., pp. 121–33.

[20] Joshua Trachtenberg, *The Devil and the Jews: The Medieval Conception of the Jew and its Relation to Modern Antisemitism* (New Haven, 1943) pp. 11–56. Robert S. Wistrich, *Antisemitism. The Longest Hatred* (New York, 1992) pp. 13–42.

[21] Ibid.

[22] Trachtenberg, op. cit., pp. 124–39. Gavin Langmuir, 'Historiographic Crucifixion', in *Les Juifs au Regard de L'Histoire. Mélanges en l'honneur de Bernhard Blumenkranz* (Paris, 1985) pp. 109–127. Rainer Erb, ed., *Die Legende vom Ritualmord: Zur Geschichte der Blutbeschuldigung gegen Juden* (Berlin, 1993).

[23] See the introduction by Robert S. Wistrich to *Demonizing the Other*, op. cit., pp. 1–12.

[24] Heiko A. Oberman, *The Roots of Antisemitism in the Age of Renaissance and Reformation* (Philadelphia, 1984) p. 117.

[25] Martin Luther, 'Von den Juden und ihren Lügen', *Luthers Reformations-Schriften*, vol. XX (St Louis: Concordia, 1890) pp. 1861–2026.

[26] Henri Zukier, 'The Transformation of Hatred: Antisemitism as a Struggle for Group Identity', in Wistrich, ed., *Demonizing the Other*, op. cit., pp. 118–30.

[27] Y-M. Yerushalmi, 'L'Antisemitisme racial est-il apparu au XX$^e$ siècle? De la "limpieza de sangre" espagnole au nazisme: continuités et ruptures', *Esprit* (March–April 1993) pp. 5–35.

[28] Ibid. Also Henry Kamen, *Inquisition and Society in Spain in the Sixteenth and Seventeenth Centuries* (Bloomington, 1985) pp. 6–43, 62–133; Ben-Zion Netanyahu, *The Origins of the Inquisition in Fifteenth Century Spain* (New York, 1995) pp. 207–512, 925–1094.

[29] B. D. Weinryb, *The Jews of Poland* (Philadelphia, 1973) pp. 185–95; Jaroslaw Pelenski, 'The Cossack Insurrections in Jewish-Ukrainian relations', in Peter Potichnyj and Howard Aster, eds., *Ukrainian-Jewish Relations in Historical Perspective* (Edmonton, Alberta 1988).

[30] Jay R. Berkowitz, *The Shaping of Jewish Identity in Nineteenth-century France* (Detroit, 1989) p. 71.

[31] Pierre Sorlin, *'La Croix' et Les Juifs (1880–1889)* (Paris, 1967); Stephen Wilson, *Ideology and Experience. Antisemitism in France at the Time of the Dreyfus Affair* (East Brunswick; New Jersey, 1982) pp. 456–584; Pierre Birnbaum, *'La France aux Français.' Histoire des Haines Nationalistes* (Paris, 1993) pp. 29–82, 102–16, 187–220.

[32] Richard I. Cohen, 'Recurrent Images in French Antisemitism in the Third Republic', in Wistrich, *Demonizing the Other* op. cit., pp. 183–195: Zeev Sternhell, *La Droite Révolutionnaire 1885–1914* (Paris, 1978) pp. 177–244; Pierre Birnbaum, *'La République Juive' de Léon Blum à Pierre Mendes-France* (Paris, 1988), and idem, *The Jews of the Republic* (Stanford, 1996) pp. 136–58, 301–17.

[33] Paul W. Massing, *Rehearsal for Destruction: A Study of Political Antisemitism in Imperial Germany* (New York, 1949); Uriel Tal, *Yahadut ve-Natzrut be-Raykh ha-Sheni* (Judaism and Christianity in the Second Reich), Jerusalem, 1975, pp. 185–234; F. Stern, *The Politics of Cultural Despair: A Study of the Rise of German Ideology* (Berkeley, 1961) pp. 267–98; Robert S. Wistrich, *Socialism and the Jews. The Dilemmas of Assimilation in Germany and Austria-Hungary* (London/Toronto, 1982).

[34] W. Boehlich, ed., *Der Berliner Antisemitismusstreit* (Frankfurt a.M., 1965) pp. 5–51, 77–90, 222–35; P. G. J. Pulzer, *The Rise of Political Antisemitism in Germany and Austria* (Cambridge, Mass., 1988) pp. 71–120; Werner Jochmann, *Gesellschaftskrise und Judenfeindschaft in Deutschland, 1870–1945* (Hamburg, 1988) pp. 30–98.

[35] George L. Mosse, *The Crisis of German Ideology. Intellectual Origins of the Third Reich* (New York, 1971) pp. 280–317. Jochmann, ibid., pp. 99–170; Shulamit Volkov, 'The Written Matter and the Spoken Word: On the Gap between pre-1914 and Nazi anti-Semitism', in F. Furet, ed., *Unanswered Questions: Nazi Germany and the Genocide of the Jews* (New York, 1989) pp. 33–53; Daniel Goldhagen, *Hitler's Willing Executioners: Ordinary Germans and the Holocaust* (New York, 1996) pp. 49–128; and Robert S. Wistrich, 'Helping Hitler', *Commentary* (July 1996) pp. 27–31 for a critique.

[36] T. Fritsch, *Antisemiten-Katechismus* (Leipzig, 1883) cited in Massing, op. cit., p. 306; Theodor Fritsch, *Handbuch der Judenfrage* (Leipzig, 1936); Jacob Katz, *From Prejudice to Destruction. Antisemitism, 1700–1933* (Cambridge, Mass., 1982) pp. 304–78, 311, 315; Lucy Dawidowicz, *The War Against the Jews, 1933–45* (London/New York, 1983) p. 96.

[37] Paul de Lagarde, *Deutsche Schriften* (Göttingen, 1904) pp. 217–47; Stern, *Politics of Cultural Despair*, op. cit., pp. 3–36.

[38] Eugen Dühring, *Die Judenfrage als Rassen-Sitten-und Culturfrage* (Karlsruhe/Leipzig 1881) pp. 46–72; U. Tal, *Christians and Jews in Germany: Religion, Politics and Ideology in the Second Reich* (Ithaca/London 1975) pp. 223–82.

[39] Houston S. Chamberlain, *Die Grundlagen des neunzehnten Jahrhunderts* (Munich, 1909) vol. I, pp. 323–546; idem, *Briefwechsel mit Kaiser Wilhelm II* (Munich, 1928) and Geoffrey C. Field, *Evangelist of Race: The Germanic Vision of Houston S. Chamberlain* (New York, 1981).

[40] Celia S. Heller, *On the Edge of Destruction. Jews of Poland between the Two World Wars* (New York, 1980) pp. 50–7. Ezra Mendelsohn, *The Jews of East Central Europe between the World Wars* (Bloomington, 1983) p. 40.

[41] Elias Heifetz, *The Slaughter of the Jews in the Ukraine* (New York, 1920, pp. 1–20, 41–74; J. Lestchinsky, *Twishn Lebn un Toit* (Vilna, 1930), vol. I, 19–53; also Baruch Ben-Anat, 'Peraot Ukraina, 1919–1921', *Kivunim* (December, 1996), 47, 10, pp. 105–39, in Hebrew.

[42] Robert S. Wistrich, *Revolutionary Jews from Marx to Trotsky* (London, 1976) introduction, pp. 1–22.

[43] For Communist attitudes to the Jews in the Soviet Union, see Edmund Silberner, *Kommunisten zur Judenfrage* (Darmstadt, 1983) pp. 138–210.

[44] Alfred Rosenberg, *Der Staatsfeindliche Zionismus* (Munich, 1938) 2nd edition; A. Hitler, *Mein Kampf* (Boston, 1943) pp. 324–5; Robert Wistrich, *Hitler's Apocalypse* (New York, 1985) pp. 154–73.

[45] Mendelsohn, op. cit., pp. 23–30, 68–71, 100–7; David Vital, *A People Apart. The Jews in Europe 1789–1939* (Oxford, 1999) pp. 837–96.

[46] E. Mendelsohn, 'Interwar Poland: good for the Jews or bad for the Jews?' in C. Abramsky et al., eds., *The Jews in Poland* (Oxford, 1986) pp. 130–9.

[47] Norman Davies, *God's Playground. A History of Poland, vol. 2* (Oxford, 1981) pp. 240–66; Emmanuel Meltzer, *Ma'avak Medini Be Malkodet. Yehudei Polin 1935–1939* (Tel Aviv, 1982); now translated into English as *No Way Out: The Politics of Polish Jewry, 1935–1939*

(Cincinatti, 1997). Pawel Korzec, *Juifs en Pologne: La Question Juive pendant l'entre-deux-guerres* (Paris, 1980) pp. 165–98, 263ff.

[48] Anna Landau-Czajka, 'The Ubiquitous Enemy: The Jew in the Political Thought of Radical Right-Wing Nationalists in Poland, 1926–1939', *Polin*, 4 (1989) pp. 169–203; idem, 'The Image of the Jew in the Catholic Press during the Second Republic', ibid., 8, (1994); Yisrael Gutman, 'The Popular Image of the Jew in Modern Poland', in Wistrich, ed., *Demonizing the Other*, op. cit., pp. 257–66.

[49] Ronald Modras, *The Catholic Church and Antisemitism in Poland, 1933–1939* (London, 1994) pp. 315, 345–6; Edward Wynot, 'The Catholic Church and State, 1935–1939' *Journal of Church and State*, 15 (1973) pp. 223–40.

[50] E. Wynot, 'A Necessary Cruelty: The Emergence of Official Antisemitism in Poland', *American Historical Review*, 76, no. 4, (October, 1971) pp. 1035–58; Jerzy Holzer, 'Polish Political Parties and Antisemitism', *Polin*, vol. 8 (Oxford, 1994) pp. 200–5; Szymon Rudnicki, *Obóz Narodowo Radykalny i Geneza i dzialalnosc* (Warsaw, 1985).

[51] Yfaat Weiss, 'Polish and German Jews between Hitler's Rise to Power and the Outbreak of the Second World War', *Leo Baeck Institute Yearbook*, 44 (1999) pp. 205–23. (Henceforth *LBIYB*). Emmanuel Meltzer, 'Antisemitism in the Last Years of the Second Polish Republic', in Y. Gutman et al., eds., *The Jews of Poland between Two World Wars* (Hanover/London, 1989) pp. 126–137; William W. Hagen, 'Before the "Final Solution": Towards a Comparative Analysis of Political Antisemitism in Interwar Germany and Poland', *The Journal of Modern History*, 68 (June 1996) pp. 351–81.

[52] Bernard Wasserstein, *Britain and the Jews of Europe 1939–1945* (London/Oxford, 1979) pp. 17–21.

[53] Henry Feingold, 'Was there Communal Failure? Some Thoughts on the American Jewish Response to the Holocaust', *American Jewish History*, vol. LXXXI, no. 1 (Autumn 1993), pp. 60–80. See also idem, *Bearing Witness. How America and Its Jews Responded to the Holocaust* (Syracuse, 1995) pp. 169–201, 225–76.

[54] Richard Bolchover, *British Jewry and the Holocaust* (Cambridge,

1993) pp. 103–20; also Tony Kushner, *The Persistence of Prejudice: Anti-Semitism in British Society During the Second World War* (Manchester, 1989) pp. 78–105; idem, *The Holocaust and the Liberal Imagination* (Oxford, 1994) pp. 146–72.

[55] Abraham Brumberg, 'The Bund and The Polish Socialist Party in the late 1930s', in Y. Gutman et al., *The Jews of Poland*, op. cit., pp. 75–96; Jerzy Holzer, 'Relations between Polish and Jewish left-wing groups in interwar Poland', in Abramsky, op. cit., pp. 140–6.

[56] Emanuel Ringelblum, *Polish-Jewish Relations During the Second World War*, ed. and annotated by Joseph Kermish and Shmuel Krakowski (Evanston, 1992) pp. 7–8.

[57] Ibid., p. 39.

[58] Ibid., p. 53. Ringelblum reproached the Poles for not actively opposing the impression that 'the entire Polish nation of all classes approved of the behaviour of the Polish anti-Semites.'

[59] Mordekhai Tenenbaum-Tamaroff, *Dapim min hadelekhah* (Tel Aviv, 1947) pp. 49–50. In Hebrew.

[60] Karski's report on Polish Jewry under Nazi and Soviet occupation, is reprinted by Norman Davies and Antony Polonsky, eds., *Jews in Eastern Poland and the U.S.S.R., 1939–46* (London, 1991). See, in particular, p. 269.

[61] Jan Błoński, *Biedni Polacy patrza na ghetto* (The Poor Poles Look at the Ghetto), Cracow, 1994, reprints Kossak-Szczucka's 'Protest' in full. See also Antony Polonsky, 'Beyond Condemnation. Apologetics and Apologies: On the Complexity of Polish Behavior Toward the Jews During the Second World War', in: *Studies in Contemporary Jewry* (Oxford, 1997) vol. XIII, pp. 190–224.

[62] Jan T. Gross, *Neighbours. The Destruction of the Jewish Community in Jedwabne* (Princeton, 2001) pp. 90–104.

[63] See Jan Gross, *Upiorna dekada: trzy eseje o stereotypach na temat Zydow, Polaków, Niemlow, Kommunistów 1939–1948* (Cursed Decade. Three Essays on Stereotypes about Jews, Poles, Germans and Communists), Cracow, 1998.

[64] Jan T. Gross, *Neighbours*, op. cit., pp. 105–110.

[65] Ibid., pp. 54–71. The quote is on page 65.

## II From Weimar to Hitler

[1] Werner Jochmann, *Gesellschaftskrise* ... op. cit., pp. 132–70.

[2] See Hans Mommsen, *The Rise and Fall of Weimar Democracy* (Chapel Hill, NC, 1996).

[3] H. A. Winkler, 'Anti-Semitism in Weimar Society', in Herbert A. Struss, ed., *Hostages of Modernization: Studies in Modern Anti-semitism 1870–1939* (Berlin/New York, 1993) pp. 196–205. (Henceforth *Hostages*).

[4] Jochmann, op. cit., pp. 171–94.

[5] Werner T. Angress, 'Juden im politischen Leben der Revolutionszeit', in Werner E. Mosse and Arnold Paucker, eds., *Deutsches Judentum in Krieg und Revolution 1916–1923* (Tübingen, 1971) pp. 235–51.

[6] Ibid., pp. 254–308.

[7] Ernst Schulin, *Walther Rathenau: Repräsentant, Kritiker und Opfer seiner Zeit* (Göttingen, 1979); Peter Loewenberg, *Fantasy and Reality in History* (New York/Oxford, 1995) pp. 108–18.

[8] Y. Arad et al., eds., *Documents on the Holocaust* (Jerusalem, 1981) pp. 15–18. (Henceforth *Documents*).

[9] Robert S. Wistrich, 'Georg von Schoenerer and the genesis of modern Austrian antisemitism', in Strauss, *Hostages*, (1993) pp. 675–88.

[10] Robert S. Wistrich, *The Jews of Vienna in the Age of Franz Joseph* (Oxford/New York, 1989) p. 211.

[11] Brigitte Hamann, *Hitler's Vienna. A Dictator's Apprenticeship* (New York/Oxford, 1999) pp. 244–5, 251–3.

[12] Robert S. Wistrich, 'Karl Lueger and the Ambiguities of Viennese Antisemitism', *Jewish Social Studies* (1983), 45, pp. 251–62; Richard S.

Geehr, *Karl Lueger. Mayor of Fin de Siècle Vienna* (Detroit, 1990) pp. 171–207.

[13] Hamann, op. cit., pp. 273–303.

[14] *Mein Kampf*, op. cit., p. 120. For the possible occult and irrational influences on Hitler's anti-Semitism stemming from sources like Lanz von Liebenfels and Guido von List, see Jackson Spielvogel and David Redles, 'Hitler's Racial Ideology: Content and Occult Sources', *Simon Wiesenthal Centre Annual (SWC)*, vol. 3, (1986), pp. 227–46; also Nicolas Goodrick-Clarke, *The Occult Roots of Nazism: Secret Aryan Cults and their influence on Nazi Ideology: The Ariosophists of Austria and Germany, 1890–1935* (New York, 1992) pp. 33–48, 90–122, 192–204.

[15] Hamann, op. cit., pp. 24–7, 38–9, 62–7; Paul Lawrence Rose, *Wagner. Race and Revolution* (London, 1992) pp. 147, 181–3; Joachim Köhler, *Wagner's Hitler. The Prophet and His Disciple* (Cambridge, 2000) pp. 191–208, 269–95; T. C. W. Blanning, 'Hitler, Vienna and Wagner', *German History*, vol. 18, no. 4 (2000) pp. 487–94. Saul Friedländer/Jörn Rüsen, eds., *Richard Wagner im Dritten Reich* (Munich 2000) especially the essay by Paul L. Rose, pp. 283–308.

[16] Margaret Brearley, 'Hitler and Wagner: the Leader, the Master and the Jews', *Patterns of Prejudice*, vol. 22, no. 2 (1988) pp. 3–21.

[17] Robert S. Wistrich, *Antisemitism*, op. cit., pp. 57–8.

[18] *Mein Kampf*, op. cit., p. 55.

[19] Ibid.

[20] Ibid., pp. 60–2.

[21] Hamann, op. cit., pp. 347–59. See also Ian Kershaw, *Hitler 1889–1936: Hubris* (London, 1999) pp. 36–69 on his period as a drop-out.

[22] *Mein Kampf*, op. cit., p. 59.

[23] Ibid., p. 512. *Documents*, op. cit., pp. 445–8.

[24] *Mein Kampf*, op. cit., pp. 445–8.

[25] Ibid., p. 65.

[26] Klaus Vondung, *Magie und Manipulation. Ideologische Kult und politische Religion des Nationalsozialismus* (Göttingen, 1971); James Rhodes, *The Hitler Movement. A Modern Millenarian Revolution* (Stanford, 1980) pp. 29–84 and Michael Ley/Julius H. Schoeps, eds., *Der Nationalsozialismus als politische Religion* (Frankfurt a.M., 1997) pp. 151–85, 229–60.

[27] Wistrich, *Hitler's Apocalypse*, op. cit., pp. 27–47.

[28] *Mein Kampf*, op. cit., p. 772.

[29] Hitler to Chvalkovsky, 21 January 1939 in *Documents on German Foreign Policy 1918–1954, Series D* (Washington DC, 1949–64) pp. 190–5. (Henceforth *DGFP*).

[30] Werner Maser, ed., *Hitler's Letters and Notes* (New York, 1974) p. 215.

[31] Ibid.

[32] Gerhard L. Weinberg, ed., *Hitler's Zweites Buch: Ein Dokument aus dem Jahre 1928* (Stuttgart, 1961) pp. 22–3.

[33] Ibid., p. 222.

[34] Wistrich, *Hitler's Apocalypse*, op. cit., pp. 43–4.

[35] Alex Bein, 'Der Jüdische Parasit. Bemerkungen zur Semantik der Judenfrage', *Vierteljahrshefte für Zeitgeschichte* (1965), pp. 121–149. (Henceforth *VjfZ*).

[36] Philippe Burrin, 'Nazi Antisemitism: Animalization and Demonization', in Wistrich *Demonizing*, op. cit., pp. 223–33.

[37] Randall T. Bytwerk, *Julius Streicher* (New York, 1983); Kershaw, op. cit., pp. 179, 560, 563–4; Fred Hahn, *Lieber Stürmer! Leserbriefe an das NS-Kampfblatt 1924 bis 1945* (Stuttgart, 1978) pp. 84ff.

[38] Robert G. Waite, *Hitler: The Psychopathic God* (New York, 1978) p. 448.

[39] Karl Dietrich Bracher, *The German Dictatorship* (London, 1991) pp. 109–133, 195–213; Jochmann, op. cit., pp. 117–54.

[40] Jochmann, ibid., pp. 265ff; Silberner, *Kommunisten ... op. cit.*, pp. 268–70.

[41] Norman Cohn, *Warrant for Genocide. The Myth of the Jewish World Conspiracy and the Protocols of the Elders of Zion* (London, 1970) pp. 138–63, 187–213.

[42] Walter Laqueur, *Weimar: A Cultural History* (London, 1974) pp. 78–109. Anton Kaes et al., eds., *The Weimar Republic Sourcebook* (Berkeley/Los Angeles/London, 1994) pp. 119–44; Robert S. Wistrich, *Weekend in Munich. Art, Propaganda and Terror in the Third Reich* (London, 1996) pp. 56ff.

[43] Bracher, op. cit., pp. 210–12; Winkler op. cit., pp. 201ff; M. Burleigh, *The Third Reich*, op. cit., pp. 106–13. See also G. J. Giles, *Students and National Socialism in Germany* (Princeton, 1985) pp. 44–90.

[44] Richard Hamilton, *Who Voted for Hitler?* (Princeton, 1982) pp. 355–419. Thomas Childers, *The Nazi Voter: The Social Foundations of Fascism in Germany, 1919–1933* (Chapel Hill, N.C., 1983) pp. 142–269.

[45] Bracher, op. cit., pp. 252–68; Henry A. Turner, *Hitler's Thirty Days to Power. January 1933* (London, 1996) pp. 135–83, shows that his victory was by no means inevitable.

[46] On the rampant anti-Semitism in the German medical community, see Robert Prockter, *Racial Hygiene. Medicine under the Nazis* (Cambridge, Mass., 1988) pp. 131–76.

[47] 'Racial Hygiene in Germany', *The Times*, 7 April 1933.

[48] Entry of 10 January 1939 in Victor Klemperer, *Tagebücher 1933–1941* (Berlin, 1995), I, pp. 456–7. The first volume was translated into English under the title *I Shall Bear Witness* and appeared in London in 1998.

[49] Ibid., p. 457. For a perceptive review of the second volume, see Daniel Johnson, 'What Victor Klemperer Saw', *Commentary* (June 2000), pp. 44–50.

[50] On German Zionism see Robert Weltsch, *Ja-Sagen zum Judentum* (Berlin, 1933) and his *Die deutsche Judenfrage. Ein Kritischer Rückblick* (Königstein, 1981) pp. 73–82; also Jehuda Reinharz, ed., *Dok-*

*umente zur Geschichte des deutschen Zionismus, 1882–1933* (Tübingen, 1981) pp. 470–549 for the reactions of German Jewry and German Zionists. The most comprehensive analysis of the general Zionist response is in Daniel Frankel, *Al pnei Tehom. Ha Mediniut Ha-Tsionit ve-she'elat yehudei Germania, 1933–1938* (Jerusalem 1994) pp. 63–154. On Nazi policy toward Zionism and Palestine, see David Yis-raeli, 'The Third Reich and Palestine', *Middle Eastern Studies, vol. 7, no. 3* (October 1971) pp. 343–53 and idem, *HaReich ha Germani ve-erets Yisrael* (Ramat Gan, 1974); also Francis R. Nicosia, *The Third Reich and the Palestine Question* (London, 1985) and idem, 'The End of Emancipation and the Illusion of Preferential Treatment. German Zionism, 1933–1938, in *LBIYB*, 36 (1991) pp. 243–65.

[51] Hjalmar Schacht, *Abrechnung mit Hitler* (Hamburg, 1949) pp. 59ff. Idem, *76 Jahre meines Lebens* (1953) pp. 44ff; Avraham Barkai, *Vom Boykott zur 'Entjudung'. Der wirtschaftliche Existenzkampf der Juden in dritten Reich, 1933–1943* (Frankfurt a.M., 1988) pp. 23–2093 is the best scholarly account of the dispossession of German Jewry.

[52] Uwe Dietrich Adam, *Judenpolitik im Dritten Reich* (1972) pp. 72–144. O. D. Kulka, 'Da'at Ha-Kahal be-Germania ha-natsionalsotsialistit ve-ha-beiya ha-yehudit', *Zion* (1975) 40, 3–4, pp. 186–290 is the most detailed study of German public opinion. On the Lutherans, Richard Gutteridge 'German Protestantism and the Jews in the Third Reich', in O. D. Kulka and Paul Mendes-Flohr, eds., *Judaism and Christianity under the Impact of National Socialism* (Jerusalem, 1987) pp. 251–70. For Catholics, G. Lewy, *The Catholic Church and Nazi Germany* (New York, 1965) pp. 268–308; Konrad Riepgen on 'German Catholicism and the Jews' in Kulka, ibid., pp. 197–226; Giovanni Miccoli, *I Dilemmi e il Silenzi di Pio XII. Vaticano, Seconda Guerra mondiale e Shoah* (Milano, 2000) pp. 118–200; Michael Phayer, *The Catholic Church and the Holocaust, 1930–1965* (Bloomington, 2000) pp. 67–81.

[53] Jeremy Noakes and Geoffrey Pridham, eds., *Documents on Nazism 1919–1945* (London, 1974) I, p. 462.

[54] Karl Schleunes, *The Twisted Road to Auschwitz. Nazi Policy towards German Jews, 1933–1939* (Urbana, Chicago and London, 1970) pp. 148–9.

[55] Adam, op. cit., pp. 114–44; Hermann Graml, *Antisemitism in the Third Reich* (Oxford, 1992) pp. 120–9.

[56] Norman H. Baynes, ed., *The Speeches of Adolf Hitler* (London, 1942) vol. I, pp. 732–4; Max Domarus, ed., *Hitler: Reden und Proklamationen 1932–1945* (Würzburg, 1962) vol. I, p. 537.

[57] Domarus, ibid.

[58] See Abraham Margaliot, 'The Reaction of the Jewish Public in Germany to the Nuremberg Laws', *Essays in Holocaust History* (Hebrew University of Jerusalem, 1979) p. 41.

[59] Ibid., p. 50.

[60] 'Isolation of Jews in Germany. Effect of New Laws', *The Times*, 18 September 1935.

[61] Margaliot, op. cit., pp. 50ff.

[62] For example Georg Kareski's interview in Goebbels' newspaper, *Der Angriff* (23 December 1935). See Margaliot, ibid., p. 50.

[63] Elie Ben Elissar, *La Diplomatie du IIIe Reich et les Juifs* (Paris, 1969) pp. 163–84; Duff Hart-Davis, *Hitler's Olympics: The 1936 Games* (London, 1986) pp. 66–88, 138–40.

[64] Helmut Krausnick/Martin Broszat, *Anatomy of the SS State* (London, 1973) pp. 51ff.

[65] Gerhard Botz, 'The Dynamics of Persecution in Austria, 1938–1945', in Robert S. Wistrich, ed., *Austrians and Jews in the Twentieth Century* (London, 1992) pp. 199–219.

[66] See Herbert Rosenkranz, *Verfolgung und Selbstbehauptung: Die Juden in Österreich, 1938–1945* (Vienna 1978) and Doron Rabinovici, *Instanzen der Ohnmacht. Wien 1938–1945 – Der Weg zur Judenrat* (Frankfurt a.M., 2000) for the subsequent dispossession, persecution, deportation and murder of Austrian Jewry.

[67] 'Berlin outbreak of Jew-baiting', *The Daily Telegraph*, 16 June 1938.

[68] David S. Wyman, *Paper Walls: America and the Refugee Crisis, 1938–1941* (New York, 1985) p. 50; Joshua B. Stein, 'Great Britain and

the Evian Conference of 1938', *The Wiener Library Bulletin* (1976) vol. XXIX, New Series, nos. 37/38.

[69] 'Nations take their stand on refugees', *Daily Express*, 8 July 1939; Paul R. Bartrop, *Australia and the Holocaust 1933–1945* (Melbourne, 1994) pp. 61–78; Irving Abella and Harold Troper, *None is Too Many: Canada and the Jews of Europe* (New York, 1983) pp. 19–37, 51–66.

[70] On American immigration policy between 1933 and 1945, see Arthur Mosse, *While Six Million Died* (New York, 1968); Saul S. Friedman, *No Haven for the Oppressed: United States Policy Towards Jewish Refugees, 1933–45* (Detroit, 1973); Monty Noam Penkower, *The Jews were Expendable: Free World Diplomacy and the Holocaust* (Urbana, Illinois, 1983); David S. Wyman, *The Abandonment of the Jews: America and the Holocaust* (New York, 1984).

[71] *The Times*, 16 July 1938.

[72] Golda Meir, *My Life* (London, 1975) p. 127.

[73] *Völkischer Beobachter*, 1 February 1939. Also, N. H. Byrnes, op. cit., I, p. 738.

## III Persecution and Resistance

[1] Helmut Heiber, '*Der Fall Grünspan, Viertelsjahrshefte für Zeitgeschichte*, 5 (1957) pp. 134–72; Michael R. Marrus, 'The Strange Story of Herschel Grynszpan', *American Scholar* (1988), 57 (1), pp. 69–79; Gerald Schwab, *The Day the Holocaust Began. The Odyssey of Herschel Grynszpan* (New York, 1990).

[2] 'Germany's Day of Wrecking and Looting', *Manchester Guardian*, 11 November 1938.

[3] Ibid.

[4] *Documents on Nazism* (Exeter, 1984) vol. 2, Document 424.

[5] Noakes and Pridham, eds., ibid.

[6] O. D. Kulka, 'Da'at Ha-Kahal' (1975) op. cit., pp. 232–42; Jörg Wol-

lenberg, ed., *The German Public and the Persecution of the Jews, 1933–1945* (New Jersey, 1996) p. 19.

[7] Saul Friedländer, *Nazi Germany and the Jews, vol. I, The Years of Persecution, 1933–1939* (New York, 1997) p. 278.

[8] Schleunes, op. cit., p. 247.

[9] See the stenographic report on the meeting of 12 November 1938 under Goering's chairmanship reproduced in Michael Berenbaum, ed., *Witness to the Holocaust* (New York, 1997) pp. 55–68 (Henceforth *Witness*). Also Peter Loewenberg, 'The Kristallnacht as a Public Degradation Ritual', in *LBIYB*, 32 (1987) pp. 309–23.

[10] *Witness*, ibid., p. 67.

[11] Ibid., pp. 60–1.

[12] Graml, op. cit., pp. 142–4; Wistrich, *Hitler's Apocalypse*, op. cit., pp. 83–7.

[13] Schleunes, op. cit., p. 165; Helmut Genschel, *Die Verdrängung der Juden aus der Wirtschaft im Dritten Reich* (Göttingen, 1966) pp. 299–300.

[14] *Witness*, op. cit., p. 55.

[15] Friedländer, op. cit., pp. 284–300.

[16] *Das Schwarze Korps*, 24 November 1938.

[17] Ian Kershaw, 'The Persecution of the Jews and German Popular Opinion in the Third Reich', *LBIYB*, 26 (1981) pp. 261ff.

[18] Hitler to Chvalkovsky, *DGFP*, op. cit., pp. 190–5.

[19] Domarus, op. cit., vol. II, p. 1058.

[20] Hans Mommsen, 'The Realization of the Unthinkable: The Final Solution of the Jewish Question', in G. Hirschfeld, ed., *The Politics of Genocide* (London, 1986) pp. 97–114.

[21] Baynes, ed., *Speeches*, vol. I, op. cit., p. 740.

[22] *DGFP*, op. cit., D-V, pp. 921–5 (memo of Schacht, 16 January 1939).

²³ Ibid., D-IV, pp. 336–41.

²⁴ Wistrich, *Hitler's Apocalypse*, op. cit., p. 85.

²⁵ Himmler and Heydrich would prefer the term 'the wish of the Führer' (*des Führers Wunsch*) when transmitting unwritten orders for the 'Final Solution', several years later. See Gerald Fleming, *Hitler und die Endlösung* (Munich, 1982) p. 64.

²⁶ Michael Burleigh, *The Third Reich*, op. cit., pp. 571ff.

²⁷ Ernst Klee, 'Euthanasie' in *NS-Staat* (Frankfurt a.M., 1983); Paul Weindling, *Health, Race and German Politics between National Unification and Nazism, 1870–1945* (Cambridge, 1989); Michael Berenbaum, ed., *A Mosaic of Victims: Non-Jews persecuted and murdered by the Nazis* (New York, 1990); Richard C. Lukas, *The Forgotten Holocaust: The Poles under German Occupation, 1939–1945* (New York, 1986); Richard Plant, *The Pink Triangle: The Nazi War against Homosexuals* (New York, 1986); and Henry Friedlander, *The Origins of the Nazi Genocide: From Euthanasia to the Final Solution* (Chapel Hill, N.C., 1995) pp. 246–302.

²⁸ Elke Froehlich, ed., *Die Tagebücher von Joseph Goebbels. Sämtliche Fragmente*, 4 vols. (Munich, 1987), vol. 3, p. 628.

²⁹ Ibid., p. 612.

³⁰ Stig Hornshoj-Moller, *'Der ewige Jude': Quellenkritische Analyse eines antisemitischen Propagandafilms* (Göttingen, 1995) pp. 3–23.

³¹ *Documents on the Holocaust*, op. cit., pp. 173–77. For Nazi ghettoisation policy in Poland between 1939 and 1941, see Christopher R. Browning, *The Path to Genocide. Essays on Launching the Final Solution.* (Cambridge, 1993) pp. 28–56.

³² For a comprehensive study, see Isaiah Trunk, *Judenrat* (New York, 1972) pp. 259–450 and for his description of the ghetto police, pp. 475–547; Philip Friedman, *Roads to Extinction* (New York/Philadelphia, 1980) pp. 539–53; Aharon Weiss, 'Jewish Leadership in Occupied Poland: Postures and Attitudes', *Yad Vashem Studies*, 12 (1977) pp. 335–65; idem, 'Judenrat', in *Encyclopaedia of the Holocaust*, vol. I (New York, 1990) pp. 762–7.

[33] Raul Hilberg, *The Destruction of the European Jews* (Chicago, 1967) pp. 664–8. See also his *Perpetrators, Victims, Bystanders: The Jewish Catastrophe 1933–1945* (London, 1995).

[34] Ibid., pp. 16–17.

[35] Hannah Arendt, *Eichmann in Jerusalem. A Report on the Banality of Evil* (London, 1994) p. 125. Also Richard I. Cohen, 'Breaking the Code: Hannah Arendt's Eichmann in Jerusalem and the Public Polemic', *Michael*, vol. XIII (1993) pp. 29–85. The first edition of Arendt's book appeared in 1963.

[36] R. Hilberg et al., eds., *The Warsaw Ghetto Diary of Adam Czerniakow* (New York, 1979) p. 70.

[37] Rumkowski's address 'Work Protects Us from Annihilation' (2 February 1942) and 'Give Me Your Children', in *Witness*, op. cit., pp. 81–6. See also Primo Levi, *The Drowned and the Saved* (London, 1999) pp. 44–51.

[38] *Scroll of Agony. The Warsaw Diary of Chaim A. Kaplan* (New York, 1954) p. 129.

[39] Ibid., p. 130.

[40] Ibid., pp. 244–5; diary entry of 20 February 1941.

[41] Ibid., pp. 202–3; 2 October 1940. In this same entry Kaplan observed that never before in Jewish history 'did we have so cruel and barbaric an enemy', nor one so evil 'that it would forbid an entire people to pray'.

[42] Dawidowicz, op. cit., pp. 312–18; Shimon Huberbrand, *Kiddush Hashem, Jewish Religious and Cultural Life in Poland during the Holocaust* (New York, 1987) pp. 175–221 for religious practice.

[43] Janusz Korczak, *Ghetto Diary* (New York, 1978) pp. 79–189; Joanna Michlic-Coren, 'Battling against the Odds: Culture, education and the Jewish intelligentsia in the Warsaw Ghetto, 1940–1942', *East European Jewish Affairs*, vol. 27, no. 2 (1997) pp. 77–92.

[44] Dawidowicz, op. cit., p. 417.

⁴⁵ E. Klee et al., eds., 'Those were the Days': The Holocaust Through the Eyes of the Perpetrators and Bystanders (London, 1991) p. 28; Dinah Porat, 'The Holocaust in Lithuania: some unique aspects', in D. Cesarani, ed., The Final Solution (London, 1994) pp. 159–74.

⁴⁶ ' "They Shall Not Take Us Like Sheep to the Slaughter!" Proclamation by the Jewish Pioneer Youth Group in Vilna,' in Documents on the Holocaust, op. cit., p. 433.

⁴⁷ Ibid. See also Avraham Tory, Surviving the Holocaust. The Kovno Ghetto Diary (Cambridge, Mass/London, 1990) notes by Dina Porat. The diary, originally written in Yiddish, provides a powerful picture of life in the Kovno ghetto, suspended between hope and despair. On the Jewish resistance in Vilna, Y. Arad, Vilna ha-yehudit be-ma'avak u ve-klyon (Tel Aviv, 1976). On Jewish resistance in general, Lucien Steinberg, Jews against Hitler (London/New York, 1978).

⁴⁸ Ber Mark, Uprising in the Warsaw Ghetto (New York, 1975) pp. 97–195 for the documents; Y. Gutman, The Jews of Warsaw, 1939–1943: Ghetto, Underground, Revolt (Bloomington, 1982).

⁴⁹ Documents, op. cit., pp. 315–16. For the objectives, appeals and reports of the Jewish underground, ibid., pp. 293–309; for SS General Stroop's final report after crushing the revolt, ibid., pp. 312–13.

⁵⁰ Reuben Ainzstein, Jewish Resistance in Nazi Occupied Eastern Europe (London, 1974) pp. 279–462 for the Jewish partisans; pp. 463–550 for the fighting city-ghettoes of Minsk, Vilna and Bialystok; pp. 551–670 on the Warsaw ghetto uprising and pp. 714–816 on the revolts in Treblinka, Sobibor and Auschwitz. Also Lucien Steinberg, Jews against Hitler, op. cit., pp. 167–292; S. Krakowski, Leḥima yehudit be-Polin neged ha-natzim (Jerusalem, 1977) – a study of Jewish armed resistance in Poland; Dov Levin, Fighting Back: Lithuanian Jewry's Armed Resistance to the Nazis, 1941–1944: (New York, 1985) pp. 167–228; N. Tec, Defiance: The Bielski Partisans. The Story of the Largest Armed Resistance by Jews During World War II (Oxford, 1993); Arno Lustiger, ed., Zum Kampf auf Leben und Tod. Das Buch vom Widerstand der Juden, 1933–1945 (Köln, 1994).

⁵¹ J. N. Porter, ed., The Jewish Partisans: A Documentary History of

*Jewish Resistance in the Soviet Union during World War II* (Lanham, Md., 1982); J. Kagan and D. Cohen, *Surviving the Holocaust with the Russian Jewish Partisans* (London, 1998) pp. 162–224.

[52] Henri Michel, 'Jewish Resistance and the European Resistance Movement', *Yad Vashem Studies*, 7 (1968) pp. 7–16; M. Novitch, *Le Passage des barbares: Contribution à l'historie de la déportation et de la resistance des Juifs grecs* (Nice, 1962); Annie Latour, *The Jewish Resistance in France* (New York, 1981); Gitta Amipaz-Silber, *La Résistance Juive en Algérie 1940–1942* (Jerusalem, 1986) pp. 62–150; Dan Michman, ed., *Belgium and the Holocaust. Jews, Belgians, Germans* (Jerusalem, 1998) pp. 3–40; Lucien Steinberg, op. cit., pp. 81–138.

[53] See René Cassin, *Les hommes partis de rien* (Paris, 1974) p. 136; Henri Amouroux, *Les Passions et les Haines – Avril–Décembre 1942* (Paris, 1981); A. Rayski, *De Gaulle et les Juifs (1940–1944)*, Paris, 1994.

[54] O. D. Kulka, ed., *Deutsches Judentum unter der Nazionalsozialismus* (Tübingen, 1997) for a unique collection of documents on German Jewry between 1933 and 1939; Konrad Kwiet/Helmut Eschwege, *Selbstbehauptung und Widerstand. Deutsche Juden im Kampf um Existenz und Menschenwürde 1933–1945* (Hamburg, 1984).

[55] See the essays by Herbert Freeden, Hajo Bennett, Joseph Walk and others in A. Paucker, ed., *Die Juden im Nationalsozialistischen Deutschland, 1933–1943* (Tübingen, 1986). Also Arno Herzberg, 'The Jewish Press under the Nazi Regime. Its Mission, Suppression and Defiance', *LBIYB*, 36 (1991) pp. 367–88; A. Paucker, 'Resistance of German and Austrian Jews to the Nazi Regime, 1933–1945', *LBIYB* 40, (1995) pp. 13–14; and his *Jewish Resistance in Germany. The Facts and the Problems* (Berlin, 1991), pp. 5–6.

[56] A. Paucker, ibid. The Zionist youth movement in Germany also became strongly anti-fascist. See Chaim Schatzker, 'The Jewish Youth Movement in Germany in the Holocaust Period', *LBIYB*, 32 (1987) pp. 157–82 and 33 (1988) pp. 301–25; and J. Reinharz, 'Hashomer Hatsair in Germany', pt. 2, 'Under the Shadow of the Swastika, 1933–1938', *LBIYB*, 32 (1987) pp. 183–229.

[57] Paucker, *Jewish Resistance*, op. cit., pp. 9, 12.

[58] E. Silberner, 'Die Kommunistische Partei Deutschlands zur Jud-enfrage', *Jahrbuch des Instituts für Deutsche Geschichte, VIII* (1979) pp. 283–334.

[59] Paucker, op. cit., p. 12.

## IV  The 'Final Solution'

[1] Götz Aly, *Final Solution. Nazi Population Policy and the Murder of the European Jews* (London, 1999) and 'The Planning Intelligentsia and the "Final Solution" ', in M. Burleigh, ed., *Confronting the Nazi Past. New Debates on Modern German History* (London, 1996) pp. 140–53. For a critique of Aly's earlier functionalism, see C. R. Browning, *The Path to Genocide*, op. cit., pp. 59–76.

[2] Richard Breitman, *The Architect of Genocide. Himmler and the Final Solution* (London, 1991) pp. 112–120.

[3] Himmler's reflections on the treatment of 'alien races' can be found in Berenbaum, ed., *Witness*, op. cit., pp. 74–6.

[4] See also Christopher R. Browning, *Nazi Policy, Jewish Workers, German Killers* (Cambridge, 2000) pp. 13–14. Hitler read Himmler's memorandum on 25 May 1940, confirming the guidelines, which he found 'very good and correct'.

[5] *Documents*, op. cit., pp. 216–18; Browning, *The Path to Genocide*, op. cit., pp. 18–20, 23–7, 127–8; Breitman, *The Architect*, op. cit., pp. 121–31.

[6] Hilberg, op. cit., pp. 260–1; *Documents*, ibid., p. 217; Breitman, ibid., pp. 121, 124–5.

[7] Leni Yahil 'Madagascar – Phantom of a Solution for the Jewish Ques-tion' in B. Vago and G. L. Mosse, eds., *Jews and non-Jews in Eastern Europe* (New York/Jerusalem 1974) pp. 315–40; see also Magnus Bre-chtken, *'Madagaskar für die Juden'. Antisemitische Idee und Politische Praxis 1885–1945* (Munich, 1997) p. 295 who argues that the Mada-gascar Plan was intended as a 'death sentence' for European Jewry.

[8] *Documents*, op. cit., p. 376.

[9] Ibid., pp. 416–17.

[10] Ibid., p. 416.

[11] Ibid., pp. 398–400.

[12] Dawidowicz, op. cit., pp. 163–4. See also Jürgen Förster, *Das Unternehmen 'Barbarossa' als Eroberungens-und Vernichtungskrieg* (Stuttgart, 1987); Hannes Heer, 'Killing Fields: Die Wehrmacht und der Holocaust', in H. Heer and K. Naumann, eds., *Vernichtungskrieg: Verbrechen der Wehrmacht, 1941 bis 1944* (Hamburg, 1995) pp. 57–77; idem, 'Die Logik des Vernichtungskrieges. Wehrmacht und Partisanen Kampf', pp. 104–56; also idem, *Tote Zonen: Die deutsche Wehrmacht an der Ostfront* (Hamburg, 1999) and *The German Army and Genocide* (edited by the Hamburg Institute for Social Research, New York, 1999).

[13] Omer Bartov, *The Eastern Front, 1941–1945. German Troops and the Barbarization of Warfare* (London, 1985) pp. 106–56 and idem *Hitler's Army: Soldiers, Nazis, and War in the Third Reich* (New York, Oxford, 1991) pp. 106–86. On Von Manstein, see Robert Wistrich, *Who's Who in Nazi Germany* (London, 1995) pp. 166–7.

[14] Omer Bartov, 'Savage War', in Burleigh, ed., *Confronting the Nazi Past*, op. cit., pp. 125–39.

[15] Andreas Hillgruber, 'Die "Endlösung" und das deutsche Ostimperium als Kernstück des rassenideologischen Programms des Nationalsozialismus,' *VJfZ*, no. 20 (1972) pp. 133–53; Eberhard Jäckel, *Hitler's World View. A Blueprint for Power* (Harvard, 1981); Wistrich, *Hitler's Apocalypse*, op. cit., pp. 67–8, 114–15.

[16] F. Halder, *Kriegstagbuch, 1939–1942* (Stuttgart, 1962–4), vol. 2, pp. 336–7; Dawidowicz, op. cit., p. 161.

[17] Dawidowicz, ibid., p. 157.

[18] Hilberg, op. cit., p. 262.

[19] *Documents*, op. cit., pp. 376–8; see also Jürgen Förster, 'The Wehrmacht and the War of Extermination against the Soviet Union', *Yad Vashem Studies* (Jerusalem, 1981) XIV, pp. 7–34; for the execution of these orders and treatment of Soviet POWs, see Christian Streit, *Keine*

*Kameraden, Die Wehrmacht und die sowjetischen Kriegsgefangenen 1941-1945* (Stuttgart, 1978) pp. 88-9, 253ff.

[20] *Eichmann Interrogated. Transcripts from the Archives of the Israeli Police*, ed., Jochen von Lang and Claus Sibyll (New York/London, 1983) p. 75.

[21] Wistrich, *Hitler's Apocalypse*, op. cit., p. 188.

[22] Philippe Burrin, *Hitler et les Juifs* (Paris, 1989) p. 138.

[23] Ibid., pp. 139-40.

[24] Krausnick, 'The Persecution of the Jews', op. cit., p. 85.

[25] Ibid., p. 111.

[26] See Breitman, op. cit., pp. 90, 139-41, 152-3, 199; Browning, *Nazi Policy*, op. cit., pp. 45-6.

[27] Christopher R. Browning, *Fateful Months: Essays on the Emergence of the Final Solution* (New York, 1985) pp. 30-1.

[28] Michael Tregenza, 'Belzec Death Camp', *The Wiener Library Bulletin* (1977) vol. XXX, New Series, nos. 41/42, pp. 8-24; Yitzhak Arad, *Belzec, Sobibor, Treblinka. The Operation Reinhard Death Camps* (Bloomington, 1999) pp. 23-9, 68-74.

[29] Hilberg, op. cit., pp. 564-6; *Rudolf Höss, Commandant of Auschwitz* (London, 1959). Deborah Dwork and Robert Jan van Pelt, *Auschwitz. 1270 to the Present* (New York/London, 1996) pp. 236-353.

[30] *Documents*, op. cit., pp. 247-8. See Christian Gerlach, 'Die Wannsee-Konferenz, das Schicksal der deutschen Juden und Hitlers Grundsatzentscheidung, alle Juden zu ermordern'. *Werkstattgeschichte*, 18 (1997) pp. 29-30. He notes that Frank's speech virtually parrots Hitler's remarks four days earlier, which Gerlach regards as the crucial moment in formalising the 'Final Solution'.

[31] *Documents*, ibid., p. 249.

[32] *Witness*, op. cit., pp. 165-71. For the background, see Christian Gerlach, 'Die Wannsee-Konferenz', op. cit., pp. 7-44; an English trans-

lation appeared in the *Journal of Modern History*, 12 (1998) pp. 759–812.

[33] *Documents*, op. cit., p. 251.

[34] Ibid. On Luther, see Christopher Browning, *The Final Solution and the German Foreign Office* (New York/London, 1978) pp. 76–81, 115–24, 158–61.

[35] *Documents*, ibid., pp. 258–60.

[36] Jeremy Noakes, 'The Development of Nazi Policy towards the German "Mischlinge", 1933–1945,' *LBIYB*, 34 (1989) pp. 291–354; Adam, *Judenpolitik*, op. cit., pp. 316–33.

[37] About 520,000 Jews were murdered in Galicia, which together with the Lublin district has been the object of a number of important regional case studies. See Dieter Pohl, *Von der 'Judenpolitik' zum Judenmord. Der Distrikt Lublin des Generalgouvernements 1933–1944* (Frankfurt a.M., 1993) and idem, *Nationalsozialistische Judenverfolgung in Ostgalizien 1941–1944* (Munich 1997) pp. 267–356; also Thomas Sandkühler, *'Endlösung' in Galizien* (Bonn, 1996) pp. 166–289 and idem his article in Ulrich Herbert, ed., *National Socialist Extermination Policies* (New York/Oxford, 2000) pp. 104–127.

[38] Letter from Minsk dated 16 December 1941. *Documents*, op. cit., pp. 408–9.

[39] Ibid., p. 394.

[40] Ibid., p. 395.

[41] Daniel Carpi, 'The Mufti of Jerusalem, Amin el-Husseini, and his Diplomatic Activity during World War II (October 1941–July 1943), *Studies in Zionism*, no. 7 (Summer 1983) pp. 101–31; Philip Mattar, *The Mufti of Jerusalem. Al-Hajj Amin al-Husayni and the Palestinian National Movement* (New York, 1991) pp. 99–107. For a translation of his articles into Hebrew, see Zvi Elpeleg, *Me-Nekudat Reuto shel Ha-Mufti* (In the Eyes of the Mufti), Tel-Aviv, 1995 and idem, *The Grand Mufti, Haj Amin al-Hussaini, Founder of the Palestinian National Movement* (London, 1994).

[42] *DGFP*, D, vol. XIII, op. cit., p. 201.

[43] Ibid., p. 202.

[44] Ibid., p. 203.

[45] Ibid.

[46] Ibid., p. 204.

[47] Ibid. For the Mufti's ringing endorsement of Hitler's attitude to the Palestine question, see *DGFP*, vol. XI (London, 1961) pp. 1153–4; for his anti-Semitism and implication in the 'Final Solution', Joseph Schechtman, *The Mufti and the Fuehrer* (New York, 1965) pp. 154–8, which included transferring Jewish children to Poland where they would be under the Nazis' 'active supervision'; also Wistrich, *Hitler's Apocalypse*, op. cit., pp. 169–70 and D. Carpi, 'The Diplomatic Negotiations over the Transfer of Jewish children from Croatia and Turkey to Palestine in 1943', *Yad Vashem Studies* (1977) vol. XII, pp. 109–124.

[48] Gerlach, '*Grundsatzentscheidung*', op. cit., pp. 25–8.

[49] Ibid. For a critique of Gerlach's theses, see C. Browning, *Nazi Policy*, op. cit., pp. 26–57.

[50] Burrin, *Hitler et les Juifs*, op. cit., pp. 140–2.

[51] Ibid., p. 141.

[52] According to secret SD reports, the German public interpreted Hitler's speech to mean 'that very soon the last Jew would be driven off European soil'. See O. D. Kulka, 'Public Opinion in Nazi Germany: The Final Solution', *The Jerusalem Quarterly*, no. 26 (Winter 1983) p. 36.

[53] Louis P. Lochner, ed., *The Goebbels Diaries, 1942–43* (New York, 1948) p. 114.

[54] Ibid., p. 138.

[55] Krausnick, op. cit., p. 120.

[56] Ibid.

[57] Hilberg, op. cit., pp. 454–6 for the background.

[58] Mario D. Fenyo, *Hitler, Horthy and Hungary. German-Hungarian Relations* (New Haven/London, 1972) p. 129.

[59] *Documents*, op. cit., pp. 344–5.

[60] Ibid.

[61] Ibid. See Breitman, op. cit., pp. 242–3.

[62] *Documents*, ibid., p. 344. Burleigh, *The Third Reich*, op. cit., pp. 659–61.

[63] *Witness*, op. cit., pp. 177ff. See also Bradley Smith/Agnes Peterson, eds., *Heinrich Himmler. Geheimreden 1933 bis 1945* (Frankfurt a.M., 1974).

[64] Yehuda Bauer, *Jews for Sale? Nazi-Jewish Negotiations 1933–1945* (New Haven, Conn. 1994) pp. 102–15.

[65] *Le Testament Politique de Hitler* (Paris, 1959) p. 89.

[66] *Nazi Conspiracy and Aggression* (Washington, DC, 1946), vol. VI, pp. 260–3.

[67] Ibid.

[68] Dawidowicz, op. cit., p. 18.

## V  Between the Cross and the Swastika

[1] *Mein Kampf*, op. cit., p. 206.

[2] *Die Rede Adolf Hitlers in der ersten grossen Massenversammlung* (Munich, 1925) p. 8.

[3] Ernst Boepple, ed., *Adolf Hitlers Reden* (Munich, 1933) pp. 55–6.

[4] *Mein Kampf*, op. cit., p. 336. Speech of 12 April 1922, in Eberhard Jäckel/Axel Kuhn, eds., *Hitler. Sämtliche Aufzeichnungen 1905–1924* (Stuttgart, 1980) p. 623.

[5] Klaus Scholder, 'Judentum und Christentum in der Ideologie und Politik des Nationalsozialismus, 1919–1945', in Kulka et al., eds.,

*Judaism and Christianity*, op. cit., pp. 183–96; and idem, *A Requiem for Hitler* (London/Philadelphia, 1989) pp. 140–81.

6 Speech in Munich, 17 December 1922, in Jäckel/Kuhn, op. cit., p. 770.

7 Ibid.

8 Ibid.

9 Ibid.

10 Baynes, ed., *Speeches*, vol. I, op. cit., p. 20 (12 August 1922).

11 Friedrich Heer, *Der Glaube des Adolf Hitler. Anatomie einer politischen Religiosität* (Munich 1968); Robert Wistrich, *Between Redemption and Perdition* (London, 1990) pp. 55–70.

12 F. Heer, *Gottes Erste Liebe* (Munich, 1968).

13 *Mein Kampf*, op. cit., pp. 564–5. Dinter, a notorious racist anti-Semite, founded the *Geistchristliche Religionsgemeinschaft* which sought to present Nazism as a second Protestant Reformation. See Kershaw, *Hitler*, op. cit., p. 298.

14 Kershaw, ibid., p. 269. Wistrich, *Who's Who*, op. cit., pp. 161–3.

15 G. Pridham, *Hitler's Rise to Power: The Nazi Movement in Bavaria 1923–33* (London, 1973) pp. 146–83; Ian Kershaw, *Der Hitler-Mythos* (Stuttgart, 1980) p. 37.

16 *Mein Kampf*, op. cit., p. 65.

17 Baynes, ed., *Speeches*, vol. I, op. cit., p. 42 (10 April 1923).

18 *Mein Kampf*, op. cit., p. 687; E. Calic, ed., *Conversations with Hitler* (New York, 1971) p. 51; Kershaw, *Hitler*, op. cit., pp. 154–5.

19 Margerete Plewnia, *Auf dem Weg zu Hitler. Der völkische Publizist Dietrich Eckart* (Bremen, 1970) pp. 94–112.

20 *Auf Gut Deutsch*, 1 (1919) p. 18.

21 Ibid., 2 (1919) p. 554. See also Dietrich Eckart, *Der Bolshchewismus von Moses bis Lenin. Zwiegespräch zwischen Adolf Hitler und mir* (Munich, 1924). The first to grasp the significance of this text and

Eckart's influence on Hitler was Ernst Nolte, 'Eine Frühe Quelle zu Hitlers Antisemitismus', *Historische Zeitschrift*, vol. 192 (1961) pp. 584–606.

[22] John Conway, 'The German Church Struggle and its Aftermath', in Abraham Peck, ed., *Jews and Christians after the Holocaust* (Philadelphia, 1982) p. 42; R. Gutteridge, 'German Protestantism ...', op. cit., pp. 227–50; Theodore S. Hamerow, *On the Road to the Wolf's Lair. German Resistance to Hitler* (Cambridge, Mass/London 1999) pp. 12–13, 52–4, 60–3, 95–6, 146–9, 151–8; Klaus Scholder, *The Churches and the Third Reich* vol. I (London, 1987) pp. 99–119, 127–45, 189–218.

[23] Doris L. Bergen, *Twisted Cross. The German Christian Movement in the Third Reich* (Chapel Hill, 1996) pp. 61–100.

[24] Eberhard Bethge, *Dietrich Bonhoeffer. Theologe, Christ, Zeitgenosse* (Munich, 1967) pp. 323, 557–9; Hamerow, op. cit., pp. 160–2, 204–8.

[25] Robert Michael, 'Theological Myth, German Antisemitism and the Holocaust: The Case of Martin Niemoeller', *Holocaust and Genocide Studies*, vol. 2, no. 1 (1987) pp. 105–22.

[26] K. Scholder, *Die Kirchen und das Dritte Reich. Vorgeschichte und Zeit der Illusionen 1918–1934*, vol. I (Frankfurt a.M., 1977) pp. 116–23; Hamerow, op. cit., pp. 195–202; Ronald J. Rychlak, *Hitler, The War and the Pope* (Huntingdon, Indiana, 2000) pp. 43–69.

[27] Konrad Repgen, 'Zur Vatikanischen Strategie beim Reichskonkordat', *VJfZ*, 31, (1983) pp. 506–35.

[28] Miccoli, op. cit., p. 286.

[29] B. Stasiewski, *Akten deutscher Bischöfe über die Lage der Kirche 1933–1945*, vol. I, 1933–1934 (Mainz, 1968) pp. 101ff.

[30] Faulhaber's sermons on the Bible appeared in English as *Judaism, Christianity and Germany* (New York, 1935). His published papers were edited by Ludwig Volk, *Akten Kardinal von Faulhaber, 1917–1945* (Mainz, 1978).

[31] Ibid., pp. 184–5; see also Michael Phayer, *The Catholic Church*, op. cit., pp. 15ff.

[32] Scholder, '*Judaism and Christianity*', op. cit., p. 191.

[33] '*Mit Brennender Sorge*': *Acta Apostolicae Sedis*, 29 (1937) pp. 145–67; for Faulhaber's draft, see Dieter Albrecht, *Der Notenwechsel zwischen dem Heiligen Stuhl und der Deutschen Reichsregierung*, I, (Veröffentlichungen der Kommission für Zeitgeschichte), A1, pp. 402–43 (Henceforth VKZG).

[34] Miccoli, *I Dilemmi*, op. cit., pp. 174–5, 178; Repgen, op. cit., pp. 209–10.

[35] Ludwig Volk, ed., *Akten deutscher Bischöfe über die Lage der Kirche 1933–1945*, VI, *1943–1945*, VKZG, Reihe Z: Quellen, Bd, 34 (Mainz, 1983), p. 675, n. 1.

[36] Miccoli, op. cit., p. 351.

[37] Ibid., p. 189.

[38] Ibid., p. 499, n. 309; *Volk* (1983), op. cit., no. 799, p. 944.

[39] Miccoli, ibid., p. 195.

[40] Heinrich Portmann, *Kardinal von Galen. Ein Gottesmann seiner Zeit*, 16th ed., (Münster, 1978) pp. 334–66.

[41] Burleigh, *The Third Reich*, op. cit., pp. 262, 400–2.

[42] H. R. Trevor-Roper, ed., *Hitler's Table Talk*, *1941–1944* (London, 1973) pp. 78–9.

[43] Ibid., pp. 6–7.

[44] Ibid.

[45] Ibid.

[46] Ibid., p. 7.

[47] Ibid., p. 79.

[48] Ibid.

[49] Ibid., p. 78.

[50] Ibid., p. 143.

[51] Ibid., p. 314.

[52] Ibid.

[53] See Alfred Rosenberg, *Der Mythus des 20 Jahrhunderts* (Munich, 1939) and Ernst Piper's essay on Rosenberg in Ley and Schoeps, eds., *Der Nationalsozialismus*, op. cit., pp. 107–125.

[54] Donald J. Dietrich, 'Catholic Resistance in the Third Reich', *Holocaust and Genocide Studies*, vol. 3, no. 2 (1988) pp. 171–61. See also Heinz Boberach, ed., *Berichte des SD und der Gestapo über Kirchen und Kirchenvolk in Deutschland 1934–1944* (Mainz, 1971) for a source of great importance covering ten years of Nazi rule and the reports the regime received from its agents concerning the Christian Churches in Germany.

[55] *Table Talk*, op. cit., p. 722.

[56] Heinz-Albert Raem, *Pius XI und der Nationalsozialismus: Die Enzyklika 'Mit Brennender Sorge' vom 14 März 1937* (Paderborn, 1979).

[57] *Actes et Documents du Saint Siège relatifs à la Seconde Guerre Mondiale*, 11 vols., 1965–1981, Vatican City. (Henceforth *ADSS*). *Lettres de Pie XII aux Evêques Allemands 1939–1945* (Vatican, 1993) p. 419. See also the summary (at times tendentious) of Pierre Blet, *Pie XII et la Seconde Guerre Mondiale d'après les Archives du Vatican* (Paris, 1997).

[58] G. Passelecq and B. Suchecky, *L'encyclique cachée de Pie XI. Une occasion manquée de L'Eglise face à l'antisémitisme* (Paris, 1995) pp. 320ff; Giovanni Miccoli, 'Chiesa Cattolica, "Questione Ebraica" e Antisemitismo fra Ottocento e Novecento nella Recente Storiografia', in Giacomo Martina and Ugo Dovere, eds., *I grandi problemi della storiografia civile e religiosa* (Rome, 1999) pp. 323–54.

[59] *ADSS*, vol. 9, Doc. 82, p. 170.

[60] Owen Chadwick, *Britain and the Vatican during the Second World War* (Cambridge, 1986) p. 205.

[61] Msgr Burzio to Cardinal Maglione, March 9, 1942, in *ADSS*, vol. 8, Doc. 298; see also Livia Rothkirchen, 'The Churches and the "Final

Solution" in Slovakia,' in *Judaism and Christianity*, op. cit., pp. 413–41.

[62] Dr Gerhart Riegner, *A Warning to the World. The Efforts of the World Jewish Congress to Mobilise the Christian Churches Against the Final Solution*. Lecture at Hebrew Union College, Cincinnati, Ohio on 17 November 1983.

[63] Chadwick, op. cit., pp. 211–12; *ADSS*, vol. 8, p. 758.

[64] Ibid., p. 213. *ADSS*, vol. 8, Doc. 507, pp. 676, 679. Only three days earlier a report from Scavizzi to the Secretary of State had informed him that over two million Jews had been killed. *ADSS*, vol. 8, Doc. 496, pp. 669–70.

[65] Chadwick, ibid. On 26 September 1942, Taylor reported to the Vatican on mass deportations and execution of Jews at special killing centres. *Foreign Relations of the United States* (FRUS), Washington DC, 1961, III, p. 772. The Polish Ambassador to the Vatican, Kazimierz Papée, had also confirmed that Jews were being murdered in camps all over Poland. *ADSS*, vol. 8, p. 497.

[66] Chadwick, p. 215.

[67] Ibid.

[68] Ibid.

[69] Ibid.

[70] Ibid. See *ADSS*, vol. 8, p. 666 for the confirmation to the Vatican by Count Malvezzi of the Institute for Industrial Research, that 'systematic massacres' of the Jews in Poland were happening daily and took on the 'most fearful and incredible proportions' (Montini's notes, 18 September 1942, Doc. 493).

[71] A Pastoral Letter by the Slovak bishops, published on 26 April 1942, had blamed the Jews for Christ's horrible death on the Cross. While observing that Jews were also human beings, it did not oppose the 'legal actions of the government in taking steps to eradicate the evil influence of the Jews'. Rothkirchen, op. cit., pp. 417–18.

[72] Sidor to Maglione, *ADSS*, vol. 8, Doc. 383, pp. 541–4.

[73] Ibid. Note of Tardini, Doc. 426, pp. 597–8. 'Ma che non possa tener a freno un sacerdote, chi lo può capite?'

[74] Menahem Shelah, 'The Catholic Church in Croatia, the Vatican and the murder of Croatian Jews', *Remembering for the Future* (Oxford, 1988) pp. 266–80; Jonathan Steinberg, 'Types of Genocide? Croatians, Serbs and Jews, 1941–5', in Cesarani, ed., *The Final Solution*, op. cit., pp. 175–93.

[75] Shelah, ibid., p. 270; Phayer, op. cit., pp. 31–40 is highly critical of the Vatican for ignoring the moral issues raised by the genocide in Croatia. So, too, is John Morley, *Vatican Diplomacy and the Jews during the Holocaust, 1939–1943* (New York, 1980) p. 165, who emphasises that the Croatian perpetrators depicted themselves 'as loyal to the Church and to the Pope'.

[76] *ADSS*, vol. 7, p. 166. See also Robert S. Wistrich, 'The Pope, the Church and the Jews', *Commentary* (April 1999) pp. 22–8.

[77] Chadwick, op. cit., p. 218.

[78] *ADSS*, vol. 9, Doc. 82, p. 170. Also note 9 in vol. 2, ibid., p. 323.

[79] *ADSS*, vol. 2, ibid.

[80] Ibid., p. 324.

[81] Pius XII to Von Preysing, 22 April 1943, *ADSS*, vol. 2, Doc. 45, pp. 138–42.

[82] Pius XII's speech was reprinted in *The Tablet* (London), 12 June, 1943.

[83] The entire speech as broadcast on Vatican Radio was published in *The Tablet*, 9 June, 1945 under the heading 'The Catholic Church and the Third Reich: Pope Pius XII Surveys an Heroic History'.

[84] Ibid.

[85] Ibid.

[86] Susan Zucotti, 'Pope Pius XII and the Holocaust: The Case in Italy', in I. Herzer et al., eds., *The Italian Refuge: Rescue of Jews during the Holocaust* (Washington, DC, 1989) pp. 254–70 and idem, *Under His*

*Very Windows: The Vatican and the Holocaust in Italy* (2001) chapters 13–16, which I read in manuscript.

[87] *ADSS*, vol. 9, Doc. 368, pp. 506ff; Miccoli, op. cit., pp. 250–262; Phayer, op. cit., pp. 97–104; Susan Zucotti, *The Italians and the Holocaust* (New York, 1987) chapter 6.

[88] *ADSS*, ibid.; Morley, *Vatican Diplomacy*, op. cit., pp. 180–1.

[89] *ADSS*, vol. 8, Doc. 165, p. 296; see also Michael R. Marrus and Robert O. Paxton, *Vichy France and the Jews* (Stanford, 1985) pp. 201–2; Miccoli, op. cit., pp. 391–7.

[90] *ADSS*, vol. 9, Doc. 317, p. 459; Miccoli, op. cit., pp. 401ff; Susan Zuccotti, 'The Italian Racial Laws, 1938–1945', in J. Frankel, ed., *Studies in Contemporary Jewry*, vol. 8 (New York, 1997) pp. 133–52.

[91] Emil Fackenheim, *The Jewish Return into History. Reflections in the Age of Auschwitz and a New Jerusalem* (New York, 1978) p. 76.

## VI   Collaboration across Europe

[1] L. Dobroszycki/S. Gurock, eds., *The Holocaust in the Soviet Union* (New York, 1993) pp. 3–73; Y. Arad, 'The Holocaust of Soviet Jewry in the Occupied Territories of the USSR', *Yad Vashem Studies*, no. 21 (1991) pp. 1–47; John Garrard, 'The Nazi Holocaust in the Soviet Union: Interpreting Newly Opened Russian Archives', *East European Jewish Affairs* (*EEJA*, henceforth), vol. 25, no. 2 (Winter 1995) pp. 3–40; Zvi Gitelman (ed.) *Bitter Legacy. Confronting the Holocaust* (Bloomington, 1997).

[2] Martin Dean, *Collaboration in the Holocaust. Crimes of the Local Police in Belorussia and Ukraine, 1941–44* (London, 2000).

[3] Ibid., pp. 60–76, 101.

[4] Ibid., pp. 75–6.

[5] John A. Armstrong, *Ukrainian Nationalism* (New York, 1963) pp. 46–7, 101–75; Hryhory Kostiuk, *Stalinist Rule in the Ukraine* (London, 1960) pp. 47–59; R. Conquest, *Harvest of Sorrow*, op. cit., pp. 219–21 and for the huge losses under Soviet domination, ibid., p. 306; also

Steven T. Katz, 'Mass Death ...' in Wistrich (1999), ed., *Demonizing*, op. cit., pp. 272–6; for the Jewish factor, see especially Taras Hunczak, 'Ukrainian–Jewish Relations during the Soviet and Nazi Occupations', in Yuri Boshyk, ed., *Ukraine during World War II: History and Aftermath* (Edmonton, Alberta 1986) pp. 39–57.

[6] T. Hunczak, 'A Reappraisal of Symon Petliura and Ukrainian–Jewish Relations, 1917–21, *Jewish Social Studies*, vol. 3 (1969), pp. 163–83; J. Klier and Shlomo Lambroza, eds., *Pogroms: Anti-Jewish Violence in Modern Russian History* (Cambridge, 1992) pp. 293–372; Baruch Ben-Anat, 'Peraot Ukraina ...', op. cit., (1996) pp. 105–39.

[7] Alexander Dallin, *German Rule in Russia, 1941–1945* (New York, 1957) pp. 107–67; A. F. Vysotsky et al., eds., *Nazi Crimes in Ukraine, 1941–44: Documents and Materials* (Kiev, 1987).

[8] Avraham Tory, op. cit., pp. 4–12; Dina Porat, 'The Holocaust in Lithuania: Some Unique Aspects' in Cesarani, ed., (1994) *The Final Solution*, op. cit., pp. 159–74.

[9] Ibid., pp. 162–6.

[10] Steinberg, 'Types of Genocide!', op. cit., pp. 175ff; for the German 'Final Solution' in Serbia and the first use of gas vans, see C. Browning, *Fateful Months* (New York, 1991) pp. 39–85.

[11] Jonathan Steinberg, ibid., pp. 176–7.

[12] Menahem Shelah, 'Croatia', *Encyclopaedia of the Holocaust*, op. cit., pp. 324–5.

[13] Ibid.

[14] Stepinac to Maglione, 24 March 1943, *ADSS*, vol. 9, annexe II, pp. 221–4 and summary of his protests by the Secretariat of State, 224–9; Morley, *Vatican Diplomacy*, op. cit., pp. 147–65.

[15] Marcone to Maglione, 8 March 1943. Doc. 130, annexe I, ibid., pp. 219–21; on Pavelic, B. Krizman, *Pavelic izmedju Hitlera i Musolinija* (Zagreb, 1980); for the Serb standpoint concerning Ustashe crimes, Vladimir Dedijer, *Jasenovac – Das Jugoslawische Auschwitz und der Vatican* (Freiburg, 1988) pp. 76–200.

[16] H. Arendt, *Eichmann in Jerusalem*, op. cit., p. 190; on massacres of Jews by the Romanian army and police on Soviet territory, Hilberg, op. cit., pp. 200–1.

[17] Eugen Weber, 'Romania' in H. Rogger and E. Weber, eds., *The European Right* (Berkeley, 1966) pp. 501–74; Emanuel Turczynski, 'The Background of Romanian Fascism', in Peter F. Sugar, ed., *Native Fascism in the Successor States, 1918–1945* (Santa Barbara, 1971) pp. 101–12; B. Vago, *The Shadow of the Swastika. The Rise of Fascism and Anti-Semitism in the Danube Basin, 1936–39* (London, 1975) pp. 55–65, 128–9; Leon Volovici, *Nationalist Ideology and Antisemitism. The Case of Romanian Intellectuals in the 1930s* (Oxford/New York, 1991) pp. 45–158.

[18] Vago, ibid., pp. 21–72.

[19] Arendt, op. cit., p. 191. For the stark details concerning Romanian massacres, see Radu Ioanid, *The Holocaust in Romania: The Destruction of Jews and Gypsies under the Antonescu Regime, 1940–1944* (Chicago, 2000).

[20] J. Ancel, 'The Romanian Way of Solving the "Jewish Problem" in Bessarabia and Bukovina, June–July 1941', *Yad Vashem Studies*, 19 (1988) pp. 187–232.

[21] Randolph L. Braham, *The Politics of Genocide. The Holocaust in Hungary*, vol. 2 (New York, 1981) pp. 743–809, 1113–20 and idem, 'The Holocaust in Hungary: A Retrospective Analysis', in David Cesarani, ed., *Genocide and Rescue. The Holocaust in Hungary, 1944* (Oxford/New York, 1997) pp. 29–46.

[22] Seredi supported the anti-Jewish laws and welcomed the removal of the 'wickedly destructive influence' of Hungarian Jews. Quoted in Y. Bauer, *A History of the Holocaust* (New York, 1982) pp. 315–16. The Papal nuncio in Hungary, Angelo Rotta, had to fight hard against such obstacles in his efforts to rescue Jews. See Phayer, op. cit., pp. 106–9.

[23] Robert S. Wistrich, 'The Jews and Nationality Conflicts in the Habsburg Lands', *Nationalities Papers* (New York, 1994) vol. 22, no. 1, pp. 119–39.

[24] N. Katzburg, *Hungary and the Jews: Policy and Legislation, 1920–1943* (Ramat Gan, 1981) pp. 262–84; Randolph L. Braham, 'Hungary: Jews during the Holocaust', *Encyclopaedia of the Holocaust*, op. cit, pp. 698–702.

[25] Nicholas Kállay, *Hungarian Premier* (London, 1954) pp. 75–6; Mario D. Fenyo, *Hitler, Horthy and Hungary* (New Haven and London, 1972) pp. 72–8.

[26] Ibid., pp. 168ff. In a conversation with Kállay in Rome on 2 April 1943, Pope Pius XII thanked him 'for having succeeded in keeping Hungary from such [Nazi] inhumanity ...' The Pope, according to Kállay, deplored the brutal German policy towards Jews.

[27] Randolph L. Braham, 'The Rightists, Horthy, and the Germans: Factors Underlying the Destruction of Hungarian Jewry', in Vago and Mosse, op. cit., pp. 137–56; Hans Safran, *Die Eichmann-Männer* (Vienna/Zurich, 1993).

[28] Nevertheless, the Allied response has been much attacked. See J. S. Conway, 'Between Apprehension and Indifference: Allied Attitudes to the Destruction of Hungarian Jewry', *WLB*, 1973/4, vol. XXVII, new series, nos. 30/31, pp. 37–48; D. Wyman, *The Abandonment of the Jews*, op. cit., pp. 237–41; for the Pope's telegram to Horthy, Rychlak, op. cit., p. 222.

[29] On Szálasi and the consequences of the coup on 15 October 1944, C. A. Macartney, *October Fifteenth: A History of Hungary, 1929–1945* (New York, 1957).

[30] On Rotta, see Phayer, op. cit., pp. 106–9 and many relevant documents in the *ADSS* relating to Hungary in 1944. Also Leni Yahil, 'Raoul Wallenberg: His Mission and His Activities in Hungary', *Yad Vashem Studies*, 15 (1983) pp. 7–54.

[31] For the Swiss press, David Kranzler, *The Man Who Stopped the Trains to Auschwitz. George Mantello, El Salvador, and Switzerland's Finest Hour* (Syracuse, New York, 2000) pp. 122–43; see also Theo Tschuy, *Dangerous Diplomacy* (Grand Rapids, Michigan, 2000) pp. 52ff, 146–207 for the story of the Swiss diplomat Carl Lutz, who saved thousands of Hungarian Jews in Budapest; on the darker aspects of indirect Swiss

involvement in the Holocaust, see Alfred Häsler, *The Lifeboat is Full: Switzerland and the Refugees, 1933–1945* (New York, 1969) pp. 33–153; Georg Kreis, ed., *Switzerland and the Second World War* (London, 2000) pp. 103–157.

³² Y. Bauer, *Jews for Sale?*, op. cit., pp. 70–1.

³³ Ibid., pp. 74–82, 98–9; Weissmandel's accusations in *Hametzar* (New York, 1960) concerning the 'betrayal' of European Jewry during the Shoah by World Jewry and the Zionist movement are refuted by Shabtai Teveth, *Ben-Gurion and the Holocaust* (New York/London, 1996) pp. 112–30.

³⁴ Bauer, ibid., pp. 98ff.

³⁵ N. Oren, 'The Bulgarian Exception: A Reassessment of the Salvation of the Jewish Community', *Yad Vashem Studies*, 7, (1968) pp. 83–106; F. B. Chary, *Bulgarian Jews and the Final Solution* (Pittsburgh, 1972) pp. 35–100; Avraham Ben-Yakov, 'Bulgaria', *Encyclopaedia of the Holocaust*, op. cit., pp. 263–88.

³⁶ Michael Bar-Zohar, *Ha Rakevot yatsou raiqot. Ha-Hatzala Hanoezet shel yehudei Bulgaria me ha-hashmada* (Beyond Hitler's Grasp: The Heroic Rescue of Bulgaria's Jews), Or Yehuda, 1999, in Hebrew, pp. 107–119, 133–7.

³⁷ Chary, op. cit., pp. 90ff, 129–183.

³⁸ Arendt, op. cit., pp. 187–8; Chary, ibid., pp. 153–4.

³⁹ Leni Yahil, *The Rescue of Danish Jewry: Test of a Democracy* (Philadelphia, 1969) pp. 31–83, 382–95.

⁴⁰ Tatiana Brustin-Berenstein, 'The Historiographic Treatment of the Abortive Attempt to Deport the Danish Jews', *Yad Vashem Studies* (1986) pp. 181–218; Hans Kirchhof, 'Denmark: A Light in the Darkness of the Holocaust', *Journal of Contemporary History* 30 (1995) pp. 431–79.

⁴¹ On the evolution of Swedish reactions, see the extensive documentation in Steven Koblik, *The Stones Cry out: Sweden's Response to the Persecution of the Jews* (New York, 1988) pp. 167–293; P. A.

Levine, *From Indifference to Activism: Swedish Diplomacy and the Holocaust, 1938–1944* (Uppsala, 1996). See also Hannu Rautkallio, *Finland and the Holocaust* (New York, 1987) for the rescue of Finland's Jews.

[42] H. J. Boas, *Religious Resistance in Holland* (London, 1945); Ds J. M. Snoek, *De Nederlandse Kerken en de Joden 1940–1945* (Den Haag, 1990) pp. 73–99.

[43] Jacob Presser, *The Destruction of the Dutch Jews* (New York, 1969); Leni Yahil, 'Methods of Persecution, A Comparison of the "Final Solution" in Holland and Denmark', *Scripta Hierosolymitana Studies in History XXIII* (Jerusalem, 1972) pp. 298ff; J. C. H. Blom, 'Persecution of the Jews in the Netherlands in a comparative international perspective', *Dutch Jewish History*, vol. 2 (Jerusalem/Assen, 1989) pp. 273–90 and idem, 'Oorlogsdocumentatie '40–'45', *Jahrboek* (Amsterdam, 1989) pp. 9–66; Guus Meershoek, *Dienuren van het gezag: De Amsterdamse politie tidjens de bezetting* (*Servants of the Authorities: The Amsterdam Police during the Occupation*), Amsterdam, 1999, describes the crucial role of the Dutch police in the deportation of the Jews to the East.

[44] Louis de Jong, 'Jews and Non-Jews in Nazi Occupied Holland', in Max Beloff, ed., *On the Track of Tyranny* (London, 1960) pp. 139–55; Gerhard Hirschfeld, *Nazi Rule and Dutch Collaboration. The Netherlands under German Occupation 1940–1945* (Oxford, 1988); also L. de Jong, *Het Koninkrijk der Nederlanden tijdens de Tweede Wereldoorlog*, vols. 1–14 (S. Gravenhage, 1969–91), which contains a great deal of information about the fate of Dutch Jewry in the Second World War.

[45] Joseph Michman, 'The controversial stand of the Joodse Raad in the Netherlands', *Yad Vashem Studies*, vol. 10, (1974) pp. 9–68; Dan Michman, 'De oprichting van de "Joodsche Raad" voor Amsterdam vanvit een vergelijkend perspectief', *Derde Jahrboek* (Amsterdam, 1992) pp. 75–101.

[46] Maxime Steinberg, *L'Etoile et le Fusil, vol. I. La Question Juive 1940–1942* (Bruxelles, 1983) pp. 83–4 points out that many of the *Ostjuden*, did not register as required by the authorities, which gave them a better chance of survival than in neighbouring Holland.

[47] R. van Doorslaer et al., eds., *Les Juifs de Belgique: De l'immigration au Génocide, 1925-1945* (Bruxelles, 1994); Martin Conway, *Collaboration in Belgium. Léon Degrelle and the Rexist Movement* (New Haven, 1993); Maxime Steinberg, 'The Judenpolitik in Belgium Within the West European Context: Comparative Observations', D. Michman, ed., *Belgium and the Holocaust* (1998), op. cit., pp. 199-214.

[48] Pierre Pierrard, *Juifs et Catholiques Français* (Paris, 1970); P. Birnbaum, *Antisemitism in France* (Oxford, 1992), pp. 109-99; Marrus and Paxton, op. cit., pp. 27-53.

[49] The relevant German documents are in Serge Klarsfeld, ed., *Die Endlösung der Judenfrage in Frankreich* (Paris, 1977) pp. 13-229; Joseph Billig, *La Solution Finale de la Question Juive* (Paris, 1977); G. Wellers, A. Kaspi and S. Klarsfeld, *La France et la Question Juive* (Paris, 1981); see also Paul Webster, *Pétain's Crime. The Full Story of French Collaboration in the Holocaust* (London, 1990); Jacques Adler, *The Jews of Paris and the Final Solution* (New York/Oxford, 1987) pp. 223-40.

[50] Richard H. Weisberg, *Vichy Law and the Holocaust in France* (Amsterdam, 1996) pp. 37-158.

[51] Jean Laloum, *La France antisémite de Darquier de Pellepoix* (Paris, 1979); on Vallat, see Marrus and Paxton, op. cit., pp. 73-120 and ibid., pp. 281-340 for Darquier's period.

[52] Ibid., pp. 106ff.

[53] P. Laborie, *L'Opinion Française sur Vichy* (Paris, 1990); Susan Zuccotti, *The Holocaust, the French and the Jews* (New York, 1993) pp. 138-56.

[54] For German intentions and French police collaboration, see the documents in S. Klarksfeld, *Die Endlösung*, op. cit., pp. 50-66, 75-195; also John P. Fox, 'How far did Vichy France "sabotage" the imperative of Wannsee?' in D. Cesarani, ed., *The Final Solution*, op. cit., pp. 194-214.

[55] Marrus and Paxton, op. cit., p. 261.

[56] Ibid., p. 269 (*FRUS* 1942, II, 710: 26 August 1942).

[57] Ibid., p. 269 (*Jewish Telegraphic Agency*, 14 September 1942); also

Geoffrey Warner, *Pierre Laval and the Eclipse of France* (London, 1968) and Fred Kupferman, *Pierre Laval* (Paris, 1976).

[58] M. Marrus, 'French Churches and the persecution of Jews in France, 1940–1944', *Remembering for the Future* (1988), op. cit., pp. 307–46.

[59] S. Klarsfeld, *Le mémorial de la déportation des Juifs en France* (Paris, 1978). Many thousands of Jews were also assisted and hidden by the French population, especially in the countryside. One Protestant village of Le Chambon-sur-Lignon smuggled several thousand Jews to safety.

[60] Renée Poznanski, *Les Juifs en France pendant la Seconde Guerre Mondiale* (Paris, 1997) p. 351 ('… le gouvernement allemand les réclame, mais dans l'intention bien arrêtée de les exterminer impitoyablement et méthodiquement'); on Jewish responses, Richard I. Cohen, *The Burden of Conscience: French Jewish Leadership during the Holocaust* (Bloomington, 1987) pp. 185–92 and Lucien Lazare, *La résistance Juive en France* (Paris, 1988).

[61] Philippe Garnier, ed., *Une certaine France. L'antisémitisme 40–44* (Paris, 1975); Jean-Pierre Azéma/François Bédarida, eds., *La France des années noires* (Paris, 1993) 2 vols; Pierre Drieu la Rochelle, *Journal 1939–1945* (Paris, 1992) pp. 54–9. This diary of a leading French collaborator illustrates well enough the pervasive and paranoid anti-Semitism of the time, though it is still relatively mild when compared to the racist ravings of Louis-Ferdinand Céline or Lucien Rebatet's *Les Décombres* (Paris, 1942).

[62] *Mein Kampf*, op. cit., p. 637.

[63] W. Scheider, ed., *Faschismus als Soziale Bewegung. Deutschland und Italien in Vergleich* (Göttingen, 1976); George L. Mosse (with Robert S. Wistrich), eds., *International Fascism* (London, 1979) pp. 1–38, introduction by George Mosse.

[64] E. R. von Starhemberg, *Between Hitler and Mussolini* (London, 1942) pp. 92–3; Meir Michaelis, *Mussolini and the Jews. German–Italian Relations and the Jewish Question 1922–1945*, (Oxford, 1978) p. 69.

[65] Leon Poliakov and Jacques Sabille, *Jews under the Italian Occupation*

(Paris, 1954) pp. 49–180. Menahem Shelach, *Ḥeshbon Damim* (Blood Account). *Hatzalat Yehudei Croatia al yiday ha-Italkim* (Tel Aviv, 1986) pp. 51–156 on the rescue of Croatian Jewry by the Italians; Susan Zuccotti, *The Italians and the Holocaust. Persecution, Rescue and Survival* (New York/London, 1987); Jonathan Steinberg, *All or Nothing. The Axis and the Holocaust 1941–43* (London/New York, 1991) and D. Carpi, *Between Mussolini and Hitler. The Jews and the Italian Authorities in France and Tunisia* (Hanover/London, 1994) pp. 102–35, 241–9.

⁶⁶ Steinberg, ibid., pp. 168–80 pointedly highlights the stark contrast between the humanitarian and relatively liberal attitudes of the Italian army and those of the Wehrmacht.

⁶⁷ Ibid. For the historical background, see the essays in Robert S. Wistrich and Sergio della Pergola, eds., *Fascist Antisemitism and the Italian Jews* (Jerusalem, 1995: International Centre for the Study of Antisemitism) pp. 13–96.

⁶⁸ Renzo de Felice, *Storia degli ebrei italiani sotto il fascismo* (Turin, 1972); Nicola Caracciolo, *Gli ebrei e Italia durante la guerra 1940–45* (Rome, 1986) pp. 42–3 quotes a survivor, Blanka Stern, who escaped to Italy: '... the Germans had psychological ways of making us Jews into an inferior race, not human any more, people without rights. When we arrived in Italy the people gave us back our sense of being human.' This is a fascinating book of interviews.

⁶⁹ Goebbels, *Diaries*, op. cit., p. 241.

⁷⁰ On the 'Final Solution' in Italy, De Felice, op. cit., pp. 389–91; F. Folkel, *La Risiera di San Sabba* (Milan, 1979); Liliana Picciotto Fargion, 'The Anti-Jewish Policy of the Italian Social Republic (1943–1945), in *Yad Vashem Studies* (1986), vol. XVII, pp. 18–49.

## VII  Britain, America and the Holocaust

¹ D. Wyman, *The Abandonment of the Jews*, op. cit., p. xv. Peter Novick, *The Holocaust in American Life* (Boston/New York, 1999) pp. 47–59 for a contrary view.

[2] Ibid., pp. 124–37.

[3] D. Wyman, 'Why Auschwitz was never bombed', *Commentary*, 65 (May 1978) pp. 37–46; Richard S. Levy, 'The Bombing of Auschwitz Revisited: A Critical Analysis', *Holocaust and Genocide Studies*, 10 (1996) pp. 267–98.

[4] Meyer Weinberg, *Because they were Jews. A History of Anti-Semitism* (New York, 1986) p. 214.

[5] Leo Ribuffo, 'Henry Ford and *The International Jew*', *American Jewish History*, 69 (June 1980) pp. 437–77; Robert Singerman, 'The American Career of *The Protocols of the Elders of Zion*', *American Jewish History* (September 1981) pp. 48–78; Albert Lee, *Henry Ford and the Jews* (New York, 1980) pp. 29–31, 46–51.

[6] Leo Ribuffo, *The Old Christian Right: The Protestant Far Right from the Great Depression to the Cold War* (Philadelphia, 1983).

[7] Ralph L. Kolodny, 'Catholics and Father Coughlin: Misremembering the Past', *Patterns of Prejudice*, vol. 19, no. 4 (1985) pp. 15–25.

[8] Richard Breitman and Alan M. Kraut, *American Refugee Policy and European Jewry, 1933–1945* (Bloomington, 1987) pp. 70–3.

[9] Weinberg, op. cit., pp. 220ff; Wyman, op. cit., pp. 14–15.

[10] Quoted in Melvin J. Urofsky, *We are One! American Jewry and Israel* (New York, 1978) p. 49; Fred L. Israel, ed., *The War Diary of Breckinridge Long. Selections from the Years 1939–1944* (Lincoln, Nebraska 1966); Breitman and Kraut, op. cit., pp. 112–45.

[11] Bernard Wasserstein, *Britain and the Jews of Europe*, op. cit., pp. 244–9.

[12] The report suggested *inter alia* that 'we may as well take down the plaque from the Statue of Liberty and black out the "lamp beside the golden door"', op. cit., p. 294.

[13] Wyman, *Abandonment*, op. cit., pp. 210–15.

[14] Feingold, 'Was there a Communal Failure?', ibid., pp. 6ff. Haskell

Lookstein, *Were We Our Brothers' Keepers? The Public Response of American Jews to the Holocaust, 1933–1945* (New York, 1986).

[15] Alex Grobman, 'Reactions of American Jewry through the American and Jewish Press, 1939–1942', M.A. thesis (Hebrew University of Jerusalem, 1978); Rafael Medoff, *The Deafening Silence: American Jewish Leaders and the Holocaust* (New York, 1987).

[16] See Yitshaq Ben-Ami, *Years of Wrath. Days of Glory* (New York, 1982); Wyman, op. cit., pp. 90–2, 253–4.

[17] Ibid., pp. 345–7 (Appendix B).

[18] Aaron Berman, *Nazism, the Jews and American Zionism, 1933–1948* (Detroit, 1990) pp. 80–9.

[19] Aaron Berman, 'Rescue through Statehood: the American Zionist Response to the Holocaust', in Cesarani, ed., *The Final Solution* (1994), op. cit., pp. 228–245; Monty Penkower, *The Jews were Expendable* (Detroit, 1988) p. 92.

[20] A. Berman, *Nazism, the Jews and American Zionism . . .* op. cit., pp. 86–7.

[21] The Riegner telegram is in Berenbaum, ed., *Witness*, op. cit., pp. 252–4; for the British response, see Wasserstein, op. cit., pp. 168–9; on the American reaction, Wyman, *Abandonment*, op. cit., pp. 42–3, 128–9. Also Walter Laqueur, *The Terrible Secret* (London, 1980) pp. 79–83 and Penkower, op. cit., pp. 64–70.

[22] Wyman, ibid., p. 90 estimates the crowd at 40,000 – a record attendance at Madison Square Garden.

[23] Stephen J. Whitfield, 'The Politics of Pageantry, 1936–1946', *American Jewish History* (1997) pp. 221–51. Ben Hecht wrote the script, Billy Rose produced, Moss Hart directed and Kurt Weill created the score. Paul Muni and Edward G. Robinson were the narrators. These stars were among the most prominent artists and entertainers of Jewish origin in America.

[24] Wasserstein, op. cit., pp. 189–94; Penkower, op. cit., pp. 98–121.

[25] Ibid., p. 196. For Canadian attitudes regarding Bermuda, see Abella and Troper, *None is Too Many*, op. cit., pp. 126–47.

[26] Wasserstein, ibid., p. 201.

[27] Ibid. For the American side, Wyman, op. cit., pp. 104–23, 341–3. It should be noted that in 1942, publicity, protest and calls for action regarding the Holocaust (especially by Christian Church leaders and MPs) were much more vocal in Britain than in the United States. A year later the position was reversed. See Tony Kushner, 'Rules of the Game: Britain, America and the Holocaust in 1944', in *Holocaust and Genocide Studies*, 5, (1990) pp. 381–403.

[28] Henry Feingold, *The Politics of Bearing Witness*, op. cit., pp. 169–201.

[29] Wyman, *Abandonment*, op. cit., pp. 288–307; Martin Gilbert, *Auschwitz and the Allies. The Politics of Rescue* (London, 1983) pp. 307–17.

[30] Gilbert, ibid., pp. 316–17.

[31] Ibid., pp. 216, 245.

[32] *Witness*, op. cit., pp. 296–304 for the documents.

[33] Ibid., pp. 298–300.

[34] Ibid., 304. McCloy's letter of 14 August 1944.

[35] Richard Breitman, 'The Allied War Effort and the Jews, 1942–3', *Journal of Contemporary History* (1985) pp. 135–57 and idem, *Official Secrets: What the Nazis Planned. What the British and Americans Knew* (London, 1999) pp. 88–109 on the British and pp. 228–30 for a comparison between Roosevelt and Churchill.

[36] Breitman, *Official Secrets*, ibid., pp. 192ff.

[37] Gilbert, *Auschwitz*, op. cit., p. 184.

[38] Quoted in Marrus and Paxton, op. cit., p. 196.

[39] Ibid., pp. 196–7.

[40] Joseph Heller, 'Roosevelt, Stalin and the Palestine problem at Yalta',

*WLB* (1977) vol. XXX, new series, nos. 41/2, pp. 25–35 (ed. Robert S. Wistrich).

41 Ibid.

42 Quoted by Berman, *'Rescue through Statehood'*, op. cit., p. 237.

43 Ibid., p. 239.

44 D. Yisraeli, *'The Third Reich ...'*, op. cit., pp. 343ff; Y. Gelber, 'Hamediniut Hatzionit Veheskem Ha-ha'avarah', *Yalkut Moreshet*, 18 (1974) pp. 23–100; Edwin Black, *The Transfer Agreement* (New York, 1984) pp. 146–53, 166.

45 D. Ben-Gurion, *Ba ma-arakhah*, vol. 3 (Tel Aviv, 1949) p. 14.

46 On the responses of the *Yishuv* and the Zionist movement to the Shoah, Yoav Gelber, 'Zionist Policy and the Fate of European Jewry, 1939–1942', *Yad Vashem Studies*, 13, (1979) pp. 169–209; D. Porat, 'Palestinian Jewry and the Jewish Agency: Public Response to the Holocaust', in R. Cohen, ed., *Vision and Conflict in the Holy Land* (New York, 1990) pp. 246–73; and idem, *The Blue and Yellow Stars of David. The Zionist Leadership in Palestine and the Holocaust, 1939–1945* (Cambridge, Mass. 1990) pp. 239–62 and the more partisan and tendentious Tom Segev, *The Seventh Million: The Israelis and the Holocaust* (New York, 1993) pp. 97–110; Mapai, Y. Weitz, *Muda'ut ve ḥoser onim: Mapai lenokhah hashoah, 1943–45* (Aware but Helpless: Mapai and the Holocaust), Jerusalem, 1994, in Hebrew.

47 Shabtai Teveth, *Ben-Gurion: The Burning Ground 1886–1948* (Boston, 1987) pp. 854–60 and idem *Ben-Gurion and the Holocaust* (1996), op. cit., pp. 221–60; see also Tuvia Friling, 'Ben-Gurion and the Holocaust of European Jewry, 1939–1945: A Stereotype Re-examined', *Yad Vashem Studies*, 18, (1988) pp. 199–232 for context and perspective.

48 Chaim Barlas, *Hatzalah Bimei Shoah* (Tel Aviv, 1975) pp. 293–5; Berenbaum, ed., *Witness*, op. cit., pp. 296ff; Gilbert, *Auschwitz*, op. cit., pp. 299–322 and Wasserstein, op. cit., pp. 309ff.

49 Quoted in *Ben-Gurion and the Holocaust*, op. cit., pp. 212–13.

50 Gilbert, op. cit., pp. 285, 304ff, 319; Wasserstein, op. cit., pp. 313–20.

[51] See Alex Weissberg, *Desperate Mission: Joel Brand's Story* (New York, 1958) and Brand's own Hebrew memoir two years earlier *Beschlichut Nidonim Lemavet* (Tel Aviv, 1956); J. S. Conway, 'The Holocaust in Hungary: Recent Controversies and Reconsiderations', in R. Braham, ed., *The Tragedy of Hungarian Jewry* (New York, 1986) pp. 1–33; Gilbert, op. cit., pp. 217–28, 240–4, 253–5; Y. Bauer, *Jews for Sale?*, op. cit., pp. 172–95.

[52] Idith Zertal, 'The Poisoned Heart: The Jews of Palestine and the Holocaust', *Tikkun*, vol. 2, no. 1 (1988) pp. 79–83 is vehemently critical; for more nuanced verdicts see Dina Porat, 'Ben-Gurion and the Holocaust' in R. Zweig ed., *David Ben-Gurion: Politics and Leadership in Israel* (London, 1991) pp. 145–70 and Tuvia Friling, *Ḥetz ba-arafel* (Arrow in the Dark). *David Ben-Gurion, Hanhagat Ha-yishuv ve-nisionot hatzalah be-Shoah* (Beer-Sheva, 1998), vol. 2, pp. 657ff on Ben-Gurion and the *Yishuv* leadership's rescue efforts during the Shoah.

[53] Wasserstein, op. cit., pp. 45, 66–9.

[54] Ibid., pp. 143–52.

[55] Ibid., p. 145.

[56] Ibid., p. 37.

[57] Quoted by Martin Gilbert, 'The most horrible crime. Churchill's prophetic, passionate and persistent response to the Holocaust', *The Times Literary Supplement*, 7 June 1996, pp. 3–5.

[58] Wasserstein, op. cit., p. 280.

[59] Ibid., pp. 275–9.

[60] Gilbert, 'The most horrible crime' (1996); for the other side of the coin and a much more critical view, see Michael J. Cohen, 'Churchill and the Jews: the Holocaust', *Modern Judaism*, vol. 6, no. 1 (February 1986) pp. 27–49.

[61] Ibid.

[62] Ibid.

[63] Gilbert, *Auschwitz*, op. cit., p. 270.

[64] Ibid., p. 305.

[65] On the mindset of British officialdom, Wasserstein, op. cit., pp. 350–5.

[66] Quoted in Breitman, *Official Secrets*, op. cit., p. 209.

[67] Ibid., p. 93; Gilbert, *TLS*, op. cit., p. 4.

[68] Breitman, ibid., p. 106.

[69] Ibid., p. 171.

[70] Ibid.

[71] Wasserstein, op. cit., p. 188.

[72] Breitman, op. cit., p. 119. He shows that the British government and its intelligence services knew about the Holocaust earlier than previously assumed. This information included reports about Auschwitz and the death camp system in Poland well before the summer of 1944, contrary to what Martin Gilbert had imagined twenty years ago. See Barbara Rogers, 'British Intelligence and the Holocaust: *Auschwitz and the Allies* Re-examined', *The Journal of Holocaust Education*, vol. 8 (Summer 1999) no. I, pp. 89–106.

[73] Laqueur, op. cit., pp. 229–38; Thomas E. Wood and Stanislaw M. Jankowski, *Karski: How One Man Tried to Stop the Holocaust* (New York, 1994) pp. 117–19, 142–7; Gilbert, op. cit., pp. 93–5; Breitman, op. cit., pp. 146–50; and the documents in *Witness*, op. cit., pp. 256–61.

[74] *Witness*, ibid., pp. 249–50. See also the heart-rending appeal of Shmuel Zygelbojm, the Jewish representative on the Polish National Council based in London, ibid., pp. 246–7. In protest against the indifference of a world 'which witnessed the extermination of the Jewish people without taking any steps to prevent it', he committed suicide in London during the autumn of 1942.

[75] Laqueur, ibid., p. 236.

[76] Ibid., p. 121 and E. Raczynski, *In Allied London* (London, 1962). Also the two comprehensive volumes by David Engel, *In the Shadow of Auschwitz. The Polish Government-in-Exile and the Jews, 1939–1942*

(Chapel Hill, N.C., 1987) pp. 157–213 and *Facing a Holocaust: The Polish Government-in-Exile and the Jews, 1943–1945* (Chapel Hill, 1993) pp. 15–167. On Karski's mission to the United States, see, ibid., vol. 2, pp. 89–94.


## VIII   Modernity and the Nazi Genocide

[1] Omer Bartov, *Murder in Our Midst. The Holocaust, Industrial Killing and Representation* (New York/Oxford, 1996) p. 4.

[2] Zygmunt Bauman, *Modernity and the Holocaust* (Oxford, 1989) is perhaps the best articulated of these efforts. For an interesting critique, see Hans Mommsen, 'Nationalsozialismus als vorgetäuschte Modernisierung', in Walter H. Pehle, ed., *Der historische Ort des Nationalsozialismus* (Frankfurt a.M., 1990) pp. 31–46.

[3] Hannah Arendt, *Totalitarianism* (New York, 1968).

[4] For the role of medicine and science, see also Robert J. Lifton, *The Nazi Doctors: Medical Killing and the Psychology of Genocide* (New York, 1986); Benno Müller Hill, *Murderous Science* (Oxford, 1988).

[5] Bauman, op. cit., p. 33.

[6] See Wolfgang Schneider, ed., *Vernichtungspolitik und Genozid im Nationalsozialistischen Deutschland* (Hamburg, 1991) for a discussion of Aly and Heim's themes.

[7] Götz Aly and Susanne Heim, 'Die Ökonomie der Endlösung?', in *Beiträge zur Nationalsozialistischen Gesundheits-und Sozialpolitik*, vol. 5 (Berlin, 1987) p. 14.

[8] Christopher Browning, *Path to Genocide*, op. cit., pp. 59ff. points out that initially the arguments of the 'productionists' in favour of economic self-sufficiency in the ghettos had the upper hand.

[9] Ulrich Herbert, 'Racism and rational calculation: the role of "utilitarian" strategies of legitimation in the National Socialist Weltanschauung', *Yad Vashem Studies*, vol. 24 (1994), p. 133.

[10] Michael Burleigh, 'A Political Economy of the Final Solution? Reflec-

tions on Modernity, Historians and the Holocaust', *Patterns of Prejudice*, vol. 30, no. 2 (1996) pp. 29–41.

[11] Dan Diner, 'Rationalization and method: critique of a new approach in understanding the "Final Solution"', *Yad Vashem Studies*, vol. 24 (1994), p. 87.

[12] Peter Longerich, *Politik der Vernichtung: Eine Gesamtdarstellung der Nationalsozialistischen Judenverfolgung* (Munich/Zurich, 1998).

[13] Louis P. Lochner, ed., *The Goebbels Diaries* (New York, 1971) p. 102.

[14] Ibid.

[15] Quoted in Matthew Cooper, *The Phantom War* (London, 1979) p. 57. See also Yehoshua Büchler, *The Extermination of the Jews Disguised as Anti-Partisan Warfare in the Occupied Areas of the Soviet Union 1941–1942* (M.A. thesis in Hebrew, Hebrew University of Jerusalem, 1989).

[16] See Tim W. Mason, 'The Primacy of Politics – Politics and Economics in National Socialist Germany', in Henry A. Turner, ed., *Nazism and the Third Reich* (New York, 1972) pp. 175–200.

[17] Albert Speer, *The Slave State. Heinrich Himmler's Masterplan for SS Supremacy* (London, 1981) p. 251.

[18] R. Höss, *Commandant of Auschwitz*, op. cit., p. 206.

[19] B. F. Smith and Agnes Peterson, eds., *Heinrich Himmler, Geheimreden*, op. cit., p. 201.

[20] Helmut Heiber, ed., *Reichsführer! Briefe an und von Himmler* (Stuttgart, 1970) p. 190.

[21] *Trial of the Major War Criminals before the International Military Tribunal* (Nuremberg, 1948) vol. 29, p. 123.

[22] Ulrich Herbert, 'Arbeit und Vernichtung: Ökonomisches Interesse und Primat der Weltanschauung im Nationalsozialismus', in Dan Diner, ed., *Ist der Nationalsozialismus Geschichte?* (Frankfurt a.M., 1987) pp. 198–236.

[23] Browning, *Paths to Genocide*, op. cit., pp. 59–85.

[24] Raul Hilberg, *The Destruction of the European Jews*, 3 vols. (New York, 1985) vol. 3, p. 994.

[25] See Bauman, chapter 4 on 'The uniqueness and normality of the Holocaust'.

[26] Mark Levene, 'Is the Holocaust Simply Another Example of Genocide?', *Patterns of Prejudice*, vol. 28, no. 2 (1994) pp. 3–26 (p. 23).

[27] Edwin Black, *IBM and the Holocaust. The Strategic Alliance between Nazi Germany and America's most powerful Corporation* (London, 2001).

[28] Henry Friedlander, *The Origins of Nazi Genocide: From Euthanasia to the Final Solution* (Chapel Hill, N.C., 1995) p. 284.

[29] C. Browning, 'The Revised Hilberg', *Simon Wiesenthal Centre Annual* (1986) p. 291.

[30] R. Hilberg, *The Destruction of the European Jews* (Chicago, 1967) p. 669.

[31] Hans Mommsen, 'The Realisation of the Unthinkable: The "Final Solution of the Jewish Question" in the Third Reich', in his *From Weimar to Auschwitz. Essays in German History* (Cambridge, 1991) pp. 224–53 (p. 250).

[32] David Bankier, 'On Modernisation and the Rationality of Extermination', *Yad Vashem Studies*, vol. XXIV (1994) pp. 109–129.

[33] Michael Marrus, *The Holocaust in History* (London, 1988) p. 40.

[34] Ian Kershaw, *The Nazi Dictatorship: Problems and Perspectives of Interpretation* (London, 1993) pp. 85–6 for a discussion of Hans Mommsen's work, which first popularised this term.

[35] Karl Schleunes, *The Twisted Road to Auschwitz: Nazi Policy Toward German Jews 1933–1939* (Chicago, 1970) p. viii.

[36] Martin Broszat, 'Hitler und die "Endlösung". Aus Anlass der Thesen von David Irving', *VJfZ*, 25/4 (1977) pp. 739–75.

[37] Mommsen, 'The Realisation of the Unthinkable', op. cit., pp. 232–3.

[38] Ulrich Herbert, ed., *National Socialist Extermination Policies. Contemporary German Perspectives and Controversies* (New York/Oxford, 2000) pp. 1–52 for the editor's introduction.

[39] Ibid., pp. 83–127 for the articles of Pohl and Sandkühler.

[40] Herbert, ibid., p. 37.

[41] See the articles by Dina Porat and Jonathan Steinberg (already referred to) in D. Cesarani, ed., *The Final Solution*, op. cit., Mark Mazower, *Inside Hitler's Greece. The Experience of Occupation 1941–1944* (London, 1993) and Jonathan Steinberg, 'The Holocaust, society and ourselves', *The Jewish Quarterly*, no. 153 (Spring 1994) pp. 46–50. Also the new book by Jan Gross, *Sąsiedzi: Historia Zagłady żydowskiego miasteczka* (Neighbours: The History of the Destruction of Jewish Shtetl), (Cracow, 2000).

[42] Tzvetan Todorov, *Facing the Extreme. Moral Life in the Concentration Camps* (London, 1999) pp. 289–90.

[43] Yitzhak Arad, *Belzec, Sobibor, Treblinka. The Operation Reinhard Death Camps* (Bloomington, 1999) p. 84.

[44] Ibid.

[45] Ibid., p. 67.

[46] Robert Wistrich, *Who's Who in Nazi Germany* (London/New York, 1995) p. 269.

[47] Ibid., pp. 278–9 for my short biography of Wirth.

[48] Arad, op. cit., p. 183.

[49] Y. Bauer, *History of the Holocaust*, op. cit., pp. 210–11.

[50] Wistrich, op. cit., pp. 241–2. See also Gitta Sereny, *Into that Darkness: An Extermination of Conscience* (London, 1977). This is the only case in which a death camp commandant revealed his feelings in lengthy interviews.

[51] Quoted in Arad, op. cit., p. 186.

[52] Wistrich, op. cit., pp. 123–4.

[53] Rudolf Höss, *Commandant in Auschwitz* (London, 1959).

[54] Todorov, *Facing the Extreme*, op. cit., p. 170.

[55] Martin Gilbert, *The Holocaust. The Jewish Tragedy* (London, 1986) p. 582.

[56] Todorov, op. cit., p. 142. Primo Levi, *The Drowned and the Saved* (London, 1989) p. 56 already noted that in the camps compassion and brutality 'can coexist in the same individual and in the same moment, despite all logic'.

[57] 'Diary of Johann Paul Kremer', *KL Auschwitz, Seen by the SS*, eds. J. Bezwinska and D. Czech (New York, 1984) pp. 214–15.

[58] Jean Améry, *At the Mind's Limits* (London, 1999) p. 31. These are powerful reflections by a survivor on Auschwitz and its realities.

[59] B. Bettelheim, *The Informed Heart* (Glencoe, 1960) p. 109.

[60] Todorov, op. cit., p. 78.

[61] Primo Levi, *The Drowned*, op. cit., p. 202.

[62] Todorov, op. cit., p. 152.

[63] Levi, op. cit., pp. 30ff.

[64] Ibid., p. 34.

[65] Ibid., p. 35.

[66] Ibid., p. 37.

[67] D. Goldhagen, *Hitler's Willing Executioners*, op. cit., p. 8.

[68] Margerete Buber-Neumann, *Déportée à Ravensbrück* (Paris, 1988) p. 53.

[69] David Rousset et al., eds., *Pour la vérité sur les camps concentrationnaires* (Paris, 1990) p. 183.

[70] For Nolte's views, see his 'A Past that will not Pass Away', *Yad Vashem Studies*, XIX (1988) p. 71. This issue reproduces the main documents of the German 'battle of the historians' (*Historikerstreit*) in the 1980s.

[71] Steven T. Katz, *The Holocaust and Comparative History* (Leo Baeck Memorial Lectures, 37, New York, 1993) pp. 3–29.

[72] Ibid., pp. 20–1.

[73] Ibid., p. 22.

[74] Olga Lengyel, *Five Chimneys: The Story of Auschwitz* (New York, 1947) pp. 110–11.

[75] Katz, op. cit., p. 24.

[76] The figures for the total number of Armenian deaths vary enormously. Katz gives a minimum number of 476,000 and a high of 776,000 fatalities (ibid., p. 17). Some Armenian historians speak of more than a million deaths. Robert F. Melton estimates that between 1915 and 1918, 1 out of 2 million Armenians were killed. See his 'The Armenian Genocide', in Alan S. Rosenbaum, ed., *Is the Holocaust Unique?* (1996), op. cit., p. 89. He adds that between 1918 and 1923 half a million more Armenians perished at Turkish hands.

[77] Pierre Papazian, 'A "Unique Uniqueness"?' *Midstream* (April 1984) pp. 14–18 and the responses by Yehuda Bauer, Helen Fein, George M. Kren, Leon H. Rappoport and Nora Levin, pp. 19–25.

[78] Robert F. Melson, '*The Armenian Genocide*', op. cit., pp. 92–3.

[79] Vahkan N. Dadrian, 'The Comparative Aspects of the Armenian and Jewish Cases of Genocide ...', in Rosenbaum, ed., ibid., pp. 104–5.

[80] Katz, op. cit., pp. 6–17.

[81] Richard L. Rubinstein, 'Religion and the Uniqueness of the Holocaust', in Rosenbaum, ed., *Is the Holocaust Unique?*, op. cit., pp. 11–18.

[82] Hyam Maccoby, *The Sacred Executioner* (New York, 1982) p. 175.

[83] Uriel Tal, 'On the Study of the Holocaust and Genocide', *Yad Vashem Studies*, vol. XIII (1979) p. 45.

## NAZISM AND THE SECOND WORLD WAR

**1933**

30 January    Hitler appointed Chancellor of Germany.
27 February    Reichstag Fire – many Communists and trade unionists arrested. New Reichstag elections.
23 March    Enabling Act grants Hitler dictatorial powers.
October    Germany withdraws from the League of Nations.

**1934**

30 June    'Night of the Long Knives' – Hitler's purge of *Sturmabteiling* (SA).
July    *Putsch* in Vienna fails but Chancellor Dollfuss is killed.
2 August    President Hindenberg dies. Hitler now Head of State. He demands oath of allegiance.
Stalin's massive purges and show trials greatly weaken Soviet military and economy (1934–1939).

**1935**

16 March    Germany resumes conscription and rearmament in violation of the Treaty of Versailles.
3 October    Italian invasion of Ethiopia.

**1936**

March    Germany reoccupies Rhineland in violation of treaties.
July    Olympic Games staged in Berlin.
October    Mussolini declares Rome–Berlin Axis.
November    Anti-Comintern Pact signed between Japan and Germany.

**1937**

November    Italy joins Anti-Comintern Pact and withdraws from the League of Nations.

**1938**

12 March    *Anschluss*.
July    Evian Conference: American and European countries meet to discuss the German-Jewish refugee problem and fail to find a solution.
September    Munich Crisis: Britain and France appease Hitler on Sudetenland to avoid war.

## The Holocaust

|        |        |        |
| ------ | ------ | ------ |
| *March* | First concentration camp opens at Dachau. | **1933** |
| *April* | The Nazis organise a national boycott of Jewish businesses and professions. | |
| | Professional Civil Service Act: Jews excluded from civil service and teaching. | |
| *May* | Goebbels, Minister of Propaganda, organises public burning of books by Jewish authors and other writers objectionable to Nazi ideals. | |
| *1 May* | *Der Stürmer*, the Nazi anti-Semitic paper revives the myth of the Jews' involvement in ritual murder. | **1934** |
| *May* | Law making non-Aryans ineligible for military service. Jewish veteran groups protest. | **1935** |
| *15 September* | Nuremberg Laws depriving Jews of citizenship and right to hold public office. Jews banned from marrying Germans in new law 'For the Protection of German Blood and Honour'. | |
| *Early* | Intensification of anti-Semitic outbreaks in Poland and introduction of quotas in Polish universities. | **1936** |
| *July* | Buchenwald concentration camp opens. | **1937** |
| *July* | Evian Conference: majority of countries refuse entry to Jewish refugees from Nazi persecution. Jewish doctors' and lawyers' licences are cancelled; Jews required to have Jewish names (to distinguish them from Aryans). | **1938** |
| *6 November* | In protest at Nazi persecution of Jews, Herschel Grynszpan shoots German diplomat in Paris. | |
| *9–10 Nov* | In response Nazis launch a nation-wide pogrom, Kristallnacht. 91 Jews killed, 191 synagogues destroyed, 30,000 Jews arrested and the Jewish community fined a billion marks as punishment for 'causing' the destruction. | |
| *12 November* | Laws to exclude Jews from economic life are instituted. | |
| *November* | Jewish children are excluded from German schools. | |
| | Emergency programme to evacuate Jewish children to Britain, France and Low Countries. | |

## THE SECOND WORLD WAR

| 1939 | | |
|---|---|---|
| | 30 January | Hitler's Reichstag speech threatens European Jewry with annihilation in the event of war. |
| | 15 March | German army occupies all Czechoslovakia in violation of Munich pact. |
| | 28 March | Franco's victory in Spanish Civil War. |
| | 7 April | Invasion of Albania by Italy. |
| | 22 May | Pact of Steel between Italy and Germany. |
| | 23 August | Soviet-German non-aggression pact and secret agreement to divide Poland. |
| | 1 September | German invasion of Poland begins the Second World War. |
| | October | Beginning of euthanasia programme in Germany which results in some 90,000 deaths. |

| 1940 | | |
|---|---|---|
| | April–May | German blitzkrieg on Denmark, Norway, Netherlands, Belgium, Luxembourg and France. |
| | 10 May | Winston Churchill becomes Prime Minister of Great Britain. |
| | June–November | Germany and France sign armistice; Battle of Britain begins; Hungary, Romania and Slovakia become members of Tri-Partite Pact (Axis Powers). |

| 1941 | | |
|---|---|---|
| | April | German invasion of Yugoslavia and Greece. |
| | 22 June | German invasion of Soviet Union. |
| | 7 December | Japan's attack on Pearl Harbor brings America into the war. Japan also attacks Hong Kong, Singapore, Philippines. |
| | 11–13 Dec | Germany and Italy declare war on USA. |

| 1942 | | |
|---|---|---|
| | September | Battle of Stalingrad begins. |
| | October–November | Battle of El Alamein: British army in Libya goes on the offensive; Rommel's Africa Corps begins its retreat which leads to its disintegration and surrender. Allies invade Morocco and Algeria. |

## THE HOLOCAUST

| | | |
|---|---|---|
| 23 *November* | All Jews in Poland are ordered to wear the star of David. | **1939** |

| | | |
|---|---|---|
| *Early* | Nazis separate Jews from general population and begin to set up ghettos in eastern European cities. | **1940** |
| *May* | 160,000 Jews sealed off in Lodz ghetto. | |
| *November* | 500,000 sealed off in Warsaw ghetto. | |

| | | |
|---|---|---|
| *March* | Auschwitz complex extended on Himmler's orders. | **1941** |
| *May* | 3,600 Jews are rounded up in Paris. | |
| *June* | Following German army advance in Russia, *Einsatzgruppen* (special killing squads) begin mass murder of Jews by shooting, gassing in vans and other means. Local police and militia assist in killings. In this way, 2 million Jews in Poland, the Baltic States and western areas of the Soviet Union were killed in the next two years. Large numbers of Slavs and other peoples were also killed. | |
| *31 July* | Heydrich receives instructions from Goering for 'The Final Solution of the Jewish Question'. | |
| *19 September* | All Jews in the Reich ordered to wear the yellow star. | |
| *29 September* | At Babi Yar 33,771 Kiev Jews killed by *Einsatzcommando* 4a. | |
| *10 December* | 4,000 Jews of Novogrudok killed. | |

| | | |
|---|---|---|
| *January* | The Wannsee Conference – Nazi officials meet to plan the annihilation of all Jews in Europe – 'The Final Solution'. Jewish resistance organisation established in Vilna ghetto. | **1942** |
| *March* | Operation Reinhardt – Liquidation of Polish Jewry begins; first transports to Belzec, Majdanek, Treblinka and Sobibor camps. Deportations to Auschwitz of Slovakian Jewry begin, followed by deportations from France. | |
| *July* | Deportations from Warsaw ghetto begin. Jewish Fighting Organisation (*Zydowska Organizacja Bojowa* – 'ZOB') is formed in Warsaw. | |
| *August* | World Jewish Congress informs British and American governments about mass murders in eastern Europe. | |
| *17 December* | One minute's silence in the House of Commons for the murdered Jews of Europe. | |

## THE SECOND WORLD WAR

**1943**

| | |
|---|---|
| *January* | Battle of Stalingrad ends with destruction of German 6th army. Hitler's dream of conquest in the East is shattered. |
| *June–July* | Allies invade Italy, Mussolini overthrown. Battle of Kursk – Red Army inflicts massive losses on Wehrmacht |

**1944**

| | |
|---|---|
| *June* | Liberation of Rome. D-Day – Allies invade Normandy. Warsaw 'Home Army' (Polish Resistance) Uprising. |
| *December* | Battle of the Bulge. |

**1945**

| | |
|---|---|
| *January* | Red Army liberates Warsaw. |
| *April* | Red Army captures Berlin. |
| *8 May* | V-E Day. |
| *6 August* | Atomic bomb on Hiroshima. |
| *9 August* | Atomic bomb on Nagasaki. |
| *15 August* | V-J Day. |

### THE HOLOCAUST

|          |                                                                                                                                                                                                                                 |
| -------- | --- |
| *March*     | Auschwitz opens its first crematorium. |
|          | Cracow ghetto liquidated: pre-war Jewish population – 60,000. |
| *April–May* | As the Warsaw ghetto is liquidated the ZOB uprising begins. Jews in the ghetto, using secret stores of weapons, fight the Germans despite being massively outnumbered. The leaders are killed and the ghetto demolished. |
| *May*       | In Novogrudok an *Aktion* kills 7,000 Jews leaving 233 alive. Three weeks later 100 of the remaining Jews escape and join partisan units. |
| *June*      | Lvov ghetto liquidated: pre-war Jewish population of Lvov – 150,000. |
| *July*      | Hitler bans all public references to the 'Final Solution of the Jewish Question'. |
| *December*  | Vilna ghetto liquidated: pre-war Jewish population of Vilna – 80,000. |

**1943**

---

|          |                                                                                              |
| -------- | --- |
| *May–July*  | Deportation of 437,000 Hungarian Jews to Auschwitz where most are gassed. |
| *July*      | Staff and 300 children from French children's homes are deported to Auschwitz. |
| *October*   | Auschwitz prisoners destroy one of the gas chambers in short-lived rebellion. |
| *November*  | Last gassings in Auschwitz. Gas chambers destroyed on Himmler's orders as Russian army approaches. |

**1944**

---

|          |                                                                                              |
| -------- | --- |
| *January*   | Budapest is liberated, including 80,000 Jews. |
|          | Auschwitz liberated by the Soviet army. |
| *April*     | Buchenwald concentration camp liberated by the U.S. army. |
|          | Bergen-Belsen concentration camp liberated by the British army. |
|          | Hitler, Himmler and Goebbels commit suicide. |
| *May*       | Nazi Germany surrenders. |
| *November*  | International War Crimes Tribunal opens in Nuremberg. |

**1945**

# Index

All Orion/Phoenix titles are available at your local bookshop or from the following address:

Mail Order Department
Littlehampton Book Services
FREEPOST BR535
Worthing, West Sussex, BN13 3BR
*telephone* 01903 828503, *facsimile* 01903 828802
*e-mail* MailOrders@lbsltd.co.uk
(Please ensure that you include full postal address details)

Payment can be made either by credit/debit card (Visa, Mastercard, Access and Switch accepted) or by sending a £ Sterling cheque or postal order made payable to *Littlehampton Book Services*.

DO NOT SEND CASH OR CURRENCY.

**Please add the following to cover postage and packing**

*UK and BFPO:*
£1.50 for the first book, and 50p for each additional book to a maximum of £3.50

*Overseas and Eire:*
£2.50 for the first book plus £1.00 for the second book and 50p for each additional book ordered

---

BLOCK CAPITALS PLEASE

*name of cardholder* ......................................

*delivery address*
*(if different from cardholder)*

*address of cardholder* ......................................

......................................

......................................

*postcode* ......................................

*postcode* ......................................

☐ I enclose my remittance for £......................................

☐ please debit my Mastercard/Visa/Access/Switch (delete as appropriate)

card number

expiry date

Switch issue no.

signature ......................................

*prices and availability are subject to change without notice*